NON LEAGUE FOOTBALL

To
VINCE

BEST WISHES
ENJOY THE FOOTBALL

NON LEAGUE FOOTBALL
My Roller Coaster Ride

Micky (Turka) Taylor

Dedication

I dedicate this book to Jacqueline, the lady I love
so much who inspired me to write this book,
my son Daniel and Zoe, grandson George
(the best), granddaughters Lauren and Emily,
great granddaughter, Jessica, Mum and Dad,
Robin (Merlin) Denman, my non-league
football family, and friends.

Contents

Foreword

Life is like a roller coaster; love is like a roller coaster; work is like a roller coaster, but non-league football is a special roller coaster and, in my book, I will explain why and how I came to write it. What you must remember is my football life spans some 60 years and a lot of things in the non-league football world have changed – some for the good, but some say not so. Can we advance so much that in the end, it destroys s the non-league tradition, for example, ground grading? Why would you need to make clubs, already struggling financially, have to get their capacity up to 3 or 4 thousand when their average gate will be no more than 300 or a thousand in a big local derby? Of course, there are no more coats down over the park as goalposts with the heavy plastic ball, no more walking up to the park in football kit of all colours, including boots if you could afford them, but at least we had a choice of what player we wanted to be and having picked teams, we could be whatever team we wanted to be; Real Madrid, Barcelona, Man. Utd., Liverpool, and of course any player you name. Now we have organised football and under 7s playing Little League football and in proper kit, being taken to the game in Mum or Dad's car and back home again. Marked out pitches some even 3g surfaces, goals with nets and a referee and don't forget the screaming Mums and Dads on the touchline, cheering their child's team on and thinking that one day they would be parents of a premiership player. In some cases, the dream becomes reality, but it's very rare today with so much import of foreign players, even into the top tier non-league level.

I had no organised football until I played for my primary school team. It was just not available; no Saturday or Sunday mini leagues and no 5/6-a-side tournaments in the 50s. Your

Saturday school football was all that you got and the occasional mid-week afternoon game, again with the school. How things have now changed for the better. The facilities for the kids now are wonderful but then, of course, there is always a downside to all things. They are the silly things in my opinion like coaches who have a badge and have never had the experience of playing the game at a decent level, but they do give up their Saturdays/Sundays and Tuesday/Wednesday nights for no financial reward. Quite the reverse - they put their own money in most cases but there is a lot more on this subject in the book. Having worked for the F.A. (Surrey County F.C. under 16/18 as coach/asst manager, I hope now you can see why I bought my ticket, got on the roller coaster, and am enjoying it still. I find it easy to enjoy and love but find it difficult to understand how the game (not always on the pitch - most of it off the pitch) has changed so much at non-league level. Looking at the money being pumped into some clubs while others have to bring out the begging bowl, I wonder how good I could have been with today's facilities; but football is full of maybes and 'might have beens'. Despite this, it never took away my love for the game. So now enjoy the ride! You won't be disappointed.

CHAPTER ONE

How I bought the ticket to ride.

So, it was on 22nd March 1948 at around 5 pm at Mayday Hospital in Croydon I was born, the only child of Violet and Tony Taylor. My name, Michael, was, I am told, given to me in respect of the Irish doctor who delivered me, but you will find in the book that I will refer to most of my experiences in the name of Micky. If Mum was alive now, she would definitely not approve of Micky. I was always going to be her Michael. We were like most in the area, poor and living in a small cottage in Laud Street, central Croydon. We had no hot water with an outside loo and frost on the windows inside in the winter. Laud Street was going to play a part in my non-league football career and also linked with a local football legend. Dad worked in a local timber sawmill, so we were never short of logs for the fire. Mum did house cleaning for a local GP and also worked in the laundry at a local hairdresser's and made the coffees for clients.

Sport was always around me, football more than any other, and Dad knew some household names who used to come in and have a cup of tea or something stronger. As kids in those days, anyone whom your parents knew very well was called uncle or aunty. One of those was footballer Pat Sayward, Aston Villa, who played in the 1957 cup final when they beat the Man. Utd. Busby Babes. It is the only time I have ever seen an F.A. Cup winner's medal, as he brought it home to show Dad. He also went on to manage Brighton. There was Roy Law, who was

Great Britain and England amateur international and holds the record appearances for Wimbledon. Again, little did I know that Wimbledon would play a part in my football career at some stage. From the boxing world, Albert Finch, British middleweight champion would visit us. All this was okay and I felt really top-drawer with these kinds of sportsmen around, but not being able to afford a pair of football boots, football never really got to me until that sad event in 1958. Dad brought me up to look after myself. This was to serve me greatly in my non-league and managerial non-league football career. Most boys down our street had bigger brothers to sort out any problems but as an only child, I got by and had a happy childhood. Dad would go to football on Saturday afternoons and watch his beloved Chelsea, but would watch other games when Chelsea were away. Dad was a good player at half-back and played for one of the best Sunday league teams in the country during the 50s. They came from Croydon and were named Heath Utd. Their home ground was Duppas Hill, bottom pitch no.1. There would be 3-4 people deep round the touchline on Sunday mornings, and occasionally on a Sunday afternoon, when they would play on the top pitch. Dad used to tell me that Roy Law's brother, Les Law was better than Roy, but not that interested in a football career, but he rated him as the best centre forward he had ever seen. Rumour had it that some sides would turn up on a Sunday morning to play Heath Utd. at Duppas Hill and if Les was playing, they would get dressed and leave and not play the game. Getting back to Heath Utd., Roy Law, the England captain and Wimbledon player would turn out now and again to play and also Brian Driscoll, who also was a friend of Dad's and went on to sign for Crystal Palace. Little did I know at the time that the name Heath and the name Les would play a very big part in my life as a non-league player/manager.

So, I guess it really looked like I was destined to buy a ticket for the non-league roller coaster ride that would go on and on.

I did not know the unforeseen circumstances that were going to lead me to buy my ticket. It was then, on 7th of February 1958, the day after the tragic Munich air crash, that I saw this strong man, my dad, who loved his football and all sport, starting to cry at the news of this terrible disaster. What I did not know at the time was that on the Saturday before Munich, he had seen the Busby Babes play Arsenal at Highbury in a thrilling game of football which the Babes won (ticket, I think, courtesy of Pat Sayward). So, it was then that I thought, what is this game of football that can have so much power over such a strong man? That is when I bought my ticket. Not on the ride yet, that comes later. You can buy a ticket for anything, but you choose when and whether you want to use it. Although I played some football over the park I was never into it as much as I was my swimming, but I did get involved in organised football from then on with my primary school team (Howard), and when I put my shirt on for the school team with pride, I knew that I was now about to board the roller coaster because everything else in my young childhood, including my swimming, was going to have to be sacrificed.

But before the swimming took a back seat to football, I still managed to be Croydon Borough champion and also got picked to swim for my county (Surrey). I was even entered for the national trials at Blackpool but the extensive training for both swimming and football was so hard, and as I have said, one had to go. Perhaps I chose the wrong sport, who knows, but all I know is that football was to win the day. Football was a team game and you could share defeat as well as glory together, unlike the swimming where, apart from relay races, you were on your own, no one to blame but yourself for losing, but self-glory for winning.

Anyway, back to football and my Saturday nights with Dad watching Match of the Day and listening to my dad's comments on the coverage of games that consisted of all of 10 minutes of the best highlights. Comments were normally aimed at the poor old ref (little did I know then that the referee was going to play a very big part in my non-league career). There were some great old-fashioned football sayings like, 'drop the shoulder and take him on', 'should have crossed the ball earlier', 'he headed that like it was a bag of cement', 'he can't trap a rat, let alone a ball', 'in the penalty area, stay on your feet and finish', 'next time you foul me, make sure I can't get up', and 'he never read that ball but then, he would have a job to read a newspaper'. It was all great fun but bringing me to love the game more and more. The day every young footballer craves came to me in the shape of non-league football. Don't forget, I had been watching Match of the Day for a while and when Dad said we were going to see uncle Roy Law play for Wimbledon, I expected this huge stadium with a large crowd, but no, not any of that was I going to see, just a ground with a couple of stands, some cover, and terracing with leaning rails. Comparing it with Match of the Day, it was a small crowd as well, but I was seeing possibly the best non-league club in the country and a crowd so passionate you could have been at any football league club, but I was at Plough Lane and about to fall in love with non-league football as well. I can't remember the exact date, but it was early 1958/9 season and the opposition was Oxford City, but it was great to see (uncle) Roy Law playing and being cheered on by the crowd. The player who stood out for me that day was a player called Eddie Reynolds, built like a brick wall and could head a ball like a bullet being fired from a gun. In fact, when Wimbledon beat Sutton United at Wembley and uncle Roy the captain lifted the amateur cup Eddie Reynolds was to set a record never to be broken as yet, he scored 4 goals and they were all with his head).

Anyway, back to the game I was watching. Wimbledon won the game and I thought if I could play at this level, I would be happy, and also get a couple of bob in my pocket which the players in the Wimbledon team were getting in the famous brown envelope (they called it boot money). Little did I know then that Wimbledon was going to play some role in my football years including returning to that same old Plough Lane with my son Daniel in 1988 to see Man. United not in a cup game but a league game. No non-league club will ever achieve that again I'm sure of that. Going back to my first visit don't forget I had only just turned 10 years old, and it would be another 3 years before I returned to Plough Lane then with dad. It was the 1961/2 season and they had signed a player from Dulwich Hamlet called Les brown. Little did I know again that Les was, in later years, going to be a big influence on my playing and managerial years, but all I knew was that I was now truly on the ride having used my ticket.

The next stage in my life was to take my 11 plus exam and you guessed it, I failed (shame the questions had not been about football or swimming I would have passed it hands down). So, it was then a change from primary to secondary modern senior school. The nearest school for me was St. Andrews at the bottom of Laud Street in Croydon and the boys I played out in the street with were all going there, but Dad insisted that I went to Tavistock School for Boys, as he possibly thought my brains were in my boots, my fist, my arms/legs and to be fair, when I went for the school interview, the headmaster, Mr Silburn, only asked how good was I at all the sports, football, boxing, swimming, cricket, not one mention of my English, maths, geography, history. I knew then this was going to be just right for me; a sporting school and the boys were from a district known in the town as Bang Hole and I knew a lot of them. Priorities first, I had to get into the school football team and have trials, as there were some very tasty first-year boys that could play a bit, and as you know, if you make the school team in the first year, you would normally go through to the fourth year before you left to go out in the big wide world to earn your living. The school was a tough place to be and you soon learnt how to look after yourself, as Dad had taught me early in my life. There were some very good remarks about the school. Some I remember very well, like 'Tavistock approved school for hooligans', 'Tavistock teaches common sense, not education', but the best was 'the school at least managed to produce 2 boys to progress to Oxford and 2 to Cambridge.... but of course, it was Oxford City F.C. and Cambridge City F.C. I made it okay in the football trials, despite my height of 5ft 3in, and was in the school team in the only position made for me - a right-winger with pace. I could take a player on and more importantly, could cross a ball so well we used to put a stick in the penalty area during practice and I could cross and hit the stick, such was my accuracy. In the first season, 26 goals in 16 games I felt was okay. We had a very good team and a centre forward called Harry (H) Worthington, who was utter class, and some other classy players too. You see, we never had any other football, so school football was the only organised game of the week. You were hungry to play; the only problem was so were all the other schools and competition was top class with both Lanfranc Boys School and Ashburton Boys being very good. The problem we had, though, was no teacher knew enough about football to educate us in formations, but the teacher who came forward to give up his Saturday mornings was history teacher, Mr Saddlebank. He was a real laugh and confessed that he did not know much and we all knew how to play so we were just to get on with it. The half-time refreshment for the team was a Polo mint (the one with the hole in the middle). What that was meant to do heaven knows; maybe he thought we had bad breath. We never had proper referees so he used to do our home games. The trouble was, he was as blind as a bat and could hardly see any of the play at all, but in general, we were all brought up to be fairly honest, so the games flowed okay until one Saturday morning.

We were playing Ingram School at home at Wandle Park, West Croydon, just beyond the slaughterhouse, that was still in use, when all of a sudden, this bull comes charging through the park gates with the men in brown coats and wellies chasing the animal. He headed towards the pitch and both teams scattered for safety until it was caught over by the bowling green. He was led back to face his fate and we resumed our game after another Polo mint. Despite this incident, I still loved the strip we were in, our colours of maroon shirts white collar, white shorts, maroon and white hooped socks. Mum had to wash that and we had to take it back by Tuesday at the latest, but we used it on the Sunday, playing over the park before it got washed. It was quite a sight to see so many different school colours on the Sunday. This book is all about non-league football and I won't, therefore, bore you with my education so I will pass that by. The first year went by so quick and we were no longer the newcomers to the big school and I soon realised that this wonderful game football brings you many friends and some enemies, but not many of them over the years. That is why I loved school for those reasons and the team was getting stronger without being coached. We coached ourselves playing the 'W' formation, which suited my position as a winger. Let me explain the system in brief. You had a centre forward, left and right-winger, two deeper players known as inside forwards right and left, behind them half-backs who played narrow, and then behind them three full-backs, one central and one right and left, who were wider out. This was a good system which worked well; it was just the poor inside forwards who had to do the fetching and carrying. So, as I said, we were getting stronger and being noticed as individuals to play for Croydon schools but none of us made it that year and despite being such a good side, we still never won anything on the football pitch. We won all the boxing, cricket, and swimming championships, but no football title. All of that held no meaning at all when something happened that would remain with me forever and with the town of Croydon and all of its schools. The horrific news came that a plane carrying Lanfranc School pupils on the 9th of August 1961 had crashed in Norway, killing 34 of our fellow pupils and 2 teachers. I say the word 'fellow' because we had played sport together between the schools and I myself knew some of the boys. So it was that terrible Man. United air crash disaster in Munich in February 1958 some three and half years earlier that had brought me into the football world and I now had a situation that left me wondering at such a young age, 13, why should things like this happen? It was a lesson in sadness for me, as I was going to have to deal with this at times in my life.

'Move on we must' is the motto so back to the school football and I got picked for Croydon schools which made Mum and Dad proud, but still no medals in school football, so maybe Croydon schools would do that for me. I was a good winger and we had a centre forward (Bobby Houghton) who could put the ball away if I could get it in to him, but despite this, not much of a run in the English schools' trophy. Bobby, though, went on to have a great football career, mainly in coaching, managing Malmo to the European cup final against Mr Brian Clough's Nottingham Forest despite losing to a single goal from Trevor Francis. As I write this book, I think he his chief coach of the Indian national team. So, time moved on again and I was preparing for work and the school team also, but Saturday junior football was starting up and this was to be the real beginning for me in non-league. Upon leaving school at the age of 15 years old, I took up a joinery apprenticeship. Others found work in Surrey Street market and the building game. This was 1963 and now the roller coaster gets going at pace. We kept in touch and a few of the Tavistock School team decided to join a proper organised team.

CHAPTER TWO

Work hard, play hard and rewards will come.

Well, this is what I had been waiting 5 years for, working, and the chance for training, and playing proper organised non-league football with my first club, Woodside Juniors. They had some of the Tavistock School side in their team and were very good players and I felt at home there. Our home ground was Ashburton playing fields, which had changing rooms (great to have a shower as we never had a bathroom at home and only one cold water tap). We also had goal nets which, to me, was like playing a cup final. I felt so important. My good friend, Steve Kember, was making his way up the ladder with Crystal Palace. He took his chance, grabbed it with both hands, and I wish it could have been me, but I had to get on with what was put in front of me and make the best of it. So, in the 1964/5 season, we played in the Croydon Minor Combination League and at 15 years old, I was raring to go and win my first trophy at football. I had plenty of them for swimming and even one for Croydon schools' cricket championship, last to bat of course and fielding on the boundary.

So, on to the football and my first season got going. I must say that I found it fairly easy with the good players around me (but I did not miss the Polo mint at half time). The segment of orange was much better. We played the easy 'W' formation that all of the boys had played at school and being a winger, as I did in my school days, it was simple, beat the man and cross the ball for the centre forward to finish off. Quite simple if you had a good one, and in Harry Worthington, we had the best around. He went on to score at least 30 plus goals in that season. A lot came off my accurate crossing and with myself chipping in with around 15 goals during that season, it blew me away with the football we played. It was only a league of ten teams, but we had won three games before the season finished and my first football plaque was to sit proudly on the shelf at home in the front room with that word 'winners' engraved upon it. The one thing I was sure of was that Mum and Dad always did the brass on Sunday and always included my plaque. Despite being a joinery apprentice, I had saved some money (thanks to Mum and Dad) and being an only child, I was able to go to Jersey that summer with a couple of the players from the team, Keith Dixon, and Andy Shuttle. It was there that I met a blonde-haired gorgeous girl called Lynne. She came from Gomersal near Cleckheaton, Yorkshire and her dad was involved in football and got me a trial with Huddersfield Town Juniors. I played against Bury and Halifax Town Juniors (then a football league side). I did quite well during these trials and they were interested in taking me on as an apprentice, (god knows how I would have got out of my joinery apprenticeship) but no need to worry, our relationship did not last that long and with it went my chance to be a professional footballer. Although she gave me the experience to love a woman more than football, this was soon to be a forgotten episode in my life. So, the 1965/66 season was upon us and after my venture up north, I re-joined Woodside Juniors way after the start of the season, but soon got back into the side and those couple of games at Huddersfield Town had given me more confidence. At Woodside Juniors, having won the league title the season before, we were not performing so well as a side and there were comings and goings with players committed to finding jobs and of course, becoming involved with girlfriends. Despite this downturn in our league form, it is funny what the cup can do to a team and how they are performing in the league, and that was exactly how it turned out to be. So much so, that we had knocked out the better sides in earlier rounds and found ourselves at the semi-final of the Croydon Minor League Cup. We considered our opposition to be inferior to us but what was to happen before the game was quite unbelievable.

On the Friday night before the Saturday semi-final, most of the team went out to celebrate reaching the final in a game that we had not even played, and in those days, not too many questions were asked if you were slightly underage for a drink. As it turned out, one of the player's friend's dad was the owner of a pub in West Norwood and we were allowed to get merry. That is exactly what we did and despite being 17 years of age, it was my first experience at being absolutely drunk. So drunk that when I got home on the no. 68 bus, I had a job to find my home in Laud Street, Croydon. I remember banging on the door and Dad answering it and laughing at my situation. I managed to get up to bed and prepare myself for the semi-final some 14 hours away. When I woke up after the room had spun round several times, it was mid-morning on the Saturday and I can remember thinking what have I done? How could I be so foolish with such an important game? But after a cold-water splash-down in the garden, I prepared myself for the semi-final. As it turned out, we really did not have to sober up at all. We were so good and so disciplined in our football (if not in our preparation), we went out and spanked our opponents 6-1. I remember having a shower after the game and going home and sleeping right round until Monday morning and facing my day at work. We were in my first cup final and learning, as all young people do, not to drink on a Friday night when playing football on the Saturday, and certainly not to that extent, whether playing football or not.

Before I get to tell you about the final, I don't know how but somewhere I have missed out my trip with Woodside Albion to Holland. That was the first time I had left England to go to a foreign country, let alone to play football. The squad was a mixture of young players and older players. I was sixteen at the time and a bit wet behind the ears, so I bought into the experience. The idea was that we were meant to go and live in with Dutch families, two players together. I was assured by our secretary, Dickie Dell, that would be the case and I would be sharing with a young guest player from Crystal Palace, who I knew well through my uncle (Tubby Harrington). The boy's name was Duncan McLane and he was going to be a good boost for the squad and myself during our week's stay, and playing in a tournament plus a couple of tour games. We left on a wet and windy Friday night on the coach to Dover and boarded the boat to Ostend. The team bus was going to be with us all week, which was great. We did have a problem on the crossing as one of the older members of the squad, Micky Pendercast, had just a little more to drink than he could handle and when the boat docked in Ostend, he was told that in that state he could not enter Belgium and would have to go back to England. That was a good start but we had to carry on to Holland and arrived around Saturday lunchtime in the Hague. We were all somewhat tired and met the families at a football clubhouse where we were going to all meet up again that evening. We were given our lodgings but they split me and Duncan up and I was taken on my own with people I had never met before, and taken to a part of the city behind a church and up some stairs to a flat. I was given the attic room that, would you believe, overlooked the Russian embassy with armed guards everywhere. I had no mobile phone in those days and to be honest, I was quite upset and a bit scared. I came to Holland to play football and found myself in what seemed to me to be a serious situation. I remember being called down from my room to have something to eat (I was not only scared but bloody starving). When I got to the dining room, the family made it quite clear that prayers were to be said before having our food. Not that I had a problem with that, it just was not something we did at home and I found it strange. If what I had put in front of me was food, then I was going to starve to death by the end of the week. I was strictly a typical English young lad who had chips with everything, eggs, sausages, spam fritters, corned beef, and a good old Sunday roast, so the meat stew with chocolate sprinkled over the top was not going down my gullet well. So, I just said I wasn't hungry and went back to my room and waited for the call to get into the car and make our way back to the football clubhouse and meet Duncan and the players. They must have thought that I was not happy as I took my belongings with me. Well, I can tell you, this was non-league football and can you think of a pro putting up with what I had just been through? I called over Dickie Dell and others of the committee and told them that if I was not put with Duncan, I would go to the British embassy and demand to be taken home. The family I was with felt insulted by my behaviour, but I got what I had been promised and was put with Duncan and in a very nice house with decent food. I was told by the committee there and then that when we got back to England, I would be reprimanded by the club for showing no respect. I told them exactly what my dad used to say, a happy player would be a good player, and during our week's stay in Holland, this was proved to be right. Despite having a niggly corn on top of my right little toe, I had a very good tournament, scoring a couple of goals, and my usual accurate crossing was getting us goals. We played every other day on top of the other couple of friendlies that had been arranged. We won the tournament, which was great, but we were no match for the other two sides. However, against a side from the Hague, we only lost with a late goal, I remember. The biggest football talking point of the week was our last game of the tour, a visit to a club called F.C. Breda. When we turned up on the team bus, we saw this stadium and thought we were going to play outside on one of the training pitches, but no, we were all thrilled to bits to be playing in such a big stadium and people paying to get in the ground to watch us. Well now, I thought of that poor old bull being led back to the slaughterhouse during the game against Ingram School at Wandle Park, as I felt we would meet the same fate. We were going to get slaughtered and we did, but we did manage to score as they rattled in seven goals past us and they were trying hard not to score any more (how decent of them). When they asked how we had got on in the F.A. cup, I did not like to tell them we had only just been entered into the Croydon Minor Combination League Cup, but I left the committee to get out of that one. So, the tour was over and now I had to go home. What a nightmare at Dover that was. At customs, we got the new shift on, so they were lively. They boarded the team bus, got the laundry baskets out which had the used kit in, bounced all our practice balls, took away some of the players' duty-free goods. I remember one of the players having to give back a bottle of whisky, which he promptly dropped so that the customs officer could not have it. All of this delayed us, but the tour had been worthwhile and some good experience in life outside of football as well. It was then time to get back to work at the joinery shop and face the outcome of the Woodside Albion committee on my behaviour in Holland. The club decided to keep it internal and give me a suspension, but I was suspended pending my future behaviour. It was more like they did not want to lose their small but clever winger and nor did the team. So, the roller coaster was just pretty well at a snail's pace after what had happened at school, and with more downs than ups, but there is plenty of time left on this ride so let's carry on.

Back to the Croydon Minor Combination cup final, and the venue was going to be Croydon arena in May 1966. I think there was another final that year as well; I remember it was England v West Germany and I certainly did not think that on my 70th year we still would not have seen them in the final again, let alone winning the World Cup. To be fair, some of the world's top footballing countries have not won it at all (Holland springs to mind).

Anyway, back to our cup final, Woodside Juniors v Mount Rovers, and despite the poor playing surface at the Croydon arena, we had such a good side that we could have played them on a rubbish tip. We beat them 3-1 and with that came my first cup winners' medal. What I do remember is that my mum kept trying to wave to me during the game and expecting me to wave back, God bless her! Some of the team, including myself, went to Margate for a holiday after England's world cup victory over the Germans. We stayed at Andy Shuttles mum's bed and breakfast in Reading Street near Margate. There was myself, Phil Quickenden, and John Fiffe. We had a great time, and I was contemplating my future playing where there was no youth football for me anymore, only the big boys' game, and what level could I play at. I was confident in my own ability, but the World Cup success for England meant that my usual wing position was going to change. As we know, Alf Ramsey adopted a new formation of 4-3-1-2, which all clubs followed (or tried to) at all levels. This meant us orthodox wingers were now going to have to put in a hard shift, tracking back, defending, then up the line to a wing position as soon as the ball changed hands. Well okay, you could cheat at park football level, but as I was to find out very soon, that was not going to happen in senior football. As if by chance really, one of the Woodside players, Keith Dixon, lived in Oval Road and in the same road was a player whose name I can't remember but what I do remember was he asked me to play for a local team called simply Power Sammers and their home ground was at a pitch called Acan Tab (ended up years later as Croydon Athletic's ground, Mayfields). So, I played on the Saturday and I did well enough for me to be asked to play again, but on a Wednesday. I told them I couldn't play on afternoons, but the manager's reply was astonishing, to say the least. He said it was a 7.30 pm kick-off and we were playing a team that had just joined the league, that club being Crystal Palace third team at Selhurst Park in a Surrey Combination League Cup pool (d). I was thrilled to bits to play there, even if the crowd was very small. We lost the game 2-1, but my best kept secret is that I scored that goal under lights at Selhurst Park. Can you imagine premiership clubs allowing those games to go on today in their cathedrals of football? Not a chance for us non-league players but I could not help thinking of my friend, Steve Kember, playing there regularly for Crystal Palace first team in front of crowds of more than 35,000. Was I jealous? Of course I was. Funny thing though, I had my day and played a few more games in a strong league and found out what pace and hard work were all about in football before I called it a day and went back to play again with my mates.

Anyway, the Woodside Juniors' side was to split up and some of us started to play for the men's first team. It was during this period I came across a footballer by the name Mick Whally, a real strong Manchester-born centre half. I became great friends with Mick and he finally got his just reward when he was invited to play for Millwall reserves in a game at the Old Den. It was a floodlit game and the opposition was Charlton Athletic reserves. Well, poor Mick collided with the post in attacking a cross from the opposition, and in doing so, broke his nose. He was taken off to New Cross Hospital and underwent surgery the following day. Some of the team went up to see him the following day, but we were soon shown the door by the sister who did not approve of chewing gum or four of us around the bed (how things have changed). Nowadays, you could take in a pet python onto the ward and no one would bat an eyelid. Mick recovered and went back to Manchester and signed for Bury in the football league and I lost touch with him after that.

Also, something was not right for me at Woodside and I decided to leave and play a bit of Sunday football while I tried to sort my football head out. It was then that one of my mates, who was also serving a joinery apprenticeship at Brixton School of Building, Pat Clayton, asked me if I would play Saturday football with him in the Redhill league for a pub side called the Clifton Arms from Caterham. It was okay and it made a change; different grounds and new friends, but a funny thing happened after a game one Saturday. I was approached to play for a Sunday side called Griffin Albion (from Merstham) and there was mention of money to be paid per game. Well, I can tell you now that I was taken aback being possibly one of the first players around that area to be in that position. It did not last long and I was on my toes and away to answer an advert for Sunday players in our local paper (the Croydon Advertiser) from Waddon Athletic Sunday team. They say fate plays a part along the way and this was fate. I met two players there, Peter Tyrrell (goalkeeper) and Ray McDermott, who were playing at Bromley at the time, or at least having trials. I asked them if it was possible for me to join them provided that they asked the manager, who was Micky Ackland. He told them to bring me along and he would take a look at me in training and small-sided games. Imagine how I felt, turning up for training at this stadium with floodlights, stand, terracing. It was like when I first went to Wimbledon with Dad some 8 years earlier, and for me, that was a new beginning and truly non-league football at its best and the roller coaster was on the up ………

CHAPTER THREE

Senior non-league football - a shock to the system.

I thought I had at long last made a breakthrough in my football roller coaster, and was sure in my mind that I was not going back to Saturday park football again as a player, and I was going to train hard and take my chance having arrived at Bromley F.C. through fate really. I knew two of their players, Peter and Ray, who got me a trial, so I thought okay, training for a couple of weeks and then a run out in the reserves. It was now the 1968/9 season and I was getting on for the ripe old age of 21 years old. When you think of that in today's football terms, and how young they start, they would have been playing since the age of seven and have been in their 12th year of competitive football, I'm not sure that is right; and will the kids burn themselves out? Only time will tell. So, arriving for my first training session and getting changed in the main stand, I felt great but had to be advised on footwear, which I thought very strange. Good job I had trainers and boots, because then comes the kick up the arse. We left the changing room and proceeded to the car park behind the covered terrace. The floodlights had been turned round so that we could train on the gravel, which was uninspiring, to say the least, but manager Micky Ackland and coaching staff tried to do the best they could, however, our chairman/secretary, Chas King, did not want us on the pitch or having the floodlights in full use, but when he was away on one of his May cruises, we trained on the pitch and had small-sided games. This was my first encounter with a non-league chairman, and there were many chairmen to come my way over the years that followed. It came as a big surprise to me when my boss, Micky, took us into the stadium. I thought it was to use the pitch because Chas King was away, but my joy was short-lived as we were made to do doggies up and down the terracing, forwards and back steps, using the leaning rails to do stretches, and after that we had to use the small cinder path round the pitch to do our running, walk one width and sprint the length of the pitch, jog one width then sprint one length and jog one width again until the ultimate was to sprint the whole pitch! This went on for at least three weeks, Tuesdays and Thursdays, and not a sniff of a game (good job I was playing some Sunday football to keep match fit). I felt like the bionic man but had to be patient. Until my name went up on the Thursday night team sheet, it was like a sentence of hard labour for me, but I knew that when my chance came, I would be fit enough to take it. That chance did come on January the 14th 1969, away in the reserve side to a team called Borough Green in the Kent Senior cup 1st round. Well, I did not know what to expect but it turned out to be a bloody nightmare. When we arrived there on the team bus, we were too early and we had to go into a pub (no alcohol allowed) and then they started to rope the pitch off as the fog began to creep in. Despite that, it was a great win, with us overcoming all the odds to win the game 2-0, so as they say, job done! The following Saturday, we played Callanders Athletic in the Kent Amateur League at their ground in Erith, with its small stand and roped-off pitch, with a playing surface that was like a bowling green, even the build-up was great. With a qualified physio doing rub downs, my legs felt great. I also learned the valuable lesson of Vaseline over the eyebrows to stop the sweat running into the eyes, and also on the knees to stop any studs cutting the knee cap. I never wore shin pads at all; I liked to be free, and for that, I would have to take my chances against some ruthless defenders, let me tell you. Now, the training paid off because the game was played at high tempo and I coped with it quite well and had my lion's share of the ball, despite the new systems being adapted since Sir Alf Ramsey's England won the World Cup. I was no longer the winger of leisure, but a workhorse for my full back, which I think I have mentioned before in the book on the system changes, but when you have in your side ex, ex Gillingham and Millwall players, it brings out the best in you and you bloody did what they demanded of you. The game ended in a 3-3 draw, in which I scored and made one (they call it assist now), but what was to stand out for me was that they had some old player playing up top, and what pace and strength he had. I was to learn, only after the game, that it was Roy Dwight, aged 36 years old who broke his leg playing for Nottingham Forest in 1959 against Luton Town in the F.A. cup final which made history. Forest won 2-1 and became the first team ever to win the F.A. cup with ten men, so this was the company I was in now, worlds apart from what I had known and the roller coaster was taking me to heights I had never known at senior level. Remember though, I had a good friend in Steve Kember, whose grandfather lived in my street, Laud Street, and Steve was doing great at Crystal Palace, gaining greatness with each game he played. So, in some respects, I was not so excited about these players with pro status who were to play against me. X Well, the manager was pleased with me after my first game and the local paper, the Bromley Times, referred to me as the Bromley Bill Bremner (don't know if it was my size or ability). A couple of weeks later, the word about the club in the reserves was the game against Cray Wanderers away, at their old ground, Grassmeade, in a league game in mid-January 1969, and in their line up, they had ex-Bromley player, Ray McDermont. In front of a large and intimidating crowd, for the first time, I was given a man-marking role on one of their better players. Being the size I am, I had to make first contact and send him flying with a tackle from behind on the heavily sanded pitch. It brought me a telling off from the ref but made the crowd go on a hate trip against me, but I loved being centre of attention and kept to my task throughout the game. On corners, it was zonal marking and I had my zone okay, but with seconds to go, Cray got a corner and delivered it out of my zone so the player who I had marked so well was not picked up in another zone and got the winner with his head. And who got the blame for the goal? Well, it could only be me; I was not happy but took it on the chin and looked forward to the next game. I had to hope my name was on the team sheet come Thursday, as I was desperate to play at home and under the floodlights. I was so glad to see my name on the team sheet after training, giving me the chance to face Stansfield in the Kent Amateur League. This was to be my home debut and it needed to go well on Saturday to catch the eye of the home supporters. Micky Ackland, my first team manager, was searching for some new blood as we were flirting near the bottom of the table, so a chance may be there. Although, is it good to come into a team that is low on confidence and morale and to some extent low on class? Well, it makes sense really with what they call a no brainer. You either try to impress with a side who were at the top and chances would be very limited, or you went with a side that were at the bottom of the league and get a chance far quicker. I decided to stay with Bromley and the chance of first-team football, but for the time being, it was reserves and the Kent Floodlight cup, and because of the position I was playing in as a winger which then became a wide midfield role (similar to what it is today), again I state it was bloody hard work. At our ground at Hayes Lane, there was a large clock situated in the middle of the main stand, which had the tunnel to the pitch and the changing rooms with showers and a bath that looked like a swimming pool. They used to start filling it up just as we went out for the second half because both the reserve team and first-team manager's tactics/ team talk would never have been heard over the noise of the taps running! Teams were only allowed 1 substitute and I was a sub for the game against Leytonstone and was over the moon to be in the dressing room with the full first team and all the trimmings that went with it. I must have warmed up so many times when the manager thought there was a bad injury, but in those days, players were built to withstand anything the opposition was to throw at them. During the second half, I was about to discover the tough world of top non-league football. The game was flowing end to end, I was picking up some passes wide to me and I was delivering the perfect cross, but another aspect in wide areas in the attacking play was for me to take throw-ins and being on the small side, it was not going to be a long throw, more a throw to the nearest white shirt. So, with the ball firmly behind my head and shoulders, from out of nowhere came an elbow to my face which connected with my jaw. Despite the blood flowing from my mouth, out came the instructions from the linesman to "get the ball in play or I'll give it to the other side". I thought of the other side; okay, if you can dish it out, be prepared to have it back in some form of revenge. The game ended quite sedately, really, and I can remember looking at that bloody clock on the main stand and praying for the game to finish. I had done well in my short time at Bromley but a strange thing was about to happen to me, which concerned my dear old mum who I idolised. I didn't know she had been tapped up by the chairman of Whyteleafe F.C., Ted (senior)Robinson, who had the antique shop in Laud Street and was always asking her to get me at the Leafe, so much so that Mum kept on at me to at least talk to him about the club. I found out during our discussions why he was known as Ted senior; it was because his son, Ted Robinson (junior) was playing at the Leafe. I remembered asking him why he wanted me to come and play when his first team were going so well in the Surrey Senior League. He said to me, "We need a wide right-sided player as cover". He also told me I would have to take a cut in money. I thought, 'Well, there is hardly any money for me at Bromley anyway, and most of that went on expenses to get to the ground to meet the bus. I also had to share a taxi home with Ray and Peter when we had long trips in the Kent Floodlit cup and would arrive back on the team bus to Hayes Lane quite late, as there were no motorways then. So, I decided to leave Bromley, but I would take with me the experience I had gained there from some very talented young players like, in particular, Roy Deadman, Ray Scrivens, and some older heads that had played at pro level. The big-time feeling was great but I must say the dressing room atmosphere in the first team and reserves was very dull in terms of 'let's get the job done and go home'. There was none of the camaraderie I was about witness in my next few non-league years, still with a good standard of team and players but I was coming up to my 21st birthday. Regarding football, I needed to decide what direction I was going to take. Work was okay as I had finished my apprenticeship and was now a master joiner, but was the non-league roller coaster going to stop for repairs................?

CHAPTER FOUR

Repairs completed - Whyteleafe and Addiscombe Social, here I come! 1969/74

By the way, the repairs to the roller coaster were completed and off we went again. As the saying goes, 'Mums are always right', but I thought the jury's out on the move to Whyteleafe. Only time will tell, but I did leave Bromley and there was one main reason, and I have to say that it was not about how Mum felt. If you remember, earlier in the book, I mentioned that Dad took me to watch Wimbledon at Plough Lane and they had just signed Les Brown from Dulwich Hamlet, and how our paths would cross some years on, well that time had come. Les was player/manager at Whyteleafe so I had to go and be introduced to him. What an instant impression he made on me! Big and strong with a great smile, he explained to me that because the first team were doing very well in the league and cup, my chances that year were going to be limited during the season, but he saw me as a prospect for the future and I had expected that. At least the first and second team trained together, just like at Bromley. He also introduced me to the second team manager, Colin Grimshaw (ex-Arsenal and Crystal Palace player) who also impressed me. Colin's team talks in the dressing room before the games were something special as he had a great football knowledge coupled with a great sense of humour. He used to start by saying "The midfield will be Freeman, Hardy, and Willis., full-backs Lilly and Skinner and up front, Bootsy and

Snudge" (I think only the older people reading this book will know these names). "Also, lads, I want you to play a fast game and get it over early as I am going out tonight, and let's have a result, win, lose or draw." He also used some classics as well; "Keep the high balls lo, and in passing, I want you to give it before you get it." (Think about that one)! It was a wonder after that lot we were able to talk tactics. So, it was to be then, after some training sessions, that I was to pull on that green shirt, white shorts and green socks and make my Whyteleafe reserve team debut on my 21st birthday in 1969 at home to Frimley Green. Dad made it to the game and, as ever, he was giving me instructions. He had no need to, as Colin Grimshaw had already told me what he expected of me, and I tell you what, I did not disappoint, as I had a stormer of a game , getting past my full-back, getting crosses in and then, the icing on the cake, got past my full back again and went for goal, cutting in and unleashing a shot that flew past the keeper and into the top left-hand corner of the net. Dad was behind that goal on the terrace and I can still see the look on his face as he clapped his hands. It was after the games we played that it kicked in for me; the thing that was missing at Bromley was the camaraderie among the players, especially at home. Some non-league fans will agree with this and some won't, but at Whyteleafe it was like one big family, including the supporters, first team and reserve team. Everyone was always around after a game having a drink and food. Sure, I believe that if you, as a player, don't put your shift in, then you deserve nothing; not every team can win all the time. I think you are tested best when you lose and it's down to how you react and cope with it. That is the same in life as a whole. Les Brown and Colin Grimshaw brought that to the table and although the first team were fairly settled with their title-winning and cup run, new players started to arrive. Many of them I ring up or meet with, even now at seventy years old. The first team went on to win the league title but unfortunately, they lost in the cup final at Walton and Hersham and were denied the double, so the 1968/9 season saw many doors open and some close on my playing career. So, it was with great optimism that after a good run in what now was becoming a very good reserve side, I was looking forward to the 1969/70 season and the beginning of pre-season under the guidance of player/manager Les Brown, who told us at a pre-season meeting, "there are no first-team players here; only training and warm-up games will determine who starts the season in the first or the reserves, along with the players who were asked to leave the club because they were considered not good enough". You see, all of Les Brown's words, and to some extent, Colin Grimshaw's, were going towards my thinking about when, or if, I would ever take up managing a non-league senior tea. Pre-season was as I thought it might be; very tough, as I had never started one with Whyteleafe and I knew of Les Brown's reputation for fitness. Of course, he was player /manager then, so he had to get fit as well, so off we would go up Whyteleafe Hill to the top, then down Salmons Lane, over the railway crossing and along the A22 to the big Caterham roundabout that had a sunken centre with passageways for pedestrians to get under this busy road. There were four entrances and Les would chalk each one with a colour and the teams were told which passageway they must score in (great fun but sometimes a bit confusing). As you know, us footballers have our brains in our boots, and some girls would say that we had our other asset in there as well, if you did not do the business! During these training sessions, Les would always finish it with the same words when he had the ball near to goal - "next goal wins!" Also, I can see him now in his shorts that were one half striped and the other plain. He also had different coloured socks on and his old Wimbledon top. After the session, it was the same routine; back to the stadium, shower, have a pint and a chat, and the one night I will never forget, as you may recall you read earlier in the book, it was announced our first pre-season game at home was to play one of the best non-league teams around which was Wimbledon. Their massive centre forward, called John O'Mara, was 6ft 3 and he could put it about as well as score goals. He went on to score 50 goals in 124 games in his time at Wimbledon; not a bad ratio. He had been at a few pro clubs as well, so you can imagine how I felt when the team sheet went up and there I was, going to play against uncle Roy. Dad was going to be there with Mum and some mates in what was a very large crowd, most of which were Wimbledon supporters coming to get a look at their team for the coming season. They were far too good for us in every department, but I had a fairly good game despite being short of service to the wide areas. This Wimbledon was more direct, playing straight up to the big man O'Mara. We lost 6-1, but I do take credit for crossing for Les to score against his old club, but Wimbledon will turn up again later in my book in another turn of fate. I was getting used to signing autographs at the Leafe, and before at Bromley as well, and that is why still to this day, my signature is near impossible to read. Funny, really, the young fans really thought we were important enough to sign their books and write a message...... Playing Wimbledon was, after all, a game in preparation for the coming season, and let me tell you now, that if any non-league or any other football fan dare think that the Surrey Senior League was a weak league, I can assure you that some of the sides in that premier league 1969/70 would have been able to at least hold their own in the national south or national north leagues of today, and the introduction of a premier and first division made competition even stronger, with the likes of Bracknell Town, Malden Town, Westfield, our local rivals, Merstham. Also, some of the previous season's championship-winning side had left but with that brought an influx of new players who would you believe, have kept in touch and celebrated my various birthdays for some 50 years now. Some of them were at my 70th birthday this year, 2018, and like my 60th and 65th, all played at Whyteleafe's ground (which now has a 3G surface).

These were players like Micky Bannatyne, John Davidson, John Comoford, Eddie Mark, Roy Kilby, Micky Vaughan, Steve (Shovel) Showler and John (Fingers) Kennedy, but there was one player that was going to stand out for all kinds of reasons during my 4-year stay at the club. His name was Barry Smith. When I parted company with the club, I was never to see him again and to this day I don't know whether he is still alive. Of course, all the other players mentioned were going to remain my friends until this day, but Smithy was a typical old-fashioned centre forward who was as brave as a lion and in order to put the ball in the net, he went into areas that players today would not go near, and in that Surrey Senior League that took some doing. The near post and far post did not exist to him because when I put the ball in from the wing, he just went for it. I lost count of how many times the ball ended up in the opponent's net with Smithy wrapped round one of the posts. As always, he picked himself up, raised his arm to the crowed, wiped the blood from his nose on his shirt and proceeded to the edge of the semi-circle to start all over again. As I said, we were great mates off the pitch, but on it we were always at each other; "what type of cross was that?" and other comments, and in reply I would say, "My old girl could have put that in the net; you're so slow you will catch a cold; by the time you reach the penalty area it will be Christmas"; but the best one was in a game against Malden Town who were very hard to penetrate at the best of times. I put this peach of a through ball into the path of his run and he never made it. So, I shouted, "Smithy, you have to read the game and the pass!", to which one of our supporters, Banksy, shouted out at the top of his voice, "He couldn't read a fucking newspaper, let alone a quality pass like that!" Banksy was always there on the terrace in his wheelchair with a blanket over him and a bottle of rum. They said he had six months to live after the Second World War, but there he was, 1969, still cheering us on! Well, such was Barry Smith's charm that he fell about laughing and when the ball was out of play, he grabbed it and took it over to Banksy and said, "Well, what could you do with it?" Without a word of a lie, he took his blanket off, stood up and kicked it and said, "I made contact and I'm in a fucking wheelchair!" There was no more to be said on that; Smithy got the message.

Also, I had a problem with him when it came to games and training. Because he lived near me and had a company car, he would offer to pick me up, which was great, but I was, and still am, a stickler for time and he was always late. The reason was that his wife, Carol, used to hide his boots and tease him until the last moment, and it came to a point where he had to leave a spare pair at my house which, would you believe, I used to keep clean for him! The other thing about Smithy was that on the way home from training he would always stop by at the then Blue Orchid Dance Hall in Purley, and he would say to me, "there is always a girl waiting at the bus stop that would love a lift home in a nice warm car". Sure enough, there always was, and he would drop me off home first and I assume he then dropped her off, but I leave the rest to your imagination.... all the players knew about his after-training antics and we used to listen to his stories before a game. You see, that is non-league football for you, no media around you in those days. You could do what you liked and no one took any notice.

Whyteleafe was a great club to play for and apart from getting expenses, we played for the love of the game and I spent 4 happy years there on that non-league roller coaster, in and out of the first team. I have to say, though, we had a very good reserve side and so to be left out of the first team (or dropped as they used to say, or today it is called rotation) although disappointed, you were at least still going to play with some decent footballers and anyway, who wanted to travel with the first team as only one substitute was allowed and that had to be through injury not tactical. As the league had only around 14 teams, you had to get in as many games you could. As I said before, I was to meet some very good footballers that also remained friends; they were not all like Barry Smith, all football and sex; they liked football, sex and a drink but always gave their best on the park, Les Brown made sure of that. The 1969/70 season was going okay, but it was all about Bracknell Town who were one of the better sides and were pretty well solid. They had a couple of ex-Reading pros and a nice slope (to their advantage) and good crowds. For us at Whyteleafe it was a long bus trip; I remember having to get changed on the bus once because we were late getting there and late to everything on the pitch, as well losing 3-0 and having a shit journey back.

I must mention now a player who took over the reserves as player/manager and a man who I have always held in high regard and was a true Whyteleafe legend Syd Maddox, who sadly passed away in 2014 and I was at the funeral with a few of the boys from the seventies who had those same feelings about the man. Syd was aged about 35 and still playing when I was under his wing when on reserve duties. He was not as funny or as tactical as Colin Grimshaw, but he was very much a disciplinarian on and off the pitch. He played at right full back and really believed he had the energy to make those overlapping runs, but you have no idea the amount of time I had to bloody cover for him when all I wanted to do was play high up the park and deliver the ball or should I say whip the ball in because that was my trademark. Even though I say it myself, I could cross a ball like a bullet out of a gun and with the accuracy of a crack marksman. Some of the boys who are still alive today will talk of those crosses when we meet up. Anyway, back to Syd Maddox and his management and playing still at that age; he would sometimes dwell on the ball having received it short from the keeper. I loved having the ball to feet and I could make my decision either to beat my full-back or play a one-two or cut inside and go for goal.

The non-league roller coaster was about to hit a big dip, the first of many in this book, so let me explain what happened to cause this dip. First, I have to say that, for my size, I was a fiery little bugger on the park and I admit that one day it got the better of me and I did something that even today I think about and really regret. I think the game was against Camberley Town reserves and Syd had got the ball and started to advance up the park. I was screaming for the ball and still it never came, so I did the unthinkable and ran down the park to Syd and took the ball from his right foot and said to him, "if you can't do fuck all with the ball, then I'm having it and I will show you what to do with it!" I can see the look on his face now and having realised what I had done to a fellow teammate and team manager, I can tell you I was dreading the final whistle and the dressing room, but as they say, you do the crime you must do the time. It was good that we won, which I thought would soften the blow from Syd, but no, Syd tore into me and threatened to take me outside and give me a good hiding. God, what the opposition thought must have gone something like this; if they are at each other when they win, what must it be like if they lose? Syd did forgive me but I could never forgive myself for that, and even at his funeral, it came back to haunt me; that was until I started writing this book and thought this silly act of mine was not so silly after all. It made me think that what was happening to me was simple, I wanted to be in control in football, just as I was at my job, being a master joiner and manager of a big joinery works at Kingston at such a young age. Also, this being in control thing was going to take me from playing football into managing a football team, but not for some years to come as you will read later. If you like, just think of the roller coaster and I wanted to be the man who held the brake that controlled the coaster for the remainder of my life.

Anyway, back to the good old Whyteleafe and life under Syd and Les. The season went okay; we finished seventh in the league and the reserves were about mid-table in the reserve division, but we won more games than we lost so there was something to build on for the next season, 1970/71, which saw some new sides come into the league and some leave, including the champions, Bracknell Town. For the new clubs, Woking Reserves, Surbiton Byron, and Mascot Sports, pre-season was much the same, and as any player at non-league level will tell you, it had to do be done to get match fit, but as always, players used to come and get fit and then go on holiday. I used to think there was no point in that but then we were not under contract and certainly not the club's property. Les liked a good pre-season and training was not all running. We would try and get a few good pre-season games under our belt, but I must say that two of the games were quite eventful for me. Up the road in Caterham, there was a psychiatric hospital called St. Lawrence's and the club were invited to go up and play the staff in an evening game at their sports club on what I must say was a very good surface but we felt should have been roped off for the game. Some of the patients were allowed to attend the game and a few of them were allowed to come to our home games as well, which was nice, despite sometimes supporting the away side because they liked their colours.

As you know, I was a wide player and as I was going down the wing, one of the patients picked up our physio's water bucket and delivered its contents straight into the front of my body, which gave everybody a laugh. Despite it being a warm evening, I was not able to carry on as I was drenched head to toe and was substituted and headed back to the changing rooms, still in shock but laughing about the situation. Needless to say, it made for a good drink with the doctors and nurses, who were over the moon we had come up to play the hospital. By the way, we won 6-0, but the score was irrelevant to the evening...

So, on to the next pre-season game, and this time I was to be in trouble but I think it was my dad who caused me to take the action I did. My grandad passed away shortly after Dunkirk and therefore I never got to see this lovely man, only the photos and stories Dad would tell me. I'm still in possession of his army tags and prayer book and photo of him in uniform. The thing with Dad was, he would never forgive the Germans and brought me up to feel the same way. So, what do you think happens? Our next pre-season game was at home to a German touring side from Munich. So, you can imagine Dad's instruction to me - "Get stuck in at them, son!" As strange as it seems, I was lucky that the referee who the club got to do the game was a man who lived locally to where Mum and Dad lived and ran the off licence around the corner so I knew him quite well. His name was Ray Hearn, a well-respected man who was known to many as being a perfect gentleman. As he arrived at the ground, he saw me and wished me well for the game that evening. Kick-off had to be early as we did not have floodlights, unlike today where all of the clubs in non-league above step 6 must have them to get the number of games in. So, the Germans arrived for the game and we exchanged banners and took to the field in front of a good crowd. I was only on the pitch for about ten minutes, when I saw my chance. As they broke away, I gave chase to catch their left-back full on, straight through him. I never knew I could tackle like that! I put him out of the game, but all I remember was ref Ray Hearn running towards me waving his finger before he got to me and saying, "Michael, if I did not know you, you would be straight off, but instead I'm going to ask your manager Les to take you off to cool down". I was not bothered; I had carried out Dad's wishes, but Les Brown didn't put me back on again as he thought I might try again. We won the game 3-1 and that was a good night's work put to bed. So, as you can see, pre-season can be fun, unlike the season before when Wimbledon played us off the park, but it was a learning curve for all of us.

Back to the season at hand, and if you think that what I had done to that German player was bad, then I can also tell you that the Surrey Senior League made that tackle look like it had come out of a Micky Mouse cartoon! I often wondered, when I thought about writing this book, how far apart non-league football is from the premiership, championship, leagues one and two and the so-called non-league national league. I am not, and never have been, envious of them all, because our world is something special; our fans, our chairmen, our players, and of course don't forget the managers, are a close-knit family. We don't all want to sit in pubs or indoors watching football on television; we go out to watch our local clubs, stand in the cold, drink the weak tea, have the hot dog or burger spread with sauce from one of the massive containers and served with love from the volunteers in the kitchen. Sorry for this slight diversion, but I did not want to give you a game by game account of my roller coaster ride, otherwise it would have become bigger than the encyclopaedia! So, back again to the coming season, 1970/71, and the start of the season after all the pre-season preparation. There were four or more warm-up two of which I have described; the other games were not worth the mention, same old stuff, 20 players all getting part of a game and perhaps three changes of formation...as I stated earlier, the league was going to be stronger and we had to improve on last season's position or we would not have progressed. I think that is fair comment and during my managerial career, that was my benchmark.

I can remember the first game that season away at Malden Town, who had been improving over the last couple of years in their playing staff and what a physical approach they had. This was as tough as it gets - no need to dive, (we never looked for that) they just put you on your arse regardless and begged the referee for forgiveness, but to be fair, they were a good side and they turned out to be worthy champions of the league. As for Whyteleafe, we finished in eighth place, one down on the year before which has to be said is not progress. I played in the reserves for quite a bit of the season but when I did get my chance, I did something quite amusing. When the team sheets went up on a Thursday night after training, I was down as No. 12 for the first team and noticed the reserve team were away to B.A.C. Weybridge, so I did no more than scrub my name off the first team and put a reserve player's name in my place. You may ask why, but I can tell you now; there was not, throughout my playing and managerial career, a better surface to play football on (and I have been on the pitch at the old Wembley in an F.A. capacity), so much so that you could not miss the opportunity to play there. Les Brown had seen what I had done and, although not that pleased, he told me to go with the reserves and enjoy my game. As I have said before, it was never a glittering playing career for me in senior football but it was preparing me for management, which at the time had not even entered my head. We won the game at Weybridge and I scored a fine goal, cutting in from the left and unleashing one of my specials to the top corner. The keeper had no chance! I didn't score many goals, but when I did, they were top drawer. I was the provider and did that job well so that others could grab the glory, but that was my trademark. That was to follow me over the next few years at senior level and into Sunday football, but during that season, 70/71, I noticed that our first team manager Les was losing his legs and enthusiasm and I was proved to be right when he announced that he was to retire at the end of that season, despite some very good players coming through the ranks. Also, he loved playing his cricket for Oxted and they tell me he was a very good batsman. So, it was to be as the season ended that, after the championship-winning season, things were beginning to go downhill as they sometimes do. Some clubs do maintain their place at the top, but remember, the players were getting older and it was time for change… From a player's point, it was all down to who was going to replace Les Brown and be able to follow in his footsteps. Some players stayed on, such as Malcolm Gates, the ever-present Vic Burge and newcomers Micky Bannatyne, Bobby (I love me) Langton, and some of the other quality players, which was a bonus for the new manager, whoever it was going to be, so we waited for the announcement all thinking it was going to be a well-known name in non-league football as we thought the club had done their homework and had picked their man from many applicants. However, it was far from it; the manager-to-be was a chap called Bill Ferry, (a London cab driver) so it was with caution that the playing staff returned in July 1971 for pre-season training under Mr Ferry and his first-team coaching staff for another crack at winning the Surrey Senior League in 1971/72, although it was going to be extra tough as four new sides had come into the league and one of them was Farnborough Town (the Real Madrid of the Surrey Senior League premier) or so they thought until they met some of the sides in the league. There was also Chessington United (first division champions), Virginia Water, and another local derby in Horley Town, so pre-season training started and were we in for a transformation or what, and I have to say not for the better by a country mile.

Along with the players, I was wondering whether he or his coaching staff had ever been in football management at any level, let alone that of a senior club. So, I have to tell you of some of the sessions he put on. The best one for me was his Grand National - we had some flat ground above the bank behind the Church Road end goal that had some lighting, although at the pre-season we did not need the light, so what Mr Ferry decided to do was have a row of high cones and oil drums opposite each other with a piece of wood across them. The length of the course was about 50 yds and the width of the jump was about 6ft and there was about 6 yds between each jump, giving about 8 fences (or hurdles) in all, so you went on the jumps and then sprinted back to the start to do it all again. The big problem with all this was the ground was not that even and you would not even play a small-sided game up there, let alone what we were doing. I remember saying to him at one of these sessions, "Bill, we are footballers, not fucking racehorses and we are going to have injuries doing this type of thing on that surface!" All the players felt the same way so he decided to scrap that type of exercise and we continued road-running again. I was always going to moan about training unless I had the ball at my feet, but we never saw much of it, just hard work. I remember we had a full-size pitch practice game and for some unknown reason, Mr Ferry decided to play himself and placed himself at left-back in opposition to me as I was playing on the right wing. So, as was normal for me, I took the ball down the wing and who was waiting for me as the last player on my way to goal? You've guessed it, Mr Ferry, so as I took the ball around him, he lunged out at me with what I can only describe as a leg-breaking tackle, after which I hit the ground. After some treatment, I got up and made my way over to him to show my feelings over the tackle. He came in for a barrage of abuse from me and I launched a right-hander at him (good job it never cleanly connected). His reaction was to send me off to cool down; the game ended and he came over to give his explanation for the tackle and I was all ears. He said he made the bad tackle to see how I would react and to find out if I had control of my temper. My reply was quite simple as I made my case for my actions. I said to him, "In a game, by the time I had received treatment for a challenge like that, you would have been in the safety of the changing rooms, sent from the field of play and out of my sight!" He accepted that reply and we became somewhat closer as player and manager, to the extent that I was to see first-team football under him unlike with Les Brown who gave me limited first-team football...The roller coaster was about to become a bit scary and I will tell you why before I go back to Bill Ferry and the start of the 71/72 season with Whyteleafe.

One of my teammates, Barry Smith, and newcomer Micky Bannatyne asked me to play in the summer (Croydon summer pub football league) for a pub called The Harp, which was in Handcroft Road next to the newly built Handcroft estate. All games were played on Mitcham Common and I met some great characters playing for The Harp. One of those was Joey Penfold, who was well-known to the market boys and to most of the town. I can see Joey now, still riding his horse down Mitcham

Road with his kit on, coming over to the pitch, jumping off and tying the horse up and taking up his position on the pitch. It was like something out of a Western movie! Some of the other pubs were the Canterbury Arms, the Wheelwrights, and many more which have now been demolished. Some of the players were top class senior players and some of the boys came from Surrey Street market, but one thing was certain; if there was any nonsense like late tackling or hurting players, you were going to have to be brave as it could easily turn into a war. Inside alone you had Ray Bates, Bumble Bates, Terry Clarkson, and of course Joey Penfold, and there were some big family names in there as well. We went on to win the league and arrived back with the trophy to a great party that lasted well into Sunday evening. One thing, though; I used to feel sorry for the referees when we had one because they could not control the games as it was so intimidating. I was only to play one season, but as a player, it certainly toughened me up to face any big-time Charlie you were going to meet in the Surrey……

So, the scare was over and the coaster was back on track as normal, so back to Whyteleafe and Mr Ferry. Funny as it may seem, I did quite well in the rest of the pre-season, which included a game at Redhill at the memorial ground and that famous old stand which, in my opinion, should have been listed and kept as a history of Redhill F.C. Anyway, I found myself in the first-team squad and could not help thinking either the manager is mad or I must be a good player, so I decided to take the option that I was good and that we had some kind of bond, but as any non-league player or fan will tell you, the first game of the season was always a nervous time. Unlike today in football where they produce a league table after one game (how silly is that), most of the teams after 1 game are on the same points whether it be three, one or zero. Well, in my playing days, you never saw a league table until after at least 3 games which gives managers and players a good idea how things are going to go.

After all, that season there were 17 teams in the league, which meant that one of the clubs was without a game every week.

The season got underway under our new manager, Mr Ferry, and it was soon quite obvious that the manager was not up to the job at this level, but I have to say that the team spirit was still there and we did the best we could and ground out some results early on. But how do you follow a man like Les Brown and the inspiration he would instil in you? We all knew somehow, he would be back in the manager's office and changing things for the better, after all, we had suffered a bitter blow in the F.A. Amateur Cup qualifying round losing 4-2 away at Buntwood Lane, the home of Mascot Sports despite them being the underdogs. There was something about myself and the way I was playing that told me that my future in the game may be in management, as I thought if, can manage a side then why can't I do it? Someday, but not yet, as I was only 23 and still had 40 years in the non-league game left in various roles.

There will be a lot more for you to read and a bloody lot for me to write about that roller coaster ride! At the time, I was managing a big joinery works in south London and I seem to want to have that same leadership in football, so back to our manager and the rumours were flying about the club about his future. As the old saying goes, there is no smoke without fire and sure enough, in early October 1971, he got his P45 and as predicted, back came Les Brown and with it my first-team football for a while. We were also back to the crazy gang that we called Syd Maddox's reserve side, but what fun we had and we enjoyed our football under his guidance because Syd knew his football and we had a shape and tactical awareness instilled in us, which was to stand me in good stead for when it came my turn to manage a reserve side. Although I did not know it at the time, reserve team management is a tough job, having a mixture of players dropped from the first team, trialists, and a youth team and getting them as a unit.

It was at this time that a couple of players came to the club and one of them was Eddie Mark. Myself and Eddie hit it off straight away, on the pitch and off the pitch, and what's more, we still ring each other and meet up and you're talking about a friendship of over 45 years. It was the same with John Davidson and Micky Bannatyne from Whyteleafe. So, in a nutshell then, the 1971/2 season continued and Merstham and Farnborough Town, Westfield and Malden Town were fighting it out for the league title, but a couple of interesting events did happen that season; we beat the Real Madrid of the league, Farnborough Town, in the Surrey Senior League final played at Wimbledon's Plough Lane ground. To lift that cup for the first time in the club's history was great and what a party we had that night back at the club, and I mean all the players. reserve and first team. because that's how we were, just one big family.

I had a fairly good season again, supplying and scoring goals in the first team and reserves, mostly reserves, but something happened in a reserve game over at Virginia Water that was talked about for ages at the club and it concerned me and my short fuse. I was having a bit of a special game where I was taking on my full back and beating him for fun. He was not happy with the situation and started to tug my shirt every time we passed. We never dived in those days; we kept on our feet, crossed or shot. This went on until I passed him one time, he tugged my shirt and the sleeve came off in his hands, so with that, I thought, "the ref ain't going to do anything but I will!" I took it upon myself to first take my shirt off, shorts off, socks as well and gave them to him saying, "you've wanted my shirt all afternoon, well now you can have the fucking lot!" So, there is little me, standing on the pitch with no strip on and holding my boots and in only my jockstrap for all the crowd to see. The crowd were in complete hysterics and all this time the ref was playing on until he saw me, he quickly ran over to me and summoned for a blanket from the clubhouse to cover me up.

I explained my action and he understood and sent me off, would you believe, for indecent exposure in front of spectators, and the big full back stayed on the park without even a caution! For a while, had left me wondering whether I wanted to play this game anymore with complete fools taking control of games, but I was to come against worse in management as you will read later.

It had not been a bad year for the roller coaster and certainly not a bad one for Merstham as they went on to win the league, beating Farnborough to the title by two points and leaving them to find pastures new in the Spartan League for the following season, so that season was over and a league finish of 12th despite winning a trophy, which was not good enough.

On to the 1972/3 season and a good pre-season training and playing and some new players to keep us on our toes. Also, Les and Syd stayed on as managers and for me, there was going to be a turning point on my rollercoaster ride. Being at Whyteleafe was okay but I needed something to happen as I was beginning to get a bit stale. It was getting a bit like you have to when it should always be you want to, and I think any ex or present non-league footballer will have gone through that period at some stage of their careers. Let me get back to what happened in the 1972/3 season that made it special for me as a player. It was really nothing to do with Whyteleafe; it was Sunday football as well as playing for the Leafe that captured me and brought back that missing sparkle. Eddie Mark, whose Dad Johnny Mark, and Roy Kilby's Dad Alf Kilby, had been approached to form a side for Addiscombe Social who, for years, had been kicking around in the Croydon Sunday league, winning nothing, so most of the younger Whyteleafe players decided to play; keeper Dicky Vincent, Roy Kilby, Billy Lennox, Eddie, Barry Smith and myself, along with some other top-class players. We were put in Division one of the Croydon Sunday League. I can say now, with hand on heart, that with that side and its class, we would have seen off most of the Surrey Senior League clubs, including Whyteleafe, and I can say that this reflected in our final table finish of 1972/3, finishing in 12th spot again and Westfield winning the title by 3 points from Chobham. Although I loved playing senior football and all that goes with it, the season was going to be all about Addiscombe Social and the class of '72, and I strongly believe that side were the best around and would have held their own in a good level of senior football anywhere in the country, although a few years later, I had the same situation with a team, but this time as a player/manager.

Anyway, back to the Social and after all, most of us were senior players and had no problem with gelling together with some of the existing players as they had their qualities as well. One player stood out for me. Every successful non-league side had to have one or maybe two, but in Micky (Cruncher) Cronin, we had one who used to frighten me just watching him tackle, let alone thinking of being on the end of one, but I must be fair to Micky; he could give the simple ball and that's all he needed to do. After you have put your body on the line, why would you want to give it away to the other side? Fucking pointless in my opinion, but what a perfect gentleman he was, because after he had put one of those crunching tackles in, he would offer the player his hand to get him back on his feet to leave the pitch or to continue the game. That was his trademark and we all loved him despite being among such class. I bet managers Johnny and Alf would put his name on the team sheet before any other!

So you might ask the season went for this class of '72 and I would just say perfect, as you would expect with our brand of passing, movement, and defending that included our Mr Reliable keeper, Dickie Vincent, I might as well go through the squad, or at least most of them. Full backs included Billy Lennox, who was so classy and could time his tackles to perfection along with great distribution and the girls loved him. the other full-back and our skipper, Jimmy Dunne, was as solid as they come and a football brain to match any non-league full back I have seen.

Sadly, Jimmy passed away in his twenties. Next is Roy Kilby, the son of joint manager Alf, and what a centre back he was; great heading ability, defending and attacking the ball, and he was as solid as they came. I don't think a bus would have got past him, let alone a footballer. He was always in control. Then, what more could you have wanted in your midfield than Micky Vaughan and Kenny Bourne? What some clubs would do now to have those two playing and producing utter class with every touch of the ball! Mind you, Micky was a moaner and you could never do anything right by him, such was his standard and his Chelsea upbringing. Kenny was a player who could run the show against the best and having him play behind me was great because I always knew I was going to see plenty of the ball. He loved those little give and goes we played that often put him through on goal, but he also had a good up-bringing with Crystal Palace. Our centre forward was Eddie Mark, son of the other joint manager, Johnny, but as with Roy Kilby, he was never picked because of that. Eddie was great to play with as his runs into the box were timed to perfection and he was braver than a lion. He scored goals for fun, but he needed one thing and that was the service, and who do you think gave him that? You are quite right! It was me, the author of this book, Micky (Turka) Taylor, because I could cross a ball as good as any pro and with so much accuracy that when he scored from one of my many crosses, (Dracula would have hated me), he would shout out as he came running over to me, "We've turked them, Micky", so he dropped the name Micky and from then on I became Turka. It was one of my trademark accurate and speedy corners that enabled us to beat favourites for the cup, Oregon F.C., in the semi-final when Dickie Boovill rose at the far post to send it like a bullet into the net to put us in the final, and that name Turka stuck and is used by many of my great friends 45 years on when phoning me and meeting me. I could go on and on about the players and sorry to the players that I missed out at my time with Addiscombe Social F.C. first team. Oh, I just remembered a certain Steve(Shovel) Showler; he would never forgive me as I'm still speaking to him on the phone, again 45 years on, and by the way, we won the league and cup double in 1972/73, so now you know why the class of 72 were just too good and who knows what we could have gone on to achieve?

For some of us, it would only last one season, but I had other ideas within the club as I saw the chance to get involved in management. I asked the club secretary, Dave Potter if I could player-manage the 2nd team as they were struggling, and so I took charge for the 73/74 season and we were playing in the Croydon Sunday league division two and I knew I had a tough job on my hands but handle it I did and we finished about mid-table. I was not building a 2nd team, but my own side at the club, and went out and got the players that I required to get success. It was hard to player-manage on Sundays and play senior football on the Saturday, but I always remember thinking this is where you want to be and you have to start somewhere. Over the next couple of seasons, I was going to make a name for myself as you will read.

The roller coaster was really at a high now so back we go to Whyteleafe's 1973/74 season. We were still playing in the Surrey Senior League and to make things harder, another new club that was joining league would go on to make history and also play a part in my playing career the following season. That club was Epsom and Ewell and their manager, Pat O'Connell, was the former Fulham player who had taken part along with some very good players including a prolific goal-scorer, Tommy Tuite, Trevor Lee, Phil Walker and Willy Bennett, who I would have the pleasure of managing in the future. They finished second in the league to champions Westfield but still managed to win the league cup. We were still under the guidance of Les Brown, first-team manager, and Sid Maddox in the reserves, and for me, it was going to be another season of some first-team football coupled with reserve football. Despite all of the comings and goings of players, we had a bond between the first team and reserves alike and a camaraderie that went with it. Unfortunately, in a lot of cases today in non-league football that does not happen. The clubhouse on a Saturday evening was always full of the players and even if the reserves or first team were away, they would return to the clubhouse to have a drink and share their views on the day's events. We also became friends with each other and mixed socially with our wives/girlfriends, but as hypocritical as it may seem, when I started into management it was far different from playing in terms of enjoying myself on a Saturday evening. In my view, the only way you enjoyed yourself was by not losing. So, we did have that culture which is often termed 'win, draw or lose, let's have a booze'. As the season passed, the first team and reserves were having a better season than previously and the first team finished in 6th position above our fierce rivals, Merstham, and the reserves were again above mid-table.

CHAPTER FIVE

Roller coaster in for repairs again but soon fixed.

The roller coaster was now fixed again. It was goodbye to Whyteleafe and off to Epsom and Ewell, a guest of Frinton Rovers and my first management success. For me, season 1974/75 was the season of change, for although the management at Whyteleafe stayed the same, I had other ideas. I felt that, despite my limited chances with the first team, it was time for me to move. I knew a couple of players at Epsom and Ewell who asked me to come over and play in the reserves as the first team at Epsom were doing very well and the reserve side was quite stable and although I hated the slope at West Street, the stadium was a lot better. Did I dare to think that I could push my way into the successful first-team squad? I persuaded another Whyteleafe player and a great friend of mine to come over with me, that player being Eddie Mark, and we settled down and waited for our chance. It was quite obvious after a while that Pat O'Connell, the manager, had a first-team squad settled and, with his connections, we had little or no hope of being in the first team, but I knew a great bloke on the Waddon Estate who happened to be the manager of a well-known local side and a playing surface that you would die for. That team was Frinton Rovers and every now and again I would go missing from Epsom and Ewell and play in some of Frinton's more important games. This culminated in Frinton Rovers winning the Surrey Intermediate Eastern League title. Despite only playing a handful of games,

I qualified and received my league winners' medal. I will come back to Frinton later in the book.

In non-league football, you have to be open-minded about these things, and Epsom's manager, Pat O'Connell, was justified because Epsom and Ewell first team went on to win the league, scoring over 100 goals, and also appeared at Wembley in the first ever F.A. Vase final, where they were beaten by 2 goals to 1 against Hoddesdon Town. They were still my club and I felt very proud of their achievement. Little did I know then that I was going to have my moment at Wembley in the future. I must also keep you up to date with my management career taking shape; my first success was at the ripe old age of 27, in the Croydon Sunday league, and as I said I intended to build a side and I did it. I brought in some good players of quality and although I won't mention them all, a few names spring to mind. There was Dixon Gill, who himself was going to go on to better things with Croydon F.C., ending up as their chairman, both the Whant brothers, Graham and Martin, and a capture from Merstham, Micky Povey. Now, Micky was the same height as me, 5ft 2ins, and whenever I played against Merstham we would have a right old go with each other, with neither one of us giving way. I still don't know to this day how I managed to sign him and play Sundays, but I did and he made a big difference to the side which saw us be promoted to division one that season. I have saved one player till last for a reason - I have seen some very talented non-league players during my 55 years in the game, but I had a player called Ricky Bascombe who came to me via Dixon Gill who had this habit of bringing me players. Ricky was the fastest player I have ever set my eyes on and top skill as well. Let me tell you about his party piece! At the end of each game, win or lose, he would stand next to the goal and run the full length of the pitch at full speed and never would any player dare challenge to beat him! We had a problem with him in as much as he was a naughty boy, which had cost him, I believe, a promising football career with Crystal Palace. It was only minor stuff, but pro clubs would not allow that. I did, and now and again, he spent Saturday night in Croydon nick (police station) and we would have to go up there and ask them if they would release him to play!

Anyway, back to Saturday football and it was goodbye to Epsom and Ewell and the 1975/6 season saw a move to Merstham, as Dixon Gill had told me it was a good set up and a very nice playing surface. I met with first-team manager, Fred Setters, who impressed me, along with reserve team manager, Tony Brown (I think). I teamed up with Steve Showler, who was to remain a great friend of mine and still is to this day, and would you believe it, the one and only Ricky Bascombe! There were also some other players there who had good reputations; Micky Povey, who I have already spoken about, Charlie Buckman, Peter Lewis, along with a good squad of players, but it dawned on me that I would have to face Whyteleafe, my old club, at some stage that season which would be interesting, not forgetting that Merstham had been Surrey Senior League champions in the 1971/2 season so it was hardly a step backwards for me.

Again, though, it was all about first team and reserve football for me and never being able to make a regular first-team spot my own. Then the penny dropped for me because, as I said earlier in the book, the game's systems were changing, but I still wanted to be that old-fashioned winger playing in the more advanced role and avoiding the offside trap but staying wide patrolling the touchline waiting for the ball to come so I could go past my full back and whip one of my speedy crosses in. That was why my chances were becoming more limited regarding first-team football as in the reserves, you never had a set pattern to play; you were the leftovers and made up the team in all kinds of positions.

I am glad that, with my management skills, I insisted that whatever formation was played in the first team was played throughout the club, right down to the youth team, so any player stepping up would not be confused and could settle in right away. First team manager, Fred Setters, was no mug and I learnt from him as I had with Les Brown back in the good old Leafe days, but now came my big chance to finally make a name for myself. Sadly this was not as a player, but my dream of player-managing a championship-winning side came in that season 1975/6 as Addiscombe Social 2nd team became champions of the Croydon Sunday League 1st division and I joined the elite band of player/managers that had won a championship as a player and gone back and done it all over again as a player/manager at any standard of football. Really, I had no reason to complain about limited first-team football at Merstham, as it was obvious my thoughts were clearly hell-bent on doing what I wanted to achieve, and the icing on the cake came when I received the trophy, along with my captain, Martin Whant, from the great Dave MacKay of Spurs and Scotland, and also John Jackson, the Crystal Palace goalkeeper.

Anyway, back to Merstham and the 1975/6 season. Not for the first time, I was starting to think this was no longer fun for me on the pitch, although we used to have some great evenings after a game in a pub outside the ground called The Griffin, but my love for Merstham was beginning to get cold, and when that happens, your play suffers as well. Mine did, and I became angry and, for a little guy that is not good, I can tell you. Us short players were trouble and that was clearly summed up in one incident away to champions-elect, Wandsworth Town, at Kimber Road, just down the road from the famous Youngs brewery at Wandsworth. The roller coaster really took a big dip there because, again, I was a naughty boy and I feel I had every right to be. It was a close game, but they were a very physical side and were very direct, whereas we tried to play. By this time, I had knuckled down to Fred's formation and played in a wide right-side midfield position. I was getting up and down the park okay and was getting in my trademark crosses and having some digs on goal when their opposing midfield player decided to throw his weight around, and in a fifty-fifty ball, decided to launch himself at me with studs as high as the top of my chest and scraping them down to my waist. All hell broke loose between the sides and I managed to kick him in the groin in retaliation, sending him down onto the grass. The referee came over, and as usual, the perpetrator didn't get spoken to; he went straight for me and sent me off for violent conduct, which seems to happen all the time in non-league! Now we were down to 10 men, and instead of going to the dressing room, I decided to put my top and bottoms on and see the game out in the dugout. Wandsworth got on top and, as far as I can remember, scored a late winner. It was not to end there because as the teams were leaving the field, before anyone could catch me, I had gone up and laid into the player who had caused horrendous marks on my chest. Things then quietened down and I had my shower and made a quick exit from the ground so as not to cause any further trouble and to head straight for Mayday Hospital, Croydon, for a check-up.

Then I waited for the charges to be brought against me. I was charged by the Surrey F.A. for violent conduct and bringing the game into disrepute, a charge that I was not happy with, and upon seeing my doctor and showing him my chest, he made the remark that he had never seen anything like the stud marks down my chest and said he would back me in my appeal, providing me with a doctor's note stating that such things should not happen on a football pitch, or anywhere, come to that. So bad were my cuts and bruising that it was a few weeks before I was able to play again, provided I was allowed to. I know this seems very hypocritical but I decided not to attend the appeal as I felt that my punishment had already been determined and the referee's report was so over the top you would have thought he was on Wandsworth Town's committee. I was suspended for three weeks and fined £10. All this really was just another sign that maybe my senior playing days were coming to an end, even at an early age. With my work, the training was becoming harder and I felt it was time to step away from senior football and join Frinton Rovers but let me tell you straight away that although they were an intermediate club, they were full of players like myself who could have made good senior players but the interest had gone and they were now playing for the love and the fun of the game and still at a decent level.

Frank Renton persuaded me to join Frinton permanently for the 1976/7 season at the club, but I didn't need much persuading as the clubhouse and playing surface were immaculate and there was a professional approach from the management, coaches, and committee. We had the nickname of The Seasiders after the town of Frinton-on-Sea. We had one player by the name of Jimmy Fitzpatrick who I met on my 70th birthday with some of the other Frinton players and our partners. Jimmy is now a very prominent MP for Poplar and Limehouse and as a gesture for my 70th birthday, he invited us to the House of Commons for a special and memorable private tour, including the members' bar and the terrace bar. Was politics on the agenda that day? Not a hope in hell's chance! It was all about non-league football. I remember my first full season well and I had a good season and, as I have said, some very good players and a first-rate manager, Frank Renton, or to most just Big Frank, but I must admit that our first home game was a bit of a knockback for me, simply because we were part of Thornton Heath Sports Club and cricket took up the start of the season, so we could not play on that great playing surface that groundsman Bobby Broomfield had prepared for at least a couple of weeks, so I played my first home game against Ashtead F.C. on Figges Marsh, a park pitch near Tooting. I remember it was a 2-2 draw and the changing rooms were across a busy main road which was pretty hard to get across. I thought well, what a comedown from playing in stadiums and senior football. After a while, I got used to the standard and it was great not having to train Tuesdays and Thursday evenings.

Now it was only on Tuesdays and that was mostly with the ball. As I said earlier, some of our players were playing well below the standard they could have played at, but they were not committed enough to take that step up, which most of them could have done had they wanted to. That aside, they were a good bunch of non-league footballers who would look after each other on and off the pitch and were paid to play as well. The league was strong with teams like Welbeck United, Battersea Park Rovers, Warlingham, Fetcham and Ashtead to name a few.

I was enjoying my Saturday football and was glad when the cricket had finished and we could play our home games on that carpet of a pitch. Of course, like all things in non-league football, the bloody away teams loved the surface and we always faced a better side at home than when we played them away. Anyway, despite all that, we kept a good home record that season and again I was playing wide and providing quality balls into the box for Jack Goldie and Jimmy Fitz to finish. There were other players as well that could have, and did, play at a high level, and one such player was Terry Arnold, simply known as T.A. His footballing brain was so far ahead of the rest of the team that he would play balls from the midfield and split defences wide open, he was that good. He was not a workhorse, but his control and passing more than made up for that, and he also kept the bar in the clubhouse lively after a game as he loved a drink, as did most of the team. We would all have to take a turn behind the bar if it got very busy and Terry loved that.

We also had some very good local derbys that used to be quite lively, and top of the list was playing Welbeck United which, at some stage, would turn a bit nasty involving players and supporters alike. One incident that stood out for me was when our groundsman, Bobby Broomfield, was in plaster and on crutches. He decided to take some of their supporters on, waving his hospital crutch about on the touchline. It was like some comedy sketch, but that is non-league football in its glory - never short of action on and off the pitch! Again, just like any sport, you will always find life hard if there are good teams around in your league which there were, so like boxers, if the quality is not around, you can be world champion and that applies to horse racing, tennis, and all team and individual sports. So, am I making excuses for having a very good team and not winning anything that season? Of course I bloody well am, anyone can see that. Anyway, it was before that season of also-runs, good enough but not quite, that one of the Saturday second-team players, Bill Hicky, who managed the Sunday side called Thornton Heath United along with keeper Jimmy True, asked me if I would consider that season 1976/7 taking them over lock, stock and barrel as the interest in the Sunday side was falling away and having a job to field a side. So, I had a big decision to make in as much as I stop playing Saturdays and concentrate on player/manager on Sundays only, or forget the offer and carry on with Frinton Rovers on Saturdays. I made my mind up to take the plunge and manage the Sunday side as well as still playing Saturdays, which really set me off once again like at Addiscombe Social, but this time there was going to be no break on a managerial career that I would look back on with pride and take Thornton Heath United to a level as not seen before. The brake was off and the roller coaster was going to be running on the Heath for some time.

CHAPTER SIX

The roller coaster's ready to ride again. Dad had his Heath United and now I've got my own Heath United and a story to tell - five seasons of it!

Let me tell you now that my Heath United had a first name, and that was Thornton, as you read in the last chapter, making it Thornton Heath United. The first thing I decided to do was take us out of the Morden and District League and put us in the southern area Sunday League and appoint my new secretary, a friend of mine, Paul Radcliffe, who said he would help out for the first season. It was going to be hard coping with Saturday playing and Sunday player-managing, but I did it and this is how it started. Talk about the roller coaster? This was going to be some ride from now on.

The recruiting of new players was going to be hard, but I had enough contacts. The only problem was not having enough time, but I always had my positive hat on when it came to football and managed to get a decent side together, with players like the Whant brothers, John Comoford and Trevor Ollington. Not only was Trevor a good player but he had a fruit stall in Surrey Street market and we always had fresh oranges and bananas for before and after the game! We did have a goalkeeping problem which meant I was forever having to change keepers that season. Did I make a mistake deciding to leave the Morden and District

League? Of course I did, and that soon became evident in our first few games. Don't get me wrong; there were some good sides in the premier division, none more so than Carribb F.C. and another side called National Dynamo. They promoted the black footballer but none of us had a problem with that as we had a good relationship with them, after all, we were there to play football not to judge their colour or their ethnic origin but I must say we used to have some banter with the black sides over kick-off times. I would always play the sides from Brixton, Southwark, Peckham, Lewisham at home on a 9.30 kick off Sunday morning, as I knew they loved to party on a Saturday night. In return, they used to put us on Sunday afternoon kick-offs at places like Southwark Park, Brockwell Park and now you can see why I had made a mistake. My players wanted to play Sunday mornings, go in the bar, have a good drink and go home to a nice Sunday roast dinner. So, Sunday afternoon games became a problem, trying to get a side out to fulfil the fixtures. We had the best home record in the league for obvious reasons and one of the worst records away. But as I stated, everyone got on very well with each other and we had some cracking games thanks to their style of football being more flamboyant with their skill and pace and my football aimed at getting the ball out wide, getting crosses in and passing the ball all over the pitch. There is one home game I remember well - it was a cold morning and Carribb F.C. turned up in dribs and drabs, thinking they could take to the pitch with their Rastafarian hats on, only for the referee to point out that they were not allowed to do this. I must say, it was a bit of fun to actually see the black sides turn up on cold winter mornings and their reaction to having to play football at that early time in the morning. I don't know why, but I always seem to have had a habit of not putting the heating on in the away dressing room, which led to more protests. Having said that, the league was a learning curve for me as a manager and far more testing than my experience with Addiscombe Social when player-managing them to the 1st division title, so times were not so bad and, as I said, I wanted to build a team for the future and I was going to do just that.

As always in football, something is around the corner either to knock you down or lift you up. Well, thank God it was the latter of those in the early part of that season. I was going to have my knock backs as most non-league managers do, and I will tell you mine during my managerial career. Despite the first part of the season in our change to a new league being a 'win one, lose one' situation, I was summoned by my uncle Tubby Harrington to play a Saturday game for his working men's club in Croydon called Croydon Liberal Sports, of which he was a member. I was having the odd day off from Frinton Rovers now and again so I agreed to play as he'd also got me tickets for Crystal Palace matches as he was a master bricklayer for Arthur Waite, the builder, who was chairman of the Palace, so I had little or no choice with him being Mum's big brother!

The game was at home to Farnham Town at Queens Park, Caterham in the Surrey cup, and in my mind, I kept thinking why am I playing at Caterham at home when the football club was based in Croydon? The sun came out on a day that would change my life and lots of other players lives in the future. We won the game with no problem, as we had the best left-winger, I had seen in non-league football for all my playing and short managerial career. His name was Bernie Donnelly, a fiery Scot, who I approached after the game to ask him if he was doing anything on the Sunday morning. He replied that he wasn't, as he had just moved down south from Glasgow for work and was on his own in a flat in South Croydon, so yes, he was able to play for me on the Sunday morning. The rest, they say, is history. He became godfather to my only child and son, Daniel, and to this day, some 40 years on, is one of my best friends and part of the family. I played him on the Sunday and he made an instant impact, which led to the players wondering where I had found such talent. Of course, he soon settled in, having met up with fellow Scot, John Comoford. As I have said already, you have to build a team and there is no point being at the bottom of Mount Everest thinking that it looks a bit slippery - just get on and climb the bloody thing if you want to reach the top! So, that's what I tried to do at first with Thornton Heath United, and then with other sides, as you will read.

I kept building the team during a season of no more than interest really, as we never adapted to it at all, but saying that, we did make club history in reaching the Surrey Senior Sunday cup semi-final, having knocked out some good sides.

In one of our home ties I had a strange situation where my keeper, the excellent Chris Jones and a very good midfield player, Reg Gaston, informed me that if the game went into extra time, they would have to leave as they had a game in the afternoon. It was good, then, that we got the winner near the end of the game and off they went to their afternoon game. I still believe that they would have stayed and played extra time, as I told you we had to borrow keepers all that season as I must have had at least four signed.

All along the way, this Surrey cup roller coaster proved to me that we had something about us to build on and that's exactly what we did. In the semi-final, we played a side called West Clandon, who had, at that time, the majority of Woking's first team playing for them. And seeing that this was a special semi-final, they were at full strength. They say that you learn something every game in football, even more so at non-league level, and it was on that day that I learned that you could combat a classy team by having a game plan and that game plan saw us doing okay and despite us not being able to score, we restricted Clandon. To say tempers got a little bit inflamed was an understatement. They thought they were coming to our ground to have a picnic but that never happened. I also learned that day that I needed to be the stronger person in the dressing room and not only inspire my players to play but to maintain their discipline. Even now, after 30 years or so, I am still going to dig out two of my players that day who let me down badly. During half-time, we obviously made our plans for the second half and they had a very good left-winger who was more than a match for my right full-back, Trevor Hollington, and my right midfield player, John Comoford. So, during the half-time interval, they made it clear to me they were going to try and take him out of the game. Well, let me tell you now; they did exactly that and in doing so, reduced us to 9 men for the last twenty minutes of the game. First, Trevor Hollington grabbed the player and was sent off, after which John Comoford said to me, "if he's going, then I will be going soon," and the next tackle John made was to go right through the player and he got his marching orders. The left-winger had to leave the field of play but of course, they had a substitute to use. Suddenly, my despair and quick reorganisation turned into a moment of joy as would you believe, we scored! Because of the mayhem, I cannot even remember who scored the goal but I knew, deep down, that they were going to be too strong for us, and despite trying very hard to protect our lead, we were hit with two late goals and consequently lost the match. For myself, there was an element of pride and also fury. The players concerned made their apologies, but it fell on deaf ears. I was not going to have a team that was going to take the field and do exactly what they felt they wanted to do. Expressing yourself on the field of play is great, but lack of discipline, as you will read later on, was certainly not going to be tolerated, as I had shown as a player. As a player, I struggled with discipline and knew what a pain up the ass I had been to some of my managers, using that cliché 'experience counts'.

I was well into my management now and I remember a comment made by the Leeds United manager, Don Revie, when he once said, "Before you become the man or the team you want to be, it is a good idea to have the same dress code as a manager, and for the team to play in the same colours." That is why Leeds United changed to their strip of all white, to look like the great Real Madrid. Why I am saying this is because one of my favourite managers and tacticians was the flamboyant Malcolm Allison, who I copied by going to Petticoat Lane in London to buy a sheepskin coat. I also changed our strip to red, as I admired the way that Nottingham Forest had taken English football by storm under their great manager, Cloughy. Shame about the sheepskin coat; at that time, I used to smoke a pipe and left the pipe in my pocket. I thought the pipe was out, but one of my players informed me that smoke was coming from my pocket and therefore the coat never saw the end of that season. Some of the players were also not going to see another season with me as their manager because I was building my side and the dressing room was going to be mine; no smoking, don't speak until spoken to, passing the ball as to give it away is a crime, and never, never let your teammates down in a win, draw or lose situation. Keep your pride at all times, but the one thing I never stopped was a player expressing his opinion, provided it was done with me privately and not in front of my players at any time.

As for the league, we applied to join back into the Morden and District League, as the southern area Sunday league had caused so many problems. We were going to now go back to early Sunday morning kick-offs, which would also bring in much-needed revenue to the clubhouse on Sunday lunchtimes. All managers say that in the summer, one of the hardest jobs is trying to recruit for the coming season, but despite John Comoford being in my bad books, he had very good contacts at Whyteleafe. So, for the 1977/78 season, Thornton Heath United were going to be a force to be reckoned with, bringing in an influx of new players.

I also became a dad for the first time when my son Daniel was born on 6 October 1977. So, I had a Taylor now who could follow in the family tradition of non-league football. The league decided to put us in division two and if you think that was going to be easy then I can tell you, the football was of the highest calibre as the Morden and District League was probably one of the best Sunday leagues in the country. I now think the reason I pulled away to have a season in the southern area Sunday league was simply because I thought it would be an easier route to success. But as you have read, that was not the case and it was not all about the strength of the league. So, it was with great optimism and I must say, some better than average footballers, that our league campaign started. Amongst the strong teams was Norbury Athletic, who we would have some great games with. I also mention that I had one of the best left-wingers that I had seen in non-league football in Bernie Donnelly, but I also now had a right-winger in former Crystal Palace and Scotland schoolboy, Billy Patterson. All over the pitch, I had class in every position and it reminded me of Addiscombe Social in the class of 1972/73. Well, now I had the class, not as a player but as a player/manager of 1977/78. But before I begin to tell you about that memorable season, I had lost the services of my good friend Paul Radcliffe as secretary, as we agreed on only a one-year help-out season. With that in mind, I searched and found the most incredible football secretary that I think any football club would have been proud to have had. His name was Jim Wright and Jim Jim, as we called him, had artificial arms and legs. How he ever did the job I will never know, because as any football club secretary will tell you, there is a lot of form-filling, telephone calls, and meetings to attend. I never asked Jim how he did it, he just did it to an exemplary level. Also, he was always present at every game and if I could not go round his house to collect him, one of the players would, as they thought the world of him and I do believe that he was one of the main reasons, along with my ever-increasing management skills, why we had senior players that possibly looked forward more to their Sunday games than they did Saturdays.

It was a great season for us as a team and for me personally. We had our moments of laughter; one instance I can remember was when Jim Jim was on the touchline, as always, and one of the opposition cleared the ball with force, knocking poor old Jim Jim over like a skittle. You can imagine him, lying on the ground, a big grin on his face as always, as the players rushed off to get him in an upright and stable position. We also had a problem where, when Jim wanted to have a wee, we would have to take him to the toilet after the game, get his plonker out, wipe it and put it back after he had finished! I can see him now, standing at the bar after every game, (because we always came back to the clubhouse after an away game, win or lose) with a rum and coke in a long glass with a straw. One afternoon, we had had a good win in the morning and the players were in good spirits. The wives and the girlfriends were in the clubhouse for an afternoon session and so was Jim Jim. I would never accuse the boys of purposely getting Jim Jim drunk, but that is precisely what happened. It must have been around about 5 o'clock when Jim Jim fell to the floor. The situation was quite simple - his false arms were all over the place and so were his legs, so we got Jim Jim on the floor. His legs were also in a bit of a mess and we were all trying to work out how to get him to the car, and worst of all, who was going to take him and present him to his mother in this state. Well, we all decided to draw lots to see who it would be. I can't remember who took him home; it certainly wasn't me, but all I know is that when the boys knocked on the front door and his mum answered, she said in her calm-natured way, "Bring him in and I'll sort him out". How inspiring was that! As I said, this brought a very tight, close feeling amongst the players, like a family, and consequently, we made history by being Morden District second division champions in 1978, beating Manor Athletic on the last game of the season in an evening game at home in front of at least 500 spectators. Such was the magnitude of the game that both us and Manor Athletic asked the league for official linesmen and not those from either club, which was the norm for Sunday football except in the F.A. Sunday cup. What a great night that was and I truly felt I had arrived on the management scene after steering such class to the league title. Celebrations were aplenty and those boys did know how to celebrate, but for us managers, it was all about the following season.

This would then be 1978/79 and building an even better side (the road to success is always under construction) was going to be hard work, or so I thought, but there is also a true saying in non-league football – 'success will bring players to you' and that is what happened. I must add at this point that across the unmade road between our clubs, Croydon Athletic F.C. were undergoing development of their stadium and little did I know then that I was going to be a big part of that in the future as you will read later on. So, back to Thornton Heath United and the 1978/79 season... There were to be a few additions to the team and of course some of the players were stood down to play in the reserve side and the reserves who also became strong. Finally, were to be no more goalkeeping problems as John (Fingers) signed again. As in all successful teams, you have to have a very good defence and so we had Fingers and the classy David Blake at centre half, with iron man Roy Kilby as his partner and with the Whant brothers completing a strong back four. Yet, the league was always going to be about ourselves and Manor Athletic and we were always close to each other regarding points which in the end, gave them the championship by just two points and sweet revenge against us from last season. We were promoted to the premier division and the season was not all that bad as the league introduced a new cup called the Edgar Hemmingway cup, and in that cup, we met Morden Nomads in the final at Carshalton arena. We had knocked a few good sides out along the way, but the Nomads were favourites and they had players including the Pritchard brothers and a group of other talented players as well which was the norm for sides in the top divisions of the Morden and District League. The game was a very close affair but can be remembered for not only us winning the trophy at the first attempt, but the way in which we won it, which was a talking point for quite some time afterwards. As I have said earlier, our super left-winger, Bernie Donnelly, scored the winner near the end of the game and on the way back to restart the game, some words were said to him by one of the Nomad players, to which he responded with a Glasgow kiss (head butt) and received his marching orders so he was not able to collect his winner's medal until we presented it to him in the clubhouse. All that little sod wants to remember is to thank that defence of ours for holding on for those last ten minutes with ten men with the Nomads throwing everything but the kitchen sink at us. So you can imagine what a great afternoon we had when we got back to the club with the trophy and started to party, knowing that when the party was over, it was time for myself to realise the premier division was going to be a challenge that would require further strengthening of the squad, to which I did. One note for the 1978/79 season was that both my wide players had chipped in with 28 goals between them and my centre forward only on six (for some reason that did not add up).

The 1979/80 season saw me receive the biggest honour that I had been awarded in non-league football, when I was chosen by the league committee to become the manager of the Morden and District representative side. As I have said before, the league was possibly one of the best Sunday leagues in the country and I was going to have the pick of some really talented non-league footballers and gel them into a team. You will read later on in the book that representative football became one of my strongest management skills, and let me tell you now, for anybody who has ever managed a representative side, this is the hardest job in football, non-league or pro as many England managers will tell you. You can have all the talent there is available in your team selection but, unless they are playing in a formation that suits them and your mannerism gets them to want to play for you and be proud of being the best 18 players in ten divisions of football, it won't work. I will come back to representative football later but it was all about Thornton Heath United and our baptism in the premier division along with for the first time in many years the same baptism applied when we entered the football association Sunday cup competition. On entering the competition, like any good manager, my aim was to win it and also to help us in the premier division of the Morden and District League. You talk of such teams like Cenward (Nicky Foracre, manager), Wrythe Athletic (manager Colin Turner), Ranelagh Sports (manager Ray Rembridge) just to mention a few, and all of these managers had far more experience than I had. I must admit, when I looked at the league, despite having what I call a top-class side, we were going to find it hard going against such quality and that proved to be the case. I wanted to make sure was that we kept our heads above water and were not relegated or all of my good work, and that of the secretary and the players, would have been in vain. We did finish the season in a reasonable position and with another appearance in the Hemmingway Cup final, only this time we were the losing finalists (and people who know me know what I think of losers' medals).

Having achieved that in the league, I must talk about our baptism in the F.A. Sunday cup. We were drawn at home to Sun F.C. from Northfleet in Kent who were the Kent Sunday league senior division one title winners 1978/79, so we knew we would have a tough job on our hands and I felt we had picked the short straw. A lot of work had to be done to stage the game. The pitch had to be roped off. We were to have F.A. officials including the referee, Mr C Downey of Hounslow, who was to be a linesman in the F.A. cup final two years later (shows you the quality of the officials). It was a great day for the club as history was being made having been the first Thornton Heath United side to ever take part. One memory that will stick out for me was our groundsman, Bobby Broomfield, driving his Land Rover down to pitch side and allowing some of the supporters to sit on top of his racking and charging extra admission for a stand seat, otherwise, it was a simple 25 pence entrance by programme. We lost the game 2-1 and I have to lay some blame at my super left winger but fiery Scotsman, Bernie Donnelly, being suspended for this game, but is it to his credit that without him we were far less of a threat. So ended our brief encounter in this prestigious competition but the vibes were clear for all to see, that Thornton Heath United had grown up big time. Also, during the season, I must mention my appointment as representative manager of the league side. I had picked my squad and gave a call to my dear football colleague, John Rains, who was manager at Sutton United at the time, to see if he could accommodate us for a floodlit friendly mid-week. John's response was great as always, and he duly obliged by putting a full side out against us. John was not a man to mince his words and the side that I put out that night would have given any Isthmian premier division side a more than good game and the score line reflected that, as we beat them 3-1. John said to me after the game in the boardroom, "Don't ever again, Micky, bring a fucking side down here and take the piss out of my team". I replied, "Well, John, I feel so proud that you have said that to me". It was an honour, having assembled my representative side, to bring out a comment from one of the best managers in the non-league game. So sad that John was to pass away so early, but his legacy will always be at Sutton United, where he is a legend, along with brother Tony. So, having prepared ourselves with one game, it was time for competition. We were drawn against the Surrey and Hants Border League and we had no problems beating them without too much trouble. In the semi-final, we were drawn to play the Leatherhead League. I can remember this game, although I'm not clear on the score, although we progressed to the final for one reason. There was a certain player who played for Ranelagh Sports who I caused to raise a few eyebrows when I picked him for the squad. His name was Ken Bernard and he was well-known as a typical old battling centre forward. As I have said, in representative football the mix has to be right and I knew I had got the right man when a ball was slung in from the wing, leaving Kenny and the Leatherhead goalkeeper to sort it out. The ball ended up in the net as often it did with Ken, but both players had collided and were lying on the deck. Both physios were out very quickly. As the players started to pull themselves together and get up from the deck, the goalkeeper started showing signs of being in shock. Kenny was also on his feet. I shouted to my physio," Is Ken okay to carry on?" He gave me the thumbs up and as he approached me in the dugout, I will never forget as long as I live, he said, "Ken said can you look after this?" and in his hand was one of Ken's front teeth with the blood still at the root.

We would face tough opposition in a final against the South Thameside league and this would take two games both ending in draws. And so, it was decided, because the season was at an end, that we would share the cup. In fact, it had again not been a bad season and obviously not that bad a start to my representative managerial career. As I prepared my Thornton Heath United side for their second season in the premier division, I was also informed that I would remain as representative manager for the season, which again made me feel very proud. Back to Thornton Heath United and the season; I had recruited some more excellent players including Sean Dalton from Crownmeads and also Richard 'Shaft' Simpson, or as he became known to me over the last 38 years, just plain Simmo. We entered the F.A. Sunday cup again and with the players I had acquired, thought that we would give a good account of ourselves this time around. We were not setting the league alight but we were never in trouble and so it was a nice change from our league football to learn that our opponents in the F.A. Sunday cup were a team from

Oxfordshire called Elco F.C. The problem was, we were drawn away and how kind of them to say that they would put the game back for an 11 o'clock kick-off and all my players that have ever played for me know that I always needed a good length of time in the dressing room and warm up before a game. So, with that in mind, we had a coach laid on for players and supporters to leave the club at 7.30 am on a Sunday morning to go to Holmer Green F.C., who were staging the game. As you can imagine, some very tired-looking players turned up to meet the coach, which left about three-quarters of an hour late, as obviously, the boys had been out on Saturday. This game was going to be talked about for years to come, not in the score line not about the journey, but about our new kit which we had purchased from a certain Mr J Comoford and Steve Showler, who were trying to establish their selves as kit suppliers. I had thought we wanted a new kit for this game and I would give them the opportunity to supply it. Well, we arrived at the ground about 10 am and as was always our practice, players were sent out to look at the surface and decide on their footwear while we put the kit out before calling them back in. I was putting the kit out, which I quite enjoyed doing, as us non-leaguers tried to be as professional as we could. Shirt numbers had to be facing out on the pegs, socks on top of shorts on the bench below the shirt, and the warm-up top. As I was hanging the shirts up and strange for me as I am on the small side, I thought to myself this kit looks a bit small. With that, I called to one of our players to come back into the dressing room and attempt to put the kit on. He could not get his head through the neck, he had a job getting his leg through the shorts and there was no way the socks were ever going to go on his feet. I was in absolute despair and Steve Showler was actually in my side that day. All I wanted to do was rip his head off and I did call him in and spoke to him very softly; "Take a look round the dressing room, Shovel. What the fuck do you think you have given me here?" So, with that, we had to go begging

Holmer Green F.C., and luckily, they had a strip that we could play in. Great preparation, I must say, because it is times like that when you must not let the rest of the team know that you are despondent and pissed off. We have come all this way to play and win a game and then, as if the whole day was going to collapse around me, we had a referee and linesman all from Oxford, who were going to give us absolutely nothing all game. We had a dubious penalty awarded against us after just 5 minutes and that set the standard that we're going to have to accept in scoring two perfectly good goals that were disallowed. Consequently, we lost the game 1-0 and so ended another attempt at the F.A. Sunday cup. So back home we came, having lost the game, a kit that was fucking useless and work on the Monday morning – non-league football at its best! This was going to be probably my last season with Thornton Heath as I felt I needed a change after five long years and my young son, Daniel, was growing up. This also applied to the representative side, only it seemed like even with the rep. side things were going to be different. I had a job to get the players to play because we were drawn away at Guildford on a Sunday afternoon and some were involved in cup games and important league games and in a way, rightly so, their managers were not over keen for them to play. However, we did play the game and unlike the season before, the side represented nowhere near the strength of the league and were beaten in the semi-final by the Surrey and Hants Border League who were well below our standard, but worked their socks off and deservedly won the game. I resigned my position as representative manager and with that, the league decided that it would withdraw from future competitions. Even as I write this book now in 2019, I do sympathise with Paul Fairclough, the England captain/manager, who has a torrid time with getting players released to play. So, with representative football finished, or should I say for me only the beginning, it was now time to finish my business with Thornton Heath United and hand over to another manager.

Some of the players also decided to call it a day and concentrate more on their Saturday football careers rather than Sunday.

I must say they were happy years - lots of laughs and memories. There were a couple that stood out for me, the first one being the annual Boxing Day game between the Saturday team, Frinton Rovers and my Thornton Heath United. The game was always played in good spirits and with plenty of banter as all players knew each other, but there was one occasion which I will always remember and it featured a referee who was a club member called Alan Halfacre, known to many as simply 'The Mouse' having got this nickname from his squeaky voice and his facial features. In this particular game, Alan 'The Mouse' decided that this was possibly either the World Cup final or the F.A. Cup final. As players, we were not really sure, and the reason being that he went strictly by the rule book, which was not required, so can you imagine it when, in one piece of banter between the players from each side, he decided to send four players off. We rolled about laughing and the players quite rightly said, "The only fucking person leaving this pitch is 'The Mouse'!" He left the pitch, uttering the words, "and fuck you lot too" and we carried on with our game and as always, finished off with a penalty shootout. 'Mouse' was not amused and left for home. He was a great person and would help anybody, but just like some people behind the wheel of a car, when Alan put his referee's shirt, shorts and socks on with his cards and his notebook, he was like a madman let loose, so God bless him, wherever he is now.

The next memory was at the annual end-of-season dinner and dance at the Aerodrome Hotel, Purley Way, Croydon. It was always the custom that the Saturday team, Frinton Rovers, and ourselves, Thornton Heath United, would have a joint evening. You know how it goes, same old thing really; first the dinner, then the presentations of awards and then the speeches from the top table. First up was the President/chairman, followed by myself, the Sunday team manager followed by Saturday first team, second team and then the moment I will never forget. The third team manager, Tommy Liddle, decided that he could not hide his end-of-the-season feelings any longer and as he stood up, swaying from side to side (from the drink), he decided to accuse the first team and the second team managers on Saturdays of leaving his team with the dregs of players and in his exact words said, "You are nothing but a bunch of c**ts," and then collapsed onto the table into his dinner plate and was carried out by some of the members on the top table to roars of laughter from all the players. Tommy has remained a great friend of mine to this day and we often talk about that moment, although he cannot remember much. By the way, his son, Simon Liddle, turned out to be a very good non-league footballer, first playing for one of my representative sides and also became a prominent member and one of the fan's favourite players of Jeff King's successful Canvey Island F.C. You will read about both of these guys later in the book.

Another event I can remember so well was one Saturday in the early days of Thornton Heath. I used to sometimes watch Frinton Rovers play on a Saturday afternoon and if I felt we were going to be a player short on the Sunday, I would ask one of the Frinton players if they would turn out for me, and on this occasion, I asked their defender, Alan (Hoppy) Hopkinson, if he would turn up at home on the Sunday. Alan was a very old-fashioned defender, tackled hard, won the ball and delivered it long and was good in the air. So much so, you could have played him anywhere in the back four and he would put a shift in. I knew I could trust him, or I thought I could, as we all knew at the club that he liked a beer after a game and some would say sometimes before. His local was the Windmill pub, opposite Fair Green, Mitcham and the landlord must have made a fortune out of him. Myself and my secretary, Paul Radcliffe, used to get to the club early on Sunday morning to put the flags up and even roll the pitch if needed, so you can imagine my surprise when arriving at the ground that early Sunday morning, Hoppy was standing outside the clubhouse with his kit bag. I said to him, "Hoppy, you're early!" to which he replied, "Micky, I have not gone home from yesterday's fucking game yet and I'm waiting for a cab." He added there was no need to open up - some of the other Frinton boys are in there having black coffee so I should go and have a cuppa. Well, I lost my discipline hat for a moment and fell about laughing because it was a Sunday non-league scene that will live with me forever, but I must admit, despite some of the aggro and the players' capers, it was also a pleasure to manage such a group of talented players. There was no sadness and it was a fitting way to bring my Sunday playing and management career to an end with a club I had picked up from the floor and taken to the top. Even then, I stepped in to do some secretary work for them, although on a temporary basis, after Jim Jim left as well, and that was a couple of seasons after I decided to quit as manager. Although we had trophies and history-making aplenty, from now on it would be in Saturday football that I would have to prove myself and gain the reputation that I had got from Sunday football management and of course a much faster roller coaster. I am still in touch with the majority of the team, even after 38 years, except with Jim Jim. I never found out what happened to him but we gave him some happy years. That was Sunday football over with until the Surrey F.A. came knocking and my son Daniel and grandson George started their non-league football adventure. So, the roller coaster was now going in for repairs again, but this time the repairs would take a bit longer as the ride needed to go faster.

Roller coaster back in service a phone call and a new beginning; Reedham Park F.C., here I come!

Having finished with Sunday football at club level, I decided to have a rest for a while and contemplate my future, which was going to be in some capacity in Saturday football. My son, Daniel, was growing up and I needed time with him as well. I took him out quite a lot, mostly to football to watch Whyteleafe and Croydon, amongst others. I took him to Whyteleafe often to see his godfather, Bernie Donnelly, play. As for the football and my ambition to be a Saturday manager, I thought maybe the chance would never come. You see, I have never been one for a coaching badge. Just like the driving test, I believe the theory is a waste of time. Experience behind the wheel is far more important. Likewise, with football, nothing beats practical experience, no matter what the level. I was never a big-name player but had a good non-league career and made some good friends and contacts. It is very difficult to get your feet under the table unless you have some big reputation. Of course, I had a good reputation in Sunday football in managing, but what non-league club was going to take on a rookie, non-experienced in managing a Saturday club? Then, out of the blue came a phone call towards the end of the 1981 season. The call came from a club who had not won a trophy since they were formed in 1968. The name of that club was Reedham Park F.C., who played in the Surrey south-eastern premier intermediate league and the chap who phoned me was the secretary, Bob Rumble, who asked me if I would manage the first team for the season 1982/83. I said that I would give it some thought, so he asked if I could go and have a look at them on Saturday and then give him my decision. They were playing at a ground called Sparrow's Den, West Wickham, and it did not take long for me to come to a decision that with a few new faces, I thought I could turn this motley bunch into a successful side. Their approach to the match, I witnessed, was to come onto the pitch in dribs and drabs, no proper warm-up, lashing balls all over the place and showing a lack of formation and discipline. I decided to phone the secretary back on the Saturday evening as I had, by then, made a list of my requirements for the next season before taking the job. When I rang him, he was over the moon to appoint me first-team manager. I think he was a bit taken aback with my demands (which in no way gave any payments to myself or the team). He asked me then what I thought of the team to which I replied that they were probably short of three or four players to have any chance of competing for honours.

I then gave him my list. First was that we could play at Sparrow's Den. He needed to find me a flat, decent playing surface. There would be a complete pre-season training starting in mid-June. There would be competitive pre-season friendlies. The kit would be refurbished or replaced, along with plenty of footballs and training equipment provided and all players in the club would be seen as equal for the first two or three training sessions and then a first-team squad would be chosen and trained separately. I don't think Bob Rumble liked that very much, but Reedham Park were about to undergo the professional touch that I had always tried to bring to the table, and if he was not happy, then I was not the man for his team. Of course, he accepted my list; he would have been bloody daft not to after all those years in the doldrums. Remember, we were non-league and not even senior status, but there was no payment to players except, and this must be quite unique, in the signing of a player when I persuaded one of Whyteleafe's better players and my good friend, Bernie Donnelly, to come and play for me for one season only and then he could then go back to Whyteleafe. Well, Bernie wasn't too keen to step down a level or two but had had just moved into a house in Purley and, with me being a master joiner, I agreed to make and fit the wardrobes in his bedroom before he signed on the dotted line (he paid for the materials). That was going to be a massive signing for us. Also, I brought to the club the experienced Johnny Comoford and those two had an instant impact on the other players, knowing things were going to be a lot different than they had ever known. Other players, of course, heard the news and were phoning the secretary up to join the new Reedham Park. One of the new sides to join the league that season was going to be Fairchild's O.B. Another very good friend of mine, Eddie Mark, who gave me the nickname Turka which he still calls me today after all these years, was going to be playing upfront for them and they were very strong and Eddie, like myself, had that 'win at all costs' mentality. We began training up at the green opposite the Tudor Rose in old Coulsdon and players were complimentary on how professional it all seemed. Bob Rumble, the secretary, had kept his promises in giving us plenty of training equipment, balls, bibs, cones. He also found a good pitch for me for our home games at the Mount Rec, Coulsdon, where the changing rooms were very near to the pitch so that we could go in at half-time and have our cup of tea and discuss the first half and if needed, give a right bollocking. So, all was set for the new season and one must remember that having a stronger first team meant that players would drop down to form a stronger second team and second-team players would drop down to form a stronger third team and that proved to be the case. I think the word was out that

Reedham Park, in all teams, were not going to be the 'also-rans' as in other seasons.

As first-team manager, I cannot remember too many of the games but a couple, in particular, stand out for me and they were against Fairchild's, who had the better of us in the first encounter between ourselves, but we were to get revenge back at the Mount, despite my good friend Eddie Mark being furious at some of the decisions made by the linesman, but as I have said, he hated losing. One other game comes to mind involving one of my players, a super striker by the name of John Parkinson. Johnny was a classy player at that level of football and had not really got to terms with Micky Taylor's dressing room. As always, I wanted the team in my dressing room no later than an hour before kick-off, home or away, and on this occasion, John Parkinson, in his laid-back manner, strolled into my dressing room 20 minutes late. To be fair to John, whereas anyone else would have made an excuse, John promptly told me that he had been shopping with his girlfriend in Croydon, to which I remember replying, "Well, you can go and finish your fucking shopping because your shirt has gone to one of the substitutes." The game was against Limpsfield Blues and we were absolutely superb that day, beating them 10-1 away from home, which put shock waves into the rest of the league. Parky did get on during the game for the last 15 minutes and still managed to bag a hat trick but he learnt that you must never cross Micky Taylor and what he was trying to achieve.

Also, there was one other incident that really had myself, Bernie Donnelly and Johnny Comoford in hysterics before the kick-off when we played Greenside F.C. Bob Rumble had noticed that Bobby Dell, the Greenside keeper, arrived at the ground with an eye patch on. Bob came running out to me saying, "You must tell our forwards their goalkeeper has got an eye patch". Well, as I said, myself, Bernie and Johnny knew Bobby Dell very well and knew that he could be a bit of a prankster at times, as well as being a tremendous goalkeeper. To make things even more laughable, Bobby kept the eye patch on during the warm-up until the referee blew the whistle to start the game, when he removed it quickly and threw it in the back of the net. The picture on Bob Rumble's face was typical of his job as a civil servant - not a sense of humour about him - and his words to me were that he should not be allowed to do that.

But going on from the funny side of the game, there was also the serious side and this was made clear when, before a home game, I told the players quite frankly; "You are the best team in the division and when I look around this dressing room and see the likes of the goalkeeper as good as Tony (Nobby) Astle, midfield player Timmy Boxall (who sadly passed away quite young), young player Jeremy Boxall, a centre forward who scored goals for fun, Simon Boxall and his partner up front, Johnny Parkinson, along with the best winger in the league, Bernie Donnelly and a back four including Johnny Comoford, Dave Nelson and Chris Bryant, I see no reason why I should not make it quite clear that you have to win the next ten games to become champions, without involving any favours from other clubs. So, you all best believe it, because if I believe then you must too." Talk about putting yourself under pressure! But that was my trademark; it was simply called winning at all cost and I knew, looking around that dressing room, that that was possible. The new roller coaster was at a new height now and going fast and what with the second team and third team all doing great, could this be the season that kick-started my Saturday managerial career?

So off we went on the journey of those last ten games, knowing that every game was going to be a cup final and we approached it as if it was. Needless to say, we did complete those ten games without loss and became Surrey Intermediate South-eastern Premier champions, on my theory that you must have talent and hard work. Sometimes the talent goes missing, but hard work must never ever go missing. So, with that, I landed Reedham Park's first-ever trophy, but as I said earlier, I was going to make it a respected club, which I did, and the second team won their championship and the third team followed suit – what a season for Bob Rumble and his club and above all he had made the right choice in making that phone call to me some nine months earlier.

Apart from feeling great about the success in my first season, there was going to be another surprise for me when I found out that the league representative side's manager, Tony Osborne, was going to stand down. I decided to put my name forward as I liked the idea of representative football and becoming the representative manager as well. I had had experience with the Morden and District League representative side and felt confident I would get the job. We had a meeting during the back end of the season with Robin the Merlin Denman and the league secretary, Bruce Scott (whose bloody canary was flying about the bloody room, sitting on my head and then sitting on Robin's head when we were supposed to be having a serious meeting. I'm sure this doesn't happen with the F.A.) We were both appointed, myself as manager and Robin as assistant. I did not know at the time we were going to be inseparable from the minute we met. Although with different clubs, Robin with his beloved Kingswood and me with my new established Reedham Park, we had an understanding of football and we both believed in the same principles when it came to representative football. Myself and Robin had decided to attend a couple of representative games after we were appointed and I can remember at Dorking's Old Meadow Bank ground, watching the representative side in a final and seeing this chap turn up with a duffle bag, dressed in a blazer and tie (so he must have been a committee member or something) and inside that bag was the cup which was won by the Surrey Southwestern League. I said to Robin, "That fucking cup is going to have our ribbons on it next year, mark my words".

So, it was back to Reedham Park and wallowing in my first success in Saturday non-league football and everyone buying into the ideas I had about taking the club forward. What a great season, but when you have had that last sip of champagne, as a manager, you start work for the next season and as I have mentioned in the book before, that road to success will always be under construction. 1983/84 here we come. And that season I was going to have to wear two hats; one for Reedham and one for the representative side and the added pressure of managing in a division higher, which obviously comes with promotion. I also had to try to strengthen the team but I wanted to give the boys a chance and although the team was not of the class of Addiscombe Social in 1972/3 or Thornton Heath, class of 1977/8, there were some very good players that had adapted well so I had to be careful who I signed and that they fitted into the existing team. Bob had been able to move us from the pitch at the Mount to the Southern Rail sports ground in Plough Lane, Croydon which suited us. We had our own bar and clubhouse and the club could make some much-needed money through scratch cards and other things. We had the added bonus of having a floodlight grass training area, which helped with set plays and game plans and one to one with certain players, so as is usual for all non-league clubs, we started back pre-season training with high hopes of another good season. My new signings Billy Forsdick, Jay Boyd, Steve Parker and Tony Hermitage, whose dad was chairman of the famous Sutton United, one of the non-league great clubs, were going to fit in quite well. However, there was also some sadness when, after a few games into the season, my mate's agreement with Bernie Donnelly was actioned and Bernie returned to Whyteleafe F.C., which was the right thing to do as he needed to play at a higher level for our league. Also appearing on the scene was Jay Boyd's Dad, Brian Boyd (who owned his own printing business). To be fair, he offered to help out and was always around on match days to watch his son Jay play who, for that standard, (I would say on today's level would be step six) was a good player to have on board and a good captain. The football and friendship bond between myself and Robin (Merlin) Denman was getting stronger as we assembled the representative side, making phone calls and meeting to decide our squad and this was on top of our club duties - me managing Reedham, and Robin managing Kingswood Wanderers. We were treating this rep appointment with the respect it deserved and never thought the roller coaster was going to get this posh.

For Reedham Park, it was a learning season again and progression on and off the pitch as we were promoted again but not as champions. The 2nd and 3rd teams picked up trophies and so the 1st team, under my management had, in two seasons, gained two promotions and the club had a few trophies to their name. Now for the rep side and our games against the South-western league in a cup final of two legs away first, then home, and if you can remember back to when I first saw the chap from Surrey County F.A. with the cup in that duffle bag and said to Robin we were going to win that next season, well let me tell you now that over the two legs we did and our ribbons were on it. So much hard work went into it and what a good squad we had assembled. There was also some icing on the cake when I was informed that we were to travel to Burton-on-Trent to play Pirelli F.C. at their luxurious sports ground. The coach travel was paid for by the league and we travelled up early on a Saturday morning, arriving in Burton about 12 o'clock for a 3 o'clock kick-off. The players were in good spirits despite a long journey and if you could picture my face and Robin's when we were invited into the canteen, not for a light snack, but expecting my players to sit down and indulge in a two-course roast dinner prior to the game. I promptly, without sounding too rude, told them if they thought we had travelled 3 and a half hours on the coach to play for a trophy with my side having fucking consumed a roast dinner, then it was a tactical move that was not going to happen. I must say I did get some looks from the league's committee members and I am sure some of my players would have willingly tucked into the meal, but Pirelli were very understanding and our roast dinners were put on hold until after the game. We made our way into the changing rooms, played the game on a fantastic surface, played football that was a delight to watch and won the trophy by a 3-0 victory. Needless to say, the roast dinner went down a treat but I did think that the £10 per person whip-round was a little excessive and myself and Robin certainly did not think that we were going to be entertained until midnight before the coach left for home, but after such a good first season with the rep side, you have to let the players let their hair down at some stage and once again, me and Robin decided to throw our manager's hats in the dustbin for the evening

As all managers will tell you at non-league level, it is not long before you have to put your manager's hat back on again and that is exactly what we had to do at 2 am on a Sunday morning at a service station on the M1 coming home. The boys needed a stop for obvious reasons and also, in some cases, a cup of black coffee, but imagine the scene when we arrived in the café and sitting down at a long table was a group of Red Indians in full headgear with painted faces returning from a convention. My players, who obviously had had enough alcohol intake, decided to, in a friendly way, do a war dance around the Red Indians on the long table, throwing plastic knives and singing 'Three wheels on my wagon and I'm still rolling along, those Cherokees won't bother me'. Listen to the song on YouTube by the New Christy Minstrels and you'll be rolling around yourself! I looked at Robin and the league committee and thought, oh my God, this is going to kick off any minute now, but it didn't and they saw it as good humour which I am glad of. Sadly, that was not the end because, as we left to join our coach, they left and they boarded their coach and the boys decided to do a war dance in the car park, preventing their coach from leaving for a few moments. Picture it all if you can. It will live in my memory forever and I only mention the culprits in private conversations. But again, this is non-league football and not your top pro clubs. One particular player in the rep side was missing from this game. A certain Tony Williams from a club by the name of Ras United stood out for me as having that extra slice of talent that made you think he could actually go on and be a professional, so with this in mind and with my contacts, I managed to get Tony a trial with Fulham F.C., whose manager, Ray Lewington, I had made contact with and he trusted my opinion of this player, so much so that he put him straight into Fulham's reserve side in a game on a Monday afternoon against Millwall at the Old Den. I was so excited at the prospect for Tony that I decided to take my son out of school for the afternoon to go and watch the match. The game was obviously played at a much quicker pace than Tony was used to, but he was far from being outclassed and had a very comfortable game, given the fact he was playing against full-time pros. I remember standing outside the players' entrance after the game waiting for Tony and also Mr Lewington, to see what the next step would be. Lewington told me he was pleased with Tony's performance and that he would be in the side on the Friday evening against Norwich City at Carrow Road and would receive instructions where to meet the team bus. I was also invited to travel with them, but as the saying goes, and it is the same in non-league football as in pro football, it is a funny old game because what happened was the game at Norwich was called off and Tony was asked to train with the reserve team instead. For some reason and I will never know the real truth, Tony was not to return to Fulham and having had a rather strong-worded phone call from Ray Lewington, and I must say I replied with the same tone, he had his scouts out on the Sunday morning to see Tony play and waited in the car park. What happened then I can only leave you to guess but it certainly wasn't the type of thing that a professional football club were going to tolerate. So that ended Tony's brief career as a pro but did my ego a world of good to know that I had an instinct for a good player. Despite what happened, Ray Lewington was a hard man to please and Tony had managed to do that, even if only for one game. I must say this was not a matter for the Surrey South-eastern Intermediate League and so myself and Robin Denman kept our faith in Tony and included him in the squad for the 1984/85 season.

On the club front, it was going to be a tough season amongst the top flight in the Surrey South-eastern Intermediate League Premier A division, but we did manage to acquire the services of a super player by the name of Willie Bennett, who came to us via Brian Boyd and a brown envelope. Ironic that Willy had played in the first-ever Vase final against Hoddesdon Town at Wembley for Epsom and Ewell, which they lost, but it was better than I could achieve at Epsom and Ewell because I couldn't get into the squad. I also had the rep side to think about, as well as my club, as did Robin, but club football must come first if you manage both and I again recruited players to Reedham Park, as we did in the representative side. You never rest on your laurels and I would sometimes think to myself, look how far you have come in such a short space of time in managing Saturday football. Of course, in the rep football it was hard getting a team together, having no training or get-togethers before a game, but still bringing home the silverware (Gareth Southgate don't know he's been born!) As I've said before, Paul Fairclough does a good job with the non-league England C team, but only a good job - where are the trophies? It's all about winning.

So, let's get back to season 1984/85 which saw the club again propel itself even more as a well-respected and well-run football club with an ambition to go further. The premier A division was as hard as it could get and our old enemy Fairchild's O.B. had now become Coney Hall F.C., with their own ground. There was also Croydon M.O., Robin's Kingswood Wanderers, Bookham and Reigate Town to name a few. It was going to be the same for the second and third teams because they had stepped up a division as well, but as always, I loved a challenge and that's exactly what we got. We needed desperately to give a good account of ourselves as we were looking to join the Johnson Wax Surrey County premier football league at some stage in the future. It was a nail-biting season, to say the least, and it was about to be the club's most successful season in terms of trophies. We finished third in the league, level on points with Kingswood Wanderers and only two points behind the champions, Croydon M.O. but there is nothing like a good cup run. Although it is true the league is a marathon and the cup is a sprint, nevertheless, we found ourselves in the semi-final against a very strong Fetcham side who, although not doing that well in the league, were certainly having a good cup run and I was two games away from winning the Surrey Intermediate premier cup. It was a game I can remember to this day. We went behind after five minutes and, although inspiration was never in doubt, I just had a gut feeling that maybe this was not our day and even more so when we hit the bar. But we kept on and we got our reward when Keith Hewitt found the back of the net just before half-time. My hopes now had been restored and I told the boys at half-time to go for it and take their chance. That's exactly what we did and we took control, having plenty of chances to increase our lead, but it was late in the game when our centre forward, John Parkinson, put us into the final with a powerful header. There were jubilant scenes at the clubhouse after the game, but as always with semi-finals, the first thing that comes to mind as a manager is now, we have to win the final. The final itself was played at Dorking Football Club and I had less fear about the final than I did about the semi-final because we had played so well in the league and I knew we had the quality. But preparation is a big thing in cup finals as it should be for any game, really. Our opponents were Caius F.C., so we had a team coach to take the players and the fans. We arrived at the ground nice and early and I can remember the look on the players' faces in the changing rooms when from out of my pocket I took a packet of cigarettes, and a box of matches, threw them on the table and said to the boys "For the first time this season, if you feel like a fucking smoke, have one now!" and I promptly put a fag in my mouth and lit it. I didn't even smoke but the amazing thing about this little tactic was, it took all the nerves out of that dressing room and that became a reality when after only three minutes of the game we took the lead when young Jeremy Boxall scored a perfect solo goal. To say that we were in control of the game throughout was an understatement and we settled the issue just before half-time when John Parkinson scored what proved to be the decisive goal and sent our fans wild with delight, knowing that we had not only one hand on the cup, we now had both hands. I remember the boys lifting me on their shoulders and carrying me in front of the main stand, a moment I will always remember as I had worked my socks off for three years to get this football club the recognition it deserved. That night, back at the clubhouse, we celebrated not only the winning of that premier cup, but the winning of two other cups, runners-up in another two league championships, and another league runner-up place, this all achieved by the first, second, third, and fourth teams. A haul of six trophies in one season were all on show at our dinner and dance at the Aerodrome Hotel in Croydon. What a great year for the club, but of course, I had another hat to wear and that was with the rep side who again were successful in retaining the cup against the South-western Intermediate League and also winning the Surrey Inter-league cup final and another trip to Burton-on-Trent to retain our trophy, again against Pirelli football club. This time, though, there was to be no roast dinner, no £10 per man whip rounds, and no Red Indians on the M1, it was simply game won, couple of beers, and back in Croydon by 11 pm (I was now feeling so confident in my own ability and soon that would be put to the test even further).

Events of the summer of 1985 saw some changes, in as much as I had felt that on the managing side, I had taken the club as far as I possibly could and it was now time to step down and have a well-deserved rest. Also, my representative colleague, Robin (Merlin) Denman, had seen his Kingswood Wanderers get promoted to the Surrey County premier football league and also the Surrey intermediate eastern league decided to disband their representative side, but again, over the few years that we were in charge, we had won enough silverware using a fair cross-section of players within the league and as they say, more so in non-league football, all good things come to an end. So, what now for my beloved Reedham Park for season 1985/86 and what role away from the dressing room was I going to play? You've guessed it; I was silly enough to take the role of chairman. I will never know what on earth made me do that. I suppose it was really that I could not let go of my ambitions. The club had now moved to a private sports ground up at Netherne Hospital in Coulsdon. The pitch was on a slope, end to end, but the clubhouse was okay and we could begin to prepare for a higher standard of football. John Comerford took over as first-team manager and carried on the good work and progress that we had made.

I thought the job of chairman would be quite an experience and not involve too much of my time. God, how I was wrong and I must admit it is the only time, when I look back, that I do have a slight bit of sympathy for chairmen of football clubs. I never thought that, behind the scenes, there could be so many issues to have to deal with and so many meetings to attend and for obvious reasons, the job was not really suited to me and I remember receiving a phone call from my dear friend Robin telling me that the Johnson Wax Surrey premier league were going to be looking to run a representative side for the 1986/87 season and would I be interested in applying for the position? I said yes and expected to hear in the future about the date for an interview. Meanwhile, with that thought in my mind, I decided to see the season out as chairman in loyalty to the club. I must say, though, that we did have some good nights up there, fund-raising and I also had the thought of playing veterans' football. This I was able to do playing for Robin's Kingswood Vets, who were a very good side and had some quality players, including the England and Chelsea defender, Ken Shellito. But I tell you what, like all football, Robin wanted the best out of you and although he refused to enter any veteran's competitions, we played some very good sides and played at some lovely sports grounds with the food and beer laid on after. Our own ground was over at Tolworth at the Kingston Poly sports complex and that had a great surface and a good clubhouse, but like most of this book so far, there is always a memory that will come to mind and that came in the form of a fixture we played over at Phipps Bridge estate, Mitcham against the Bath Tavern, on a pitch that was flat but with hardly any grass, and changing rooms that were surrounded by barbed wire. For those who don't know about the estate, some 25 years ago it was a place of reputation for all kinds of hard fighting boys who you would not like to cross at any time, and also the Bath Tavern did not take kindly to strangers, but non-league football has a bond of its own and expecting the worst, I was quite surprised how their team behaved and how we were treated in the Bath Tavern after the game as one of the locals had the beer flowing and a good spread put on. That was vets' football… My time now had come to say goodbye to Reedham Park, who were to change their name to Netherne FC in a few years' time, but I had laid the foundations and my good friend and former player, John Comerford, was to take the club on further, along with my good friend Steve Clark, who was head of the F.A. cup competitions across the board; Vase, Trophy, Sunday cup, and was always on the TV holding and shaking that green bag with the clubs' numbers inside. How things have changed. Do we really want to know the number of our team beforehand and have some machine like the lottery? Just pick

out a ball from the bag, enjoy the excitement and that's it done. I remember the days when it was done on the radio when the famous announcement was made: "Now over to Lancaster Gate for the F.A. cup draw." What lovely times they were; Steve Clark was to pay me a great compliment in one of Reedham Park's programmes during season 1990/91 when they finally made the Surrey premier league and I quote from the programme: 'Our rise to where we are now is down to Micky Taylor, who guided the club up from the lower reaches of the Intermediate League to the top and paved the way for the club's current respect and position that it has reached.' I have kept that programme to this day but myself and Steve, as I think I have said before in the book, were to meet in very unusual circumstances and that you will read later on.

CHAPTER EIGHT

1988/89-1992/93 this roller coaster has seen its day; I'm jumping on a new and better one now in the non-league fairground and bigger times ahead in representative football.

As I said, the Surrey premier league wanted to talk to me about managing their newly formed representative side and so I went along to meet them for the interview with Robin, although he was not going to be involved to start with, as he was looking after his own side, Kingswood Wanderers. On the interview committee was the league secretary David Havenhand, Peter Adams, chairman, who was on the F.A. committee, and Reg Mendham, who was also on the F.A. committee. Well as far as the interview went, it was a done and dusted deal really, and the job was mine if I wanted it (obviously they had done their homework). I found the three of them so polite and passionate about their football at non-league level and knew that not only was I going to be the manager of a very exclusive representative side, but I felt very strongly that I did not want to let these three gentlemen down in any way. Of course, like it has been said on many occasions, representative football is not easy and the higher you go, the more quality players are involved, and also the quality of the clubs who become very protective of their players. One club was Ditton F.C., who to be fair were entitled to participate or not, but they decided to get their players involved if needed and I felt good about that. But I made it clear to the club it was not a problem for me as there were enough teams in the league to cover my playing squad if required. So, I set about my job and arranged for some friendlies.

I can always remember my first friendly in the 1988/89 season. It was a very prestigious one. We had, on the committee, obvious links with all kinds of well-connected representative sides and it was with great pride that I had to pick a squad to face the famous Royal Engineers at Staines Town. The reason I state famous is that they played in the first-ever F.A. cup final in 1872 and won the F.A. Cup in 1875. So, you can imagine that with their tradition and the fact they never played that many representative games, they were certainly going to put a good side out and I was to be tested very early on in my new job. We won the game quite comfortably. I can't remember the exact score line, but as I have said, I felt very proud to have swapped pennants, our one with the Surrey County badge and theirs with that famous old trophy, the F.A. cup. It was great also for the players who enjoyed the evening and I felt that we were going to gel quite quickly as a unit. Needless to say, the committee was also very pleased and it was to be my first pat on the back, but not my last by far. So, we continued that season and I was looking at all the clubs involved in the league and the players and knew that during the latter part of the season we would be entering the Surrey Inter-league trophy. The players came from such clubs as Frinton Rovers, my old club, Kingswood Wanderers, and Ashtead among others. Unfortunately, the first season was going to consist of only two competition games; the others were just friendlies, and that just wasn't enough to achieve what I wanted to in getting a side together as near to a club side as you could get. Hence, we didn't manage to win that trophy in our first season in representative football, although we had some good results in friendly games.

I remember playing a complete Sussex County under-21 side and earning a draw against a very talented team that included Crawley Town and Brighton and Hove Albion players. Despite this, I felt that we needed something more in the way of competition games and raised the point with my committee to see whether we could possibly get invited into a new competition called the South-eastern Inter-league competition. As I have said, my committee were very keen to take part and we were accepted. So, it was going to be a very busy 4 years in this new tough competition for me now at the helm, on a journey that would have the roller coaster having more ups than downs and it was time to buy the tin of silver polish once again. It would be very hard for me, and boring for you as a reader, if I were to take you through every game during those years of representative football, so I am going to take a season at a time and highlight certain games and stories. But I must say that getting rep sides together is not easy, as you have a problem with trying to have a training session with the chosen squad. Also, some of the clubs were not helpful in releasing players, although most of the clubs in the Surrey premier league did not have floodlights then, so I had no problem with the midweek games and the players saw themselves as being in the limelight, so to speak. I pointed out to them on many times, when they were selected to play, that I considered them to be the best twenty players out of a league that had over 300 players registered, and if that is not some kind of honour then they have no ambition at all as footballers. Luckily for me, it was the opposite, as the players and management of other clubs were not happy if their players had not been selected, which meant that I had broken the ice and made a good impact on those clubs and also their supporters as well had their views. I had a very strong code of conduct for my players which went like this: you play for me and Robin with a winning attitude because we selected and trust you; you represent your club in all you do while you are in our company, and you respect the referee and officials and the league committee at all times, and no way mobile phones must be on in dressing room before the game and for at least 15 mins after the game. If you can't do that, then I don't want you, no matter how good you think you are or we think you are.

As for our referees for these games, they were of the top quality and for a lot of our home games, we had a top-class man in the middle who I considered the best of all, Mr Ray Lewis, who had officiated in some very big pro games but was always willing to give his time to non-league football. Such was the class of the man that I remember in one game he came trotting past my dug-out and quite simply said," Micky, if you don't get hold of your No. 7 as he is getting on my nerves, then I will fucking send him off and I don't want to have to do that!" He was a players' man who would always have a laugh and a joke, and if you swore at him, he would simply swear back, providing a certain word was not used. Of course, he would get things wrong, but because of his attitude towards the teams in play, you were forgiving of him. I call that respect for each other. I wish referees would have that attitude now, instead of flashing cards about all over the place, but it must be a two-way thing as well, with benches setting examples. I can honestly say that during my managerial roles in club football, and apart from one incident when working for the County F.A., I have never given referees any verbal from the bench, as I would just simply at the end of the game knock on their door and ask to have a word. Never do it at half-time as you have too much to do in that dressing room and you know how quick that fifteen minutes goes. Plenty more on refs later on, but to this day I still have a coat that Ray Lewes had manufactured for all Surrey County youth staff with the County badge on one side and on the other side was a ref whistle with Ray's initials (nice touch).

So, it's on with the rep side and my second season and the new competition in the 1989/90 season. What was going to make it a bit more special was that my old club, Reedham Park, had been promoted and all my earlier years working as their manager had paid off and their players were at my disposal again. Never in my wildest dreams did I think our paths would cross again but they did and it was going to be to my advantage. I knew the season was going to be tough because, like any job in non-league football management, winning games keeps your job safe and a bad season might see me gone. I had no budget to work with, but also no supporters to answer to and although it was an honour for me, you still had a committee to answer to and a responsibility, to clubs who have released their players, to look after them on and off the park. I would sometimes have managers coming up to me after a game and asking, "How can you get my player to play like that when he doesn't do that for me?" and my reply was simple; "Do you really know and understand your player like I do?"

There is always a downside to anything that is good and it was that you would spend weeks watching players to fit into the team jigsaw, but you do miss that week-to-week dressing room involvement, but it was a small price to pay for success at representative level. It was going to be hard work as we had no warm-up games because all the County league sides had entered and were not willing to play you outside the competition. We started the league with a home game against the F.C.N. Music, Kent County league at Redhill F.C. and played very well that night and were comfortable in beating them. The stars were shining brightly in captain Steve Lake (Frinton Rovers), Randolph Payne (BT Telecoms) and Alan (Buster) Dorrill, (Reedham Park) among those in a very strong squad. Any manager reading this book will know what I mean when you get that feeling, just by one game, that you have something special in your hands, the way they gelled together, playing for each other, treating it as though it was their club and in a way it was going to be for at least six games during the season.

The players were really enjoying the experience playing against other County league's rep sides and the standard was high and demanding. We also had the Surrey Inter-league gup to play for but found it less demanding than County league sides and we soon took care of the Surrey Western league over two legs to reach the final of the Surrey Inter-league cup, where we were to play the Surrey Combination league at Woking F.C., but we still had three games to go in the South-eastern Inter-league and next up was away to the Middlesex league; also one of the last games to be played at the old Hounslow Town ground, which had a slope. This was a big pitch for us to play on, our football creating problems for Middlesex all over the park, but as usual, possession counts for nothing unless you put the ball in the back of the net and that night, we failed to do that. We put ourselves in the position where we had to beat both Unijet Sussex league and the Essex league to win the trophy. Our next game was to play the Essex league at Basildon town F.C. in a must-win game. Once again, we played really well, full of confidence and came away with another very good win, but this time our possession saw us through, scoring three goals with no reply and set up the final game against Unijet Sussex league which was going to be now a cup final situation. We had to win, as a draw would see Sussex as champions. The game was played at Redhill F.C., in front of a good-sized crowd. We had a management discussion and decided to play a different formation and go all out and win the game. I can remember the game very well and it featured an outstanding performance from Steve Parker (Reedham Park), who would in the future be my captain. We played very well and scored on the stroke of half-time and again, our possession was a delight to watch as we were leading and creating chances. It was obvious that Sussex had come with a plan to stop us scoring and play on the brake, which they had failed to do, but you must give them credit as, with minutes to go and with virtually two hands on the trophy, we had the game snatched from us with a late goal and little time left to get one back. Their plan had worked - play for a draw and get a draw, but we should have had the game well won before that killer goal. It was a heart-breaking night but the committee had seen the hard work we had done all season and came into the dressing room at the end and told us how proud they were and that we must go to Woking and win the Surrey Inter-league cup. Myself and Robin Denman had a canny way of dealing with disappointment: after the game, we didn't talk about coming runners-up in a prestigious tournament, but more about going to Woking and lifting that trophy and that next season we would see that our ribbons were going to be on the Tom Stabler trophy, without any doubt.

It was now coming to the end of the season and off to Woking for the cup final against the Surrey Combination football league. As often happens in non-league football, from disappointment can come success and glory and I must say again, our performance at Woking on a good surface was absolutely first class and gave us the win that we deserved and the trophy and I have one fond memory from that game and it will live with me forever. Any player, chairman or manager will know what it is like to be in a dressing room when you have just won the cup, although having said that, there are some who may never have had that experience. So, there we were with the cup in the dressing room and in walks our committee, led by our chairman of the league, the one and only Peter Adams, one of the nicest guys you could ever wish to meet in football. Peter and the committee went around the dressing room congratulating everyone, took the cup from the table and said, "Right lads, I will be back in a minute; the cup needs filling up for celebration'. The boys and I had showered and the cup was still was not back in the dressing room, Then the door burst open and in walks Peter with his famous grin as wide as the Grand Canyon, with the cup in his hands, full to the brim and stated, "I am sorry, lads, they had no champagne in the bar, so I decided to buy a bottle of whisky and fill the cup up with that." The look on my players' faces was absolutely incredible and I promptly said to Peter, "What a lovely gesture, but the boys have to drive home and cannot take any risks with such a potent drink." I don't I think any of them had ever tasted whisky. He again laughed and said, "Right, I will go and get the lads a crate of beers delivered to the dressing room and I am sure we will get rid of the whisky in the boardroom." We did get our beers and had a great ending to a great night.

What a fantastic bunch of footballers I had been lucky to work with all that season; John Richards (Springfield Hosp) Marc Fabian (Ashford Town) and Andy Boxall (Ditton S.F.C.), to name a few. Some names would change the following season, but some would be with me again for the ride. I must say I wondered what the whisky did to the cup! God only knows, but we were to find out! The season finished in a playing role for me. I was working for the Croydon Council and for some reason, the Council were asked to raise a football team to play the Surrey Street market traders in a charity game to be played at Duppas Hill recreation ground. Our Council team was made up of councillors and workers, of which I was one. The turnout for this game was amazing and the pitch had spectators on all sides, creating a great atmosphere and you could tell the Surrey Street market boys were up for it. I knew most of them and they were giving it big time weeks before the game which created the interest for people to attend the game. The mayor of Croydon was there and also the then Crystal Palace manager, Steve Coppell, to present the cup and medals to the winning side. Like most of these charity games, it went to a penalty shoot-out which we won and lifted the trophy. I still have the picture of me collecting my winner's medal from Steve Coppell. Now, the market boys wanted revenge and challenged us to a return game the following year, which we had no option but to accept. This time, they wanted the game played at Croydon arena. I knew they were going to bring in some ringers, so we did the same, which really took the edge off the reason behind it all being a charity event. Anyway, we won the game again and I remember well going up to collect my winner's medal once again, this time from the mayor of Croydon. He looked at the state of my right leg, which was cut from the knee right down the shin bone with stud marks, and stated that this was awful and he could not see the point of playing again the following year, and so that was the end of that. To be honest, I just thought he did not know much about football, as really this was sometimes the norm, in those years and before in non-league football, and as you have read earlier in the book, I had been dealt a lot worse than that.

So finally, the season over and as for the Surrey premier league, my job was safe and I was looking forward to another crack at the title in the 1990/91 season, as I was still making a name for myself at representative level. That is exactly what I did; we played in the South-Eastern Inter-League cup again and against the likes of Sussex, Kent, Middlesex, and Essex leagues. We had a new crop of players, including a very good keeper in Andy Hilton (Hersham R.B.L) and Paul Ottoway (Croydon M.O), who were going to be part of a very strong squad which I felt was stronger than the year before. I had set my sights on winning the South-east Counties championship for the first time and not let it slip through mine and Robin's fingers again. This time, the games were to be strung out a bit more and not played towards the end of the season in a mad rush, to fit them in along with the Surrey Inter-league cup. Within the league itself, there were to be changes and I will come to that when I have finished the games account of this season 90/91.

First up for us was a visit to play the Essex league at a venue called the Basildon Bowl and although not the perfect start, we came away with a 1-1 draw after being 1-0 down at half-time and felt we should have won the game. Our next game was a

Surrey Inter-league game and it was to be revenge for the Surrey Combination at Hampton F.C. as we lost 4-2. To be fair, they were the better side on the night and I remember thinking after that defeat, where do we go from here? I had treated the Surrey Inter-league cup with contempt as I was after the big one, and I had rested some of the squad players to give others a chance to impress. The lesson learned there was always play your best side or you will face defeat, which is what happened, but players and others who have known me through the years as a player and manager at non-league level will know I was always confident of turning things around and that my 'where do we go from here' soon turned into 'I tell you where we go; we remain unbeaten in two seasons in the south-east counties so continue that and we will win that trophy!' So, all attention was focused on the next South-east Counties game, a home game against a strong Sussex County league at Redhill F.C.

The game was a cracker of a match and we took the lead when the strong Tony Enever (Frinton Rovers) headed home just before half-time. I felt then that Sussex were going to have a right go in the second half at us, and that is what they did and again we were to be denied victory when they equalised in injury time, just as they had done the season before. The only difference this time was that we still had two games to play, and with other results going our way, we needed two wins to get that trophy. They were at home to Middlesex and away to Kent. The first of those games was at home to Middlesex County league at Croydon arena in a game that we completely dominated from start to finish, despite a gusty wind cutting across the pitch (nothing changes at the arena then), but we played some good football and got our win 3-0. The big game with the Kent League for the title was up and running, so in between, I was busy working with Reedham Park F.C., who were soon to become Netherne F.C., trying to form a veteran side for the 1991/92 season as I had been playing for Robin Denman's vets side, Kingswood and as was my makeup,

I wanted to take charge of my own side. So, all parties agreed and we were going to play as Netherne vets, using the home pitch on Sundays, and bring some much-needed revenue into the club.

On to the game with the Kent league to be played at my old club Bromley F.C., at the Hayes Lane ground. I must admit I was a bit nervous about the venue as I never really had the happiest of times there, but there was no need to worry as we put on a first-class performance and beat Kent and became champions and lifted that Tom Stabler trophy after two seasons in which we still remained unbeaten and that takes some doing in the company we were keeping. Those County league sides were all strong and took the competition very seriously. The roller coaster was running very nicely thank you, and also off the pitch things were starting to happen with a certain Mr Reg Mendham joining the committee, to whom I took a liking straight away, with his humour and of course his links to the Surrey F.A and what it could do for me. My old club, Reedham Park, changed their name to Netherne F.C. with my good friend, Steve Clark, taking over as secretary. (Steve had a good job with the F.A. as cup competitions director).

So off we go again; 1991/2 season and as well as the rep side, I had the Netherne vets to look after as well, which to be fair was a nice diversion and allowed me to have a game at 44 years young. Also, with the rep side, there had been many player changes from clubs to other clubs within the league, and one player in particular caught my eye. His name was Kevin Simpson, or just plain Sibbo. He had made the move from Frinton Rovers to Netherne. I have seen many good non-league players strike a dead ball, but nothing compares to Sibbo. He was lethal, and in our first South-east Counties rep game that season, away to Essex at Chelmsford City (their old ground next to the county cricket ground), he was to prove my selection spot on. The night will be remembered for more than just a football match as you will read, but first the match. It was played on a perfect surface and a very close game and we wanted to keep our unbeaten record intact. We won the game 3-0, but the night belonged to Sibbo, with two of the best direct free-kicks I think I have ever seen. I can't give you exact times, but early in the first half, all of thirty yards out, he strolled up and buried the ball in the top hand corner of the Essex net. I don't even think the goalkeeper saw it, but I certainly did! One thing is for sure; Sibbo knew what he was going to do the minute he stepped up to the ball, and would you believe, midway through the second half, this time 40 yards out, a direct free kick again and he puts the ball top right-hand corner, leaving their goalkeeper with no hope. We added a third goal in the final minutes but as I said, the night belonged to Sibbo. My son, Daniel, was with me that night, a budding 14-year-old goalkeeper with Crystal Palace, and as we had laid on a team bus, I decided that he could come to the game.

A great night was about to be turned in to a night of horror for all the players, myself and the committee members. Essex had laid on their normal healthy spread after the game and we were all on the team bus at around 10.15 pm. The boys were all in joyful mood until just after crossing the Dartford Bridge, one of the lads shouted, "I think there is smoke coming from the back of the coach!" I ran down to tell the driver who obviously pulled in on the hard shoulder. It was a very cold December evening and we were ushered off the coach just in case it caught fire. I remember the driver making a phone call and informing us that there were no drivers available to bring out a relief bus to us. By this time, it was 12.30 am and we waited and waited and at around 2.30 am, a London transport single-decker bus turned up, sent by the coach company. We transferred all our belongings and kit on to the bus, which still had on the front No. 12 Norwood Junction. Of course, the one thing that the bus had that the players found quite amusing was a bell, so you can imagine now, we are travelling round the M25 with the bell constantly ringing! The driver pulled on to the hard shoulder and his words were quite clear; "If you don't stop fucking ringing that bell, you can all get off my fucking bus!" Needless to say, the boys decided to obey his instructions and we arrived back home about 4.30 am. We had to go to work that day and my son had to go to school, but it was alright for Reg Mendham; he was retired and as I said, he had a good sense of humour and could see the funny side of it all. I think it just proves you can't always have a perfect night, but I dread to think what the atmosphere would have been like if we had lost. I always wonder how long it would have taken for your precious premiership club to have to wait for a replacement coach; probably a fleet of taxis or limousines within 20 minutes at worst. But the funny thing about all of this is that it brought the squad of players closer together and was the talking point every time we met up for a game.

We did not have to wait long for that as our next opponents were F.C.N. Kent league at Chipstead F.C. and it was, as always, a tough game. We saw ourselves being outplayed at times but kept playing our style of football which had served us so well, but it was no surprise that with the clock running down, Kent took the lead when our ever-present and reliable goalkeeper Andy Hilton failed to deal with a cross and it was slotted home at the far post. Our two-year South-east unbeaten run was under threat until that man Kevin Simpson saved the day with one of his special free kicks, 35 yds out and bang! top corner again with seconds to go.

In the Surrey Inter-league cup, I had decided, after what happened last season, to treat it with more respect and field the strongest side. So, with that in mind, we travelled to Camberley Town F.C., to play the Woking league and came away with a good 3-0 win and a performance to match. During this period, I had heard rumours that one of our committee members, Reg Mendham, was going to ask me if I would like to become involved in working for the Surrey F.A. as a scout for the under 18s and the under 16s, and so I waited for the approach. Meanwhile, games were coming thick and fast and our next South-East Counties rep game was at home to the Sussex County league at Corinthian Casuals and it was possibly our best performance to date as we took them apart 4-1. We needed just one more win against Middlesex County league to lift the title again and make history as being undefeated in 3 seasons; some achievement, even by my standards.

Away from rep football, the Netherne veteran team I was running was doing okay. We had played 6 games, won 2, lost 2 and drawn 2 and progressed in the Surrey vets cup but unfortunately, it was to be the Surrey cup that was going to be the reason for me disbanding the vets' team and seeking to play instead of running the team. The reason for this was we were playing a side called Robin Hood Rovers, who, as soon as they arrived, were complaining about the dressing rooms, and also that the pitch was not playable as it was heavy. I thought then this is vets' football not semi-pro non-league and the final nail in the coffin was when the ref gave them a penalty for handball (it was not the penalty that bothered me but the fact he sent my player off for handling the ball with intent). I mean, after all, we were playing for fun not to have players sent off when they had given up their time to play and enjoy themselves. So that was it for me; I just lost interest and called it a day and concentrated on my rep football totally.

Reg Mendham, as expected, approached me to work with the Surrey County F.A. youth and I agreed and felt quite honoured. All that remained was for me to be proposed and seconded at a Surrey County F.A. meeting in August. By the time that meeting took place, we had played Middlesex County league at Uxbridge Town F.C. and beaten them 3-0 to lift the trophy again and still keep our 3-year unbeaten tag in the competition. Things happen quite quickly in football, as you all know, and out of the blue came the news that our sponsor for the rep side, Johnson Wax, were to withdraw their money at the end of the 1992/3 season, so at least we had another season. We also got to the final of the Surrey Inter-league cup but lost 3-0 at Molesey F.C. to our old friends and enemy the Surrey Combination. No excuses, the squad had won that trophy before but were giving me the vibes that they wanted to complete a triple by winning that cup again and remaining unbeaten into the bargain...

Back to the Surrey F.A. now, and my appointment on the committee which was in August 1992. I was appointed chief scout with a view to joining the management team at some stage, but I must admit I was to become very apprehensive after talking to Reg about the F.A. It went something like this; "You will enjoy it with the F.A. We have all the best hotels and travel. Also, last season we travelled up to play Lancashire in the F.A. County youth cup final at Bolton Wanderers' ground. We had a great weekend!" he said. "We were treated like royalty - great hotel, great food; everything was just top drawer." But I was amazed because he never mentioned the game until I asked him the outcome, to which he replied, "Dear Micky, we lost 5-0, I think, but at least we had made the final," to which I replied, "If any fucking team of mine, F.A. or club level whatever, had lost like that, they would have been on the bus home on the Saturday night and fuck the reception and the hotel!" Well, you should have seen his face; it was a picture, and even he had to laugh to my response. But I realised very quickly that this was the F.A. and you must take defeat on the chin, or so they thought. I found the management teams very nice football people, Paul Midwinter and Micky Spicer, under 18s and Mike Godfrey and Brian Stone, under 16s and they made me feel welcome straight away, so I had a twofold job for that first season, especially as I had never worked in youth football and only got involved in watching my son Daniel train with Crystal Palace as a goalkeeper. However, I knew a player when I saw one, no matter what age, so I had to get out there and see what was about in the County F.A., watching plenty of southern youth league games, Surrey school games and also looking after the rep side in our final season, which was stressful, to say the least. But what we achieved with the Surrey premier rep side in that final year was quite remarkable in as much as myself and Robin still managed to keep the flame burning and just add a couple of more players to the squad which was becoming very much like a club side rather than a rep side. It was that type of thinking that was going to stand me well for the future in working for the F.A.

Our first fixture in that 1992/93 season was a tough home game against Middlesex County league at Croydon sports arena, which ended up a 1-1 draw and it was a point gained with a late goal and still unbeaten. Next up for us was a home game against our old enemy from Essex. This time we played at Redhill F.C. and we certainly had the bit between our teeth as we set about getting another 3points. The game was hard as always, but we got the early goal and that settled us down and we took control and added a second goal midway through the second half to give us a 2-0 win and go two points behind Sussex who were top. This was a familiar situation for me, in as much as we still had all to play for and keep that unbeaten record intact, but that was how the competition was; you could not afford a defeat or more than two draws or you were out of contention. Simple equation really, but for us non-league managers, a very stressful one.

So, we had Kent County league away and Sussex County league away to determine the outcome of our last season as the league's representative side. We played the F.C.N. Music Kent County league side at Tonbridge F.C. on march 30th1993, knowing anything less than a win and it would be game over as Sussex had beaten Middlesex and were waiting for us. As usual, the boys played very well and we took control early on and raced into a two-goal lead midway through the first half, but Kent had other ideas and slowly crept back into the game, adding a goal just before half-time, so I changed a few things around during the break and those changes caused them all kinds of problems in the second half. They thought that we would sit on our lead and defend what we had got, but little did they know, I always had a policy of best form of defence is attack, so with our three up front and them not being able to cope, we added a further two goals, took our three points and set up a cup final-type game with the Sussex County league at Burgess Hill F.C. on 15th April.

At this point, I was beginning to earn a reputation, within the non-league world, as a successful representative manager. I use the word earn rather than given a reputation because that normally associates with failure of not being able to manage. So, with all this in mind, we had about two weeks to prepare for our final game. There have not been many stories of my time with the rep. side, but it was to end with a remarkable situation and one that I still think of today. The lesson to be learnt is simply never believe you're beaten, but you have to accept defeat if that is the outcome. As long as you have done all you can. Non-league fans are more forgiving than professional club fans as they know you have a living to earn outside of football and at times that can be very demanding. Also, what they pay on the gate is nothing like what they would pay to watch a non-league game. So now I will tell you what happened in the two weeks before that crucial game. I had lost no fewer than four of my regular squad players through injuries and on the night, we played Sussex, I had a bare eleven players and was just hoping that we were not going to get any injuries during the game. When we arrived at Burgess Hill F.C., you could sense that Sussex County league were ready for a celebration party as a draw would give them a title. You might think that being a representative side you would be able to just pick up the 'phone to a club whose player you had in your notebook and he would promptly make himself available. It doesn't work like that. Some players are just not prepared to come and sit on the bench (you must remember there are no financial gains, only the honour) which to me was hard to accept, but they had had a long season and so were probably just wanting a rest.

And so, to the match; myself and Robin could not have wished for a better eleven players than we had in our dressing room and we knew, against the odds, they would do their best. So, in front of quite a large partisan crowd, Sussex began to put us to the sword and although you must always, as a manager, keep your private thoughts to yourself and not influence your players into negativity, as Sussex took a 2-0 lead in the first half, I did believe that they had got both hands on the trophy, but at half-time, my thoughts and Robin's were relayed to the players, that we still felt we had a chance. I made one very important change; I went with a three at the back, took one of my midfield players and put him upfront. His name is Alan (Buster) Dorrell and I remember him saying to me, "For fuck's sake, Mick, I've never played upfront in my life!" to which I replied, "They don't know that, and there is a first time for everything." So, we came out for the second half and you could sense, when we kicked off, that Sussex were a little bit alarmed by our change of formation and we scored two goals in the first 15 minutes of the second half to draw level. I knew then if we stayed positive, we could get a winner because a point was no good for us, and that winner came 5 minutes from the end from a player who 40 minutes ago had said 'I've never played upfront'. That goal was to be decisive as we again lifted the trophy, or shall I say snatched it out of Sussex's hands to finish a four-year South-east Inter-league County competition undefeated and we had won the trophy on three occasions. We congratulated the boys after the game and the committee were overjoyed – job done. I don't know if the competition carried on after that, but it had been a great ride for those 5 seasons and experience well-gained. It is a shame that such representative football at County League level has almost disappeared, although I know the F.A. do run a County league national competition, with the winners going abroad to represent England. I would have fancied our chances in that, but it was not to be. I was also now on the Surrey F.A. youth committee as chief scout and was watching on average three to four games a week, looking for that special player that would fit into the under 16s and under 18s and to be fair to both Paul Midwinter, under 18s manager, and Mike Godfrey, under 16s manager, they took note of my recommendations and it was always a pleasure when I was requested to attend the under 18s and under 16s games. I felt that I had stepped up a gear and this was going to be an exciting future despite my little conversation with Reg Mendham over being quite happy to lose a cup title 5-0. I remember quite clearly during that 1992/93 season, my son, Daniel, was a budding goalkeeper, having been with Crystal Palace and Chelsea youth, and used to travel with us just to watch the games as he was under the age to play. As we were travelling on the team coach to play Kent County youth at Gillingham F.C., 7th May 1993 Reg came up to me and said, unbeknown to the managers, "Micky, would your son like to play in goal today?" I said, "No, Reg, he is underage, he hasn't brought his boots or gloves and I think you really should consult the managers," to which he replied "If I say he plays, he plays," at which I laughed until tears were running down my cheeks thinking what on earth have I let myself in for?

CHAPTER NINE

1993 – 1998 Surrey County youth F.A. and non-league youth football

The roller coaster gets posh now but not without its ups and downs and problems. Surrey County Youth F.A. was a real tough job. How did I get involved in the national boys' club's indoor six-a-side with a boys' club that had never won anything? So, there I was getting well involved with the Surrey F.A. youth and although a lot of travel was involved, I was seeing some really good prospects playing and it was not always from the top non-league clubs that I found the best. In fact, it was quite the opposite and one example of this was a player who came from Morden Vale F.C. under 18s by the name of Steve McKimm, and he was a true leader and tough for his age. Steve went on to play for Hendon and now, in 2019, has the job at Tonbridge Angels as first-team manager and fighting, as I write this book, for a place in the Bostick league premier playoffs. There will be more examples like that, but also there were some players who were good enough but wasted their chance to progress. Some of Surrey f.a. county youth players were going to get lucky by being managed by me or being involved at senior club level at some stage in the future (talk about blow your own trumpet!).

During that year, 1993, we also had a very good under 16s squad with some players being signed up by the pro clubs; Danny Boxall to Crystal Palace, Junior Mendes to Chelsea, Ben Judge, who was to go on and have a great non-league career, but for myself it was so different than the Surrey premier rep side in as much as I kept quite a stable squad over the 5 years at the helm but with the youth side, it was always going to be change, year after year, because of the criteria. For example, under 16s had to have a birth date that met F.A. rules and the same went for the under 18s but at least most of the boys had played in the 16s the year before and of course, we could play the 16s in the 18s as well. Another rule was they had to live in Surrey or have been born in Surrey. So you can imagine, not only did I have to find players, their criteria had to be met and on many occasions, I had seen a player and recommended him to the team managers, only to find out that Wally Howard, the county F.A. secretary, had done his homework and they were ineligible to play. Sometimes, this took some explaining to some of the players and to their clubs, but the F.A. were very strict with their rules.

Of course, this does apply also when you get to the England youth level with their 16s, 17s, 18s, and 19s, but we all know if and when you did become a full international, age was no limit and you could go on and play for as many years as you were able to and were picked to play. I am not saying that it was just hard work for me; it was always hard work for the management team. having to change the sides virtually every season. Another thing that we had was what they called a selection committee but to his credit, Mike Godfrey, then the under 16s manager, had a chat with me and the outgoing under 18s management and said that we should do away with this nonsense. If we had a chief scout and of course, club nominations, why should we put a load of names forward to a committee who had not seen a majority of the players play at all? Personally, I felt that the main aim of this selection committee was to keep the balance of clubs involved i.e. Woking, Sutton United, to name a few, should have a share of the players. It was very hard to get the committee to agree to this but in the end, I think they realised it was a bit outdated and really pointless appointing a chief scout if they wanted to carry on in this manner. Mike Godfrey also was the instigator, and in my opinion quite rightly so, of having the same management team for the under 16s and the under 18s, but before this could happen, obviously it had to be addressed by the F.A. committee and voted upon and they agreed that this should now be the case from the 1993/94 season. Of course, the managers of the under 18s, Paul Midwinter and Mick Spicer, obviously felt they were being pushed out the door and after quite a successful run, decided to leave their positions. So, Mike Godfrey decided to appoint Micky Read as his assistant for both sides as Mike had been working at Carshalton along with him. He also brought me in closer to the management set-up than just doing my work as chief scout and when Micky Read was not available for any reason, I would step in and assist Godders. This move for that season saw us do quite well in both the Home Counties championships and in the F.A. County youth challenge cup.

We had success at home at Woking F.C. against a good Hampshire side, which gave us the feel-good factor and we looked forward to the draw to discover who we would get in the next round of the County Cup. We were drawn away to Essex and the game was to be played at Southend United F.C.'s ground, Roots Hall, which to be fair to Essex, was a quality venue for us. It was then that I was tested with my own man-management skills. Mike Godfrey wanted to draw me closer into the management side, so you can imagine the scene; as always, I was in the dressing room and I was asked by Godders to take a certain player, who I happened to know quite well and still do to this day, out of the changing room and onto the pitch to explain to him that he was not included in the squad for the game. I broke it to him as best as I could using my skills and the tears started to run down his face in his disappointment. I felt sad as well because it was such an opportunity to play on a professional club's ground and he was going to miss out. As we were nearing the end of our conversation in the middle of the pitch, there comes a shout from the players' tunnel; "Micky! Get that player into the dressing room now; we have a situation on our hands!" and would you believe it, our preferred centre half for that day had started a nose bleed that was uncontrollable and therefore Martin was quickly changed up and the referee was advised and we changed the team sheet on his approval. So, Martin was preparing to now go out for this all-important County Youth cup tie, but as the bell went and we were about to go out onto the pitch, our first-choice centre half's nose bleed had stopped! How things can change in football. Martin got his game and the other player was sat in the stands. You will notice that I have not mentioned any surnames so as not to cause any embarrassment.

We won the game 4-2 after extra time and progressed, which saw us play Middlesex at Enfield F.C. in the next round, where we were to win again after a quite comfortable game. We were now in a position of being in the quarter-final of the F.A. County Youth challenge cup and we were to play the very strong West Riding County Youth. This was played at our favourite home venue, the Kingfield Stadium, Woking on 12 February 1994. Unfortunately, we were beaten that day by a better side, who I think went on to win the trophy.

Going back to the Home Counties championship, we were successful in as much as we were winners at both 18s and 16s but still eluding us was that all-important, challenge cup. During all these events Micky Read had decided to leave Mike Godfrey at Carshalton Athletic and move on to Dulwich Hamlet, so Mike Godfrey asked me if I would like to get involved with Carshalton's youth team, as my son Daniel was also there as youth team goalkeeper. I decided to join Carshalton Athletic as assistant with, I think, the physio, John Franks. This was my first job in non-league senior club football management youth side, a path that would lead me to some exciting years ahead at club level, but I don't really want to harp on about the Carshalton Athletic job at this moment because this chapter is about the Surrey County F.A. but I will touch on that subject later.

One thing I must add about 1994 that was extremely remarkable - there was a new roller coaster ride and it was to do with Addiscombe Boys' Club in south London and indoor five-a-side football. A good friend of mine, Micky Southwick, who was my apprentice, asked me if I would be interested in getting a team together for his dad, Johnny, as the boys' club had never won much in the way of football competitions. He wondered if I could raise some players to register for the club and play in the Surrey Association of Boys' Clubs competitions for under 17s. So obviously with my growing connections in football, I managed to raise quite a decent side of seven players as you needed to rotate. The Surrey competition was to take place at Tolworth leisure centre and some very strong clubs were entered. They were no different from Addiscombe in as much as they too had recruited players to represent them. Even in five-a-side, you have to have quality with the ball and you certainly have to have a tactical way of playing and I was quite pleased for Johnny when we won and lifted the Surrey Boys' Club winner's trophy. This was not to be the end of the road, as we now became the representatives of the Surrey Boys' Clubs to play in the South-east Counties championship at Woking leisure centre against Sussex, London, Essex, Kent and Middlesex, again all talented sides. It was a day-long tournament and the boys were at their best and never lost a game. We became champions of South-east England and lifted another trophy. I think at this time Johnny was thinking of getting a trophy cabinet for the Boys' Club, and to my surprise, once again, we were to go to the Shoot! magazine Great Britain national finals at Nottingham University, representing the south-east of England. Johnny was over the moon and said that he would allow us to stay overnight on the Friday and we were treated to a special night at the Hilton

Hotel, Leicester, all expenses paid (what a mistake to make!). It was a long drive from south London, using the Boys' Club minibus and I was on edge already with how the players were going to behave in this posh hotel. We also had the Leicester rugby team staying at the hotel before travelling down on the Saturday to play Bath in the Pilkington cup final at the home of rugby that was Twickenham. I must say, what a great bunch of lads. I chatted to them along with some of my players, and they were really interested in us reaching the national final. Because of them, we had the media all over the place and I think some of the boys thought that the media were there for us as well; good job they were not because after a meal, we sent the boys to their rooms and me and Micky Southwick decided to have something to eat and a drink on our own in peace and quiet, or so we thought. That was when a member of the reception team came over and told us about a problem with the boys. I say there was a problem - they were playing fucking football in the corridors, and as you can imagine, I went mad at them and threatened to leave and not let them play in the finals. They also had pay-tv on in the rooms without informing me and I dread to think what they were watching, but the night ended with peace and quiet, thank God. On the Saturday morning after early breakfast, we were off to Nottingham for a rather big challenge and my thoughts were how were we going to cope with that and the pressure of playing against the best in Britain. We duly arrived at Nottingham University all in good spirits and totally amazed at the indoor stadium which had, running alongside one length of the pitch, tiered seating for spectators. After seeing what facilities were like, we then got to see the group that we had been drawn into. In our group, we were going to have to play the best club in Wales, the best club in the West Country, and the best club in the Midlands. Unfortunately, only two clubs would go through to the semi-final out of two groups, so it almost seemed laughable really that we faced the possibility of all the travel and arrangements that we had to make and it could be all over after three ten-minute games. To be fair to the lads, they tried very hard and we did manage to win one and draw one of our games, but as I have said before, lose a game and you are virtually out. Don't forget, we were in an age group of 16 to 19-year-olds and we lost our game to a very strong Welsh side who in fact were under 19s. We were all done by 2 pm and on our way back down the motorway, but it was a great experience for the lads.

I knew, deep down, that I would like to give it a go again the following year. I spoke with Johnny and he had no problems with us entering the competition again in 1995. I also decided to recruit another couple of players and so the squad was stronger for the 1995 tournament. Again, we had to go through the same process, which we did by winning the Surrey championship, then representing Surrey in the South-East Counties championship and winning that, History repeats itself as we again got to the Great Britain five-a-side finals and again the venue was Nottingham University. I must mention the names of the squad that I took to Nottingham: Danny Taylor, Stephen Hall, Barry Kingsford, Kojo Ohene, Martin Beard, Jamie Sinclair, and Leon Dillon. Assisting me was John Franks, who I was working with at Carshalton Athletic Youth, as most of these players were with us at Carshalton and John was quite interested to come and see the tournament. I decided that this time there were to be no special treats the night before in any posh hotel and we were going to stay at the Holme Pier Point sports centre, also in Nottingham. It was a great venue for us to be staying in on the Friday because we had recreational facilities for the boys such as pool, snooker, darts, table tennis and also for myself, Johnny Franks and Micky Southwick, we had a bar. I can remember the evening very well., We had been to the tournament the year before and the mood was more relaxed and of course, there was plenty to keep the players occupied. So, they had their evening meal and their various energy drinks, soft drinks, and water and decided to set up various tournaments. It was great to see them enjoying themselves, so I took to the bar and let them get on with it, giving them a deadline of 10 pm to go to their rooms. I must admit, on I probably had a few more drinks than I should have done. It was then that I got involved in the pool table tournament and in my merry state, I promised any player that could beat me I would get down on my hands and knees and tell them they were the greatest. Now, if ever there was a big-time Charlie it was Martin Beard, now a headteacher, and who do you think beat me? You've guessed it – it was Martin Beard. The boys were in hysterics as I knelt down and looked up at Martin and told him that he was the greatest. I remember saying to him "Let's hope you are tomorrow". On the Saturday morning after breakfast, almost like déja vu, we made the short trip to Nottingham University. This time we were a year older and stronger and you would not believe the opposition we were going to have to face. In our group was the best from Northern Ireland, the best from Wales, and the best from Scotland. I remember saying to the lads, "Quite an easy group, then?" We played our first game against the champions of Scotland and we got our first win. The same happened with the champions of Northern Ireland and we found ourselves suddenly facing Wales again, only this time for a place in the semi-final – no going home early this time, I thought to myself. Well I was proved right and the boys played magnificently and we beat the champions of Wales. Therefore, we were drawn in the semi-final to play the winners of group A which consisted of the champions of the south of England. By this time the seating area was packed and inside the sports hall, the noise was quite deafening. The south of England had quite a few supporters but I had a side that loved all that type of attention. The game was so close that it was always going to be a sudden death goal that was the outcome. I can clearly remember that during that period of sudden death, our prolific scorer, Stephen Hall, broke loose and finished it to put us in the final of Great Britain where we would face the champions of the north of England. I had watched them during the day and they were a real quality side. The boys were up for it and the game was played at a furious pace. Barry Kingsford hit the post, the ball came out kindly for the North of England, they went down the other end, finding the back of our net and lifting the trophy. The boys were quite distraught having come so close, but I told them I was so very proud of them to even think that we were the second-best in the whole of Great Britain, and certainly, Johnny felt the same way. The game was videoed, which I got changed to DVD and sometimes still, I watch that final and how unlucky we were. We had a long journey home and four of the players, Barry Kingsford, Danny Taylor, Jamie Sinclair and Leon Dillon, were playing on the Sunday morning, 11 am kick-off at Corinthian Casuals F.C. in the final of the Surrey cup against Aldershot Town for their beloved Selsdon Juniors. They won the cup final and then I had to drive my son from that game over to Slade Green F.C., where he played for the league representative side in an inter-league trophy final. Unfortunately, they lost that game, but I can't imagine many people in management at non-league level have travelled far and wide and experienced so much in probably the longest weekend I've ever had. Needless to say, work for me and school for my son was a no-no for us on Monday morning.

I hope you enjoyed this special little roller coaster but it is now back to the Surrey F.A. and a different roller coaster again. The year was 1995 and I had now become assistant to Mike Godfrey with both age groups. I also managed to get my good friend, Dave Martin, onboard to make up the management team and also recruited my friend, Robin Denman, as scout along with the ever-present Brian Stone (kit man) and Micky Bullen, the physio, and a bloody good one at that! We were very lucky to have a man on board that was brought in by Godders to look after = catering in general, for the management on away trips and at home. His name was Paul Reynolds, known to all as Mars Bar. I got on great with Paul and admired the professional way that he went about his business, never missing a trick and looking after us all like we were royalty. To this day, I don't know what happened to him after I left the F.A. I believe he has now passed away.

That year was a first for me for a couple of reasons; one, I had my first experience of travelling away with the County F.A. and two, I played my last competitive game at the ripe old age of 47 and I will tell you more about that later. After beating Berks and Bucks 1-0 away at Thatcham Town F.C. in the first round of the F.A. County Youth cup, we were handed a game away to Oxfordshire in the 2nd round to be played at the Rover car plant sports ground, Oxford, a game in which we won with plenty to spare. We were now in the third round and creeping towards the final but the draw gave us a tough away trip to Cornwall or 'the Royal Duchy' as they liked to be called and that meant a two-night stopover. I must say in true Mike Godfrey fashion, we prepared for the game by having a Sunday training day/get together at the famous Charterhouse public school near Guildford. The facilities were great and it was there that I met a coach who had a great impact on me. His name was Colin Lippiatt and he was working with Geoff Chapple at Woking at the time. What a great coach and a gentleman, and he was always available to us when we used to have our Sunday meet-ups with the squad. I remember him saying to me, "Micky, I don't want you to think I am here interfering with your plans. I was asked to come along and help and give some advice." Sadly, he has since passed away at a very young age, God bless him.

As I said, the training days were great and the boys loved it and also being looked after by our catering manager, Mars Bar. Believe it or not, I used to love taking the goalkeepers aside and coaching them and for me at the height of 5ft 3ins that seemed a bit strange to them, but nothing beats experience. While my son, Daniel, was being coached as a keeper at Chelsea by Dave Collyer and at Crystal Palace along with Jimmy Glass, I was making notes. Also, one of the best keeper coaches I ever saw was at Carshalton Athletic where my son was playing in the youth team and his name was Ron Wilson. So it was that after a few moments, the keepers knew what I was on about. It always amazed me was they never had goalkeeping coaches at the senior clubs they were playing for, but I know that has changed now and quite a few clubs do have a goalkeeping coach.

So, back to the game in Cornwall and the third round and the dramas that went with it. For my first trip away, myself and Dave Martin were in the building trade so meeting the team bus at 1 o'clock on the Friday at Met Police Imber Court was a problem. With the county allowing us to do so, we decided to make our own way down to Newquay as the game was to be played at Newquay F.C., and we stayed at the Gull Rock Hotel on the seafront. Dave went by car and I went on the train to St. Austell and got a cab from there to be in time for a late dinner and meet the team who seemed in high spirits, and Mike Godfrey and the blazer brigade, or old cobwebs as we used to call them. I roomed that night with one of the players' Dads, Peter Kingsford whose son Barry was in the squad, but it was no problem as I knew Peter very well and we always had a laugh when we were together.

The lads went off to their rooms and the management team went up to the bar. It was said that it was always Dave Martin and me left at the end, as we would discuss the game and make our minds up as to the players we all wanted, Godders included. On the Saturday morning of the game, 7th January 1995, we all had breakfast and relaxed for a while before having a brisk walk with all the squad and management team along the front. Then it was back to the hotel for our pre-match meeting. What happened while we were out seemed, at the time, quite unusual. The delegation team, headed by Whally Howard had gone down to Newquay F.C. to measure the pitch to make sure it was of the correct size for the game to take place and I remember thinking, if it isn't, then too bloody late now. Or was it just to show their faces and enjoy some Cornish hospitality? Back at the hotel, the boys were getting ready for the game whilst me, Dave, and Mike Godfrey sat down to pick the team and the subs. One player in particular to mention was Steve Lewington (Dulwich Hamlet) the son of Ray Lewington, ex-Chelsea player, manager of Fulham, and other footballing roles including assistant to Roy Hodgson, the England manager. With the team picked, plus the substitutes, and the cobwebs duly arriving back from their excursion to the ground, the players were coming down from their rooms to assemble and to board the coach for the short journey to the ground for a 2.30 pm kick-off. We arrived at the ground nice and early, around 1 pm and we found to our surprise that the quality of the playing surface should have been of more concern than the size of the pitch. Also, the dressing rooms were too small for our entourage. Micky Bullen, our physio, always had a fold-up couch for any last-minute rub-downs and with this in place, it was very cramped indeed.

As I said before, I used to warm up the goalkeepers, and for this reason, I used to wear my green top with my initials on. On seeing it, some of the early Cornish fans likened me to our very own Cornish pixie! I replied to them, in a nice way, "You'll be laughing on the other side of your face come 4.30!" (It's always good to have some banter). I can also remember being in the changing room with the players having had their warm-up and Godders asking Mars Bar if he would go and get a tray of tea for the management team. So, off he duly went to collect the teas. I must admit he was gone rather a long time and I could see Godders getting agitated as he wanted to have his say to the lads before myself and Dave had our pennyworth, so with that, he had slammed shut the dressing room door which had been left open for some fresh air. But who do you think was coming to the door at that time? None other than Mars Bar with a tray full of teas, who was hit by the tray when the door was slammed shut! I have heard some language in dressing rooms in my time, but when it comes from a posh-speaking type of person, it becomes even funnier! There he was, covered from head to toe in tea, all over his best new suit, County tie and white shirt, threatening to kill Godders. The boys were in hysterics and it took the nerves away. So, with that situation over, we took to the park to a very robust Cornish side and a very boisterous crowd who made it very clear that we should get back to England. This wouldn't go down well these days, especially with racist remarks frowned upon! Myself and Dave Martin's response to that was two fingers up and "Who pays your bloody pensions!"

We took the lead through Steve Lewington but that was short-lived, as Cornwall scored two quick goals and a comedy led to their third just before half-time, when the ball was not cleared properly and remained in the air, only for goalkeeper Danny Burgess (the Sutton United keeper) to punch it into his own net when it finally came down. We had a good old sort out at half-time as usual because Godders was a great organiser and very professional, but he didn't have that player/man management or the anger of a dressing room that myself and Dave Martin had, so strong words were said by myself and Dave and we gave a better account of ourselves. Our keeper, Danny Burgess, was suffering from concussion and was replaced by a substitute, the Woking keeper, Justin Gray. We came out in the second half looking the stronger of the two sides and it was deserved when we pulled a goal back through striker Steve Lewington again. The final minutes were frantic but we could not find that equaliser to take us into extra time and therefore we were knocked out.

As usual, we had to attend the after-match reception at a very posh hotel before the lads could go back to our hotel and get changed and have a night out. So, we arrived back at our hotel for what we thought was going to be a nice quiet evening of deliberation while the lads went out into Newquay to enjoy their Saturday night. They were not treated as losers in such a way as they had given all they could on a difficult pitch. So as per the norm, the hierarchy had their little corner in the hotel bar, Godders and Mars Bar decided to retire early and it was me and Dave again, having a good drink. It must have been by now ten or eleven in the evening and as the cobwebs were leaving to go to their rooms, Whally Howard informed me and Dave that we must stay up until every player had reported back to the hotel and gone to their rooms. Myself and Dave were not too concerned at having this role, but when the clock got round to well past midnight, I was beginning to think of my early rise and the train home from St. Austell. The boys were coming back in groups and I can clearly remember one of the lads (not to be named) about to go up to his room wearing just his shirt, shoes, and boxer shorts. We called him over with smiles on our faces and asked him where his trousers were, to which he replied, "I was round the back of MacDonald's having fun with a young Cornish lady when the boys in the cab shouted for me, so I ran and got in the cab, holding my wallet. Me and Dave were in stitches and said to him, "Good job you've got your tracksuit to wear home tomorrow!" The last two players came in, so we checked the list and were just about to go to bed when the night porter came over to us and said that there was a call from the local police and one of us needed to come to the phone. I decided to take the call. A police officer informed me there had been some kind of disturbance in the town during the evening and they were aware that a group of lads from London were involved, so and they were going to come to the hotel in the morning to take statements. I acted very quickly as I knew that there would have been chaos with the hierarchy and the coach would have been delayed. I said to the officer, "I will come down to the station in the morning and give you a statement if that is acceptable". He agreed that would be okay and that is how we left it. I'm glad

Dave had the car but he wasn't very pleased when I told him we had to be at the police station at 9 am and then get the bus to St. Austell station for my train home to London. Dave was true to his word and we told the night porter we needed breakfast at 7 am. Considering it was already 1.30 am, it didn't give us much time to sleep off what could only be described as a very tiring day. So, early on the Sunday morning, myself and Dave ate breakfast and Dave drove me to the police station. Dave was going to go back to the hotel to make the apologies for me having to leave early, but of course, that was not the real reason. We went into the police station and explained to the desk sergeant on duty the situation and the phone call from the night before and that we were prepared to make a statement. He smiled at us and said in his very broad Cornish accent, "I have nothing in the book from any police officer on duty last night about any fracas in the town involving your footballers and they have all left their night shifts now". He apologised for our inconvenience but we were just relieved that no action was to be taken and it was a secret that myself and Dave kept all that season. I still had to catch a bus to meet my train. This was another problem, as in those days, buses seemed to run when they wanted to and if the changeover driver didn't fancy it, the bus would turn round and come back. So just imagine, after all the events of the previous night and the morning, I arrived in a sleepy village called St. Enoder. If the bus driver could wake up the other bus driver, I could continue my journey to St. Austell to get to Paddington by train on which I had a reserved seat. When we got to this little village, the bus driver said he would try his hardest to wake up the changeover driver and I can still see the driver going up to this cottage and banging on the door for the exchange driver. He then came back to me as I was the only one on the bus and informed me that old Fred would be along as soon as he was ready. He finally arrived drove the bus to St. Austell and I made my train to Paddington with just two minutes to spare, only to find when I boarded the train that the reservation system had failed and all seats were unreserved. For my pain and suffering, I had to stand for two and a half hours to Exeter before getting a seat. I can remember Dave Martin ringing me on the Monday evening to tell me that one of our players, an Italian lad who shall remain nameless, had one of his eyebrows shaved off. The hierarchy did have their enquiry after all as the player's father, who had made the trip, was adamant that his son would never play for the F.A. again. Dave informed me that the rest of the players kept tight-lipped and we never did find out who had done this. Despite that disappointment, we did manage to win the Home Counties under 18s championship.

Now back to earlier when I said I had two memorable events in 1995 concerning football and you've read the first. The second one was about playing again and I was asked to play for the G.M.B. Union South-east side in a semi-final, which we won, and we were now in the final and the big surprise for me was that in my last ever competitive game at the age of 47, I was going to play at the lovely ground called Craven Cottage, the home of Fulham Football Club as Fulham were being sponsored by the G.M.B. at the time. We played the Southern G.M.B. and the game went into extra time and a penalty shootout. It was my turn to take a penalty and what happened next was quite unbelievable as I put the ball in the perfect area near to the post, only to see this goalkeeper dive and the ball hit him on his head on the way into the net. Thank God that they missed theirs and we scored ours again to give me my last ever winners medal, which I have on display to this day. It's all good fun this non-league football don't you think?

So, I think we should now get on to the 1995/96 season and another crack at that F.A. County Youth cup. Also, it was going to be a season that saw me take up my first senior position at a club (other than a youth team position), as reserve team manager at Croydon Athletic, which I will tell you all about later in the book, and let me tell you now, are you in for some hell of a ride of a true non-league club and their goings-on!

Again, the name Carshalton Athletic youth team keeps cropping up and although Mike Godfrey had left the club to concentrate more on the County F.A., I decided to stay as I got on very well with John Franks, the manager, We had some great moments Which I have told many people about over the years. We had a female physio who came to the club to gain some work experience. I can't remember her name, but I think it was Helen. She was a lovely person and when she was on duty for the first time at a game and I introduced her to the players she said to them, without any shyness, "Right, let's get it over with let's have your trousers and your pants down because I've seen it all before!" Needless to say, all the players froze there and then. I don't think I had ever heard them so quiet. One of the most common pre-match scenarios is that players all love to be pampered in some way, having a rub-down on their legs, groin, and other parts of their body which needed loosening up, but on this night, not one player entered the physio's room and it was quite funny really to see the players actually doing their own rub-downs rather than see the female physio.

The next story was when we were playing Gillingham F.C. away at the Priestfield Stadium, Gillingham, and it was in the John Ullman cup. We had a team bus for the trip as it was an evening game and I can remember one of our young star players, Barry Kingsford, being told that he was going to be playing in an unfamiliar role at right-back. He then refused to board the team bus. I spoke to his father, Peter, and asked him if he would have ten minutes with him in private and if he couldn't change his mind then the bus was leaving without him. In the end, Barry decided that he would travel on the team bus and play in the unfamiliar position. We had a great game with Gillingham that night and the ironic thing about the whole evening was not the fact that we gave them a great game and lost 3-2 only minutes from the end of extra time, but what I remember it for was what a great game Barry had and he learnt those big words called discipline and teamwork. He went on to have a good career in non-league football, making many appearances in Carshalton's first team and also played under me at Croydon F.C., and he remains a great friend of my son to this day.

Another moment was when one of our players, a big black lad called Mark Clark, was in the showers and the players sprayed Deep Heat into his underpants. The scene when he put his underpants on after his shower was absolutely hysterical. Clarky was running around the dressing room like a madman! As any footballer will know, there are certain areas you just do not put Deep Heat on. It is a great memory and I can still picture the scene even today. I was never far from their pranks as well; nearly every game, I would have to go home sometimes with no socks, sometimes with no club tie and even no underpants. They were always returned to me the following week or at training (I can't imagine that happening in the premiership, can you?) Having said that, I have heard very many stories about the crazy gang called Wimbledon F.C. and I truly believe that they were the nearest full-time professional club to non-league football outside of non-league.

So now I must get back on to Surrey and the 1995/96 season. I must apologise to readers of this book if I keep hopping about, but there are so many tales to tell and as mentioned many times, the quest for the F.A. County Youth cup was always top of the list. Once more, we had assembled a very good squad of players, including some very good under 16s from the season before, and some of our players had just crept in under the age barrier. Mike Godfrey, myself and Dave Martin were very confident that we had something very special and could bury that ghost of losing to Cornwall the season before in the first round and all that stuff that went with it. So, to kick the season off, we assembled the squad for a training day and get-together on Sunday 3rd September

1995 at Charterhouse Public School and another chance to work with Colin Lippiatt again. I enjoyed every moment of sharing our thoughts about non-league football and the future, and the players also enjoyed his company. I must admit that sometimes I found it a bit tiring having the reserve team at Croydon Athletic and also the youth team and of course the County F.A. youth under 18s/16s but I was glad to be involved in all of it. I am sure that the training days were a great benefit to the players as they felt they were in good hands and being well looked after as Mike Godfrey would not have had it any other way, as his main role was not so much a dressing room person, like myself and Dave Martin. We had a few Home Counties games to play, one of those being home to our old enemy, Sussex F.A., who we beat, and Middlesex F.A. away, who we also beat, before our F.A. County Youth cup 2nd round game away at Oxfordshire F.A. on 18th November 1995 at the Rover sports and social club in Oxford. We won the game without too much trouble, but it was a bit disappointing that we could not have the overnight stay that would have given us a bit more bonding. However, we were through to the third round at home to Devon F.A. at Molesey F.C. on 6th Jan 1996.

No disrespect to Molesey, but it was not my favourite ground as the place always lacked any kind of atmosphere, although it was a big pitch which suited us even though the surface was not great. It was a game we needed to win and, although the conditions were the same for both sides, it was a tough game against a very physical Devon side. It suited them better with their long-ball tactics, but we had a good side and we soon settled down and played our football and took control of the game. We ended up beating them with plenty to spare. Now we were into the 4th round and a home draw against the Liverpool F.A. at Met Police ground, Imber Court, on 6th Jan 1996 and things were about to hot up as we had plenty of drama and, in some way, sadness as well, which unfortunately has not gone away in football. Again, we were at full strength but this time on a perfect surface against a very good Liverpool side (who we had watched in their previous game).

On to the game itself now, and I could sense early on that a couple of our players were not at their best. Consequently, Liverpool took full advantage and scored two goals in the first half and I must say it was probably our worst performance since I joined the management staff. So, it was with great relief that the half-time whistle blew and we were able to get the boys back into the changing room. For obvious reasons, I will not mention any names here, only to say that they were being racially harassed by a couple of the Liverpool players. Obviously, I have no proof of this, only what my players had told me, and these situations can often be denied by the opposition. Now let's get one thing straight here; I am a strict 'sticks and stones may break my bones but names will never hurt me' person, so my response to my under 18s was quite simple and I give it to you as it was said in the dressing room at half-time; "We are a team; we look after each other and for those Liverpool players who caused problems, you have to go out and fucking sort them out. I'll sort the ref and the fucking linesman out. We are not going to be beaten by that type of tactics."

By the time Dave Martin and Mike Godfrey had also had their say, there was a red mist in the dressing room. We had actually got the players fuming and I wanted an early response. So, we started the second half and, from the moment we kicked off, I could sense that we were on a different level in terms of our will to win the game. I myself was out of the dugout telling the linesman to be aware of any situation, and within 15 minutes of the second half, we were level at 2-2. Tackles were flying in all over the place, and fair ones at that, and now I had a different sense that we were going to go on to win this game and that's exactly what happened. We scored another 2 goals to put us 4-2 up and we even missed a penalty. I'd say that was job done, no need to talk to the referee about what had gone on at half-time or at the end of the game. We gave them the perfect answer in how to deal with these situations. At the end of the game, in the dressing room, there were overwhelming scenes of joy, but I wasn't finished yet. I said to the lads, "When we go to the after-game reception at the hotel, 'fucking make 'em have it, and send them back up the M1/M6 with their Tails between their legs!" I know that we only had a problem on the pitch and not with spectators, and I do know that obviously, in non-league football there can be problems from the terraces, but I think you must stand up and be counted and the real answer is to try and be unaffected and go on and win the game and that's precisely what we did. We hurt Liverpool more than any committee could have ever done.

So enough said about that for the moment. All I was glad about was that, at the end of the day, justice had been done and we were in the semi-final of the F.A. County Youth cup to face Durham F.A. or the Berks and Bucks F.A.

Now comes the big shock for me personally. On the Sunday morning, we had an under 16s game at which our same management team was present and I was confronted by a member of the F.A. committee. I thought that I was going to get a little pat on the back for our great fight back and win, but no, not the F.A. I was told there would be a letter in the post to me as they had had a meeting after the Liverpool game and decided that I was in breach of the F.A. committee's standards of conduct. I obviously asked why I was going to get a letter and I was told that it was because I spent most of the second half out of my dugout talking to the linesman and what they called 'inciting my players to go to war with the opposition'. I explained to them what had gone on and how we had addressed it at half-time. I said, "While you were in the board room at half-time, drinking your whisky and eating your cucumber sandwiches, the management team were having to sort this problem out!" They were disgusted to have heard of such goings-on. They wanted to report Liverpool and I said, "No, they have been hurt enough and now you can stick your fucking job up your ass as I feel you have insulted me." They tried as hard as they could to get me to change my decision, which I eventually did, but they still had to send me a letter warning me about my future conduct. That is why I still maintain that the abbreviation F.A. can be interpreted in any way or form you like. I received the letter and acknowledged it, but never did I apologise for my actions.

The next thing on the management team's mind was the all-important semi-final against Durham and how we were going to approach the game. As I have said before, we had a management team and backroom staff who were very professional in their approach to the finest detail. Our kit man, Brian Stone, was great, as was our physio, Micky Bullen, and our scout Robin (Merlin) Denman and of course, not forgetting our catering manager, Paul (Mars Bar) Reynolds. The management team of Godders, myself and Dave Martin were a great team and who needs these silly bloody coaching badges, as some coaches just hide behind them, not having any experience at all and they land good jobs. (This subject has always been a thorn in my side.) When asked to take it, I just bluntly refused.

Anyway, I knew that Durham were playing at home to Berks and Bucks in their quarter-final at Spennymoor Town F.C. in the northeast of England. You may remember that they beat my 5-aside team in the national final with a sudden-death goal so it brought back a bad memory. I was going to make the long trip to watch the quarter-final and what a long day it was, starting by leaving home at 7.am, up to London to King's Cross, then the train to Durham. I had a long trip ahead of me and plenty of time for thought, more so on my outward journey as I knew my head would be full of the winners of the game I was going to see and spending time looking at my notes. I started to think about our players and what they had achieved in being picked to play for their County F.A., and out of all the players, they were the best 18 in our county, and that went for the under 16s as well. The next step could only be playing for their country! I said to them on many occasions that it is with pride they must wear that shirt (as you won't see any of these in replica in the sports stores). They were not paid to play but must play for us, the management team, as though it was like your own club. Also, the supporters we had were very special as most of them were family members. There were the scouts too, from many big clubs, so I think that message was clear as I had experienced all of this when my son, Daniel, had played in goal for Surrey schools and Surrey youth and been captain for Croydon schools on some occasions. it was just then that I thought, 'what the hell am I doing on this train doing a 550-mile round trip to watch our opposition in the semi-final in action?' But once again it soon made me realise how professional we were in our approach.

I was now entering the world of non-league scouting and although I did not know it then, it was going to keep me involved later on in life with my football and I would say that most scouts find it easier to watch a certain player rather than a team. I arrived in Durham to get the bus to Spennymoor. Durham played just as I thought a north-east side would; always a direct approach and they had little trouble in beating Berks and Bucks as they played a 4.4.2 formation, which was ok for us. They also went man to man marking on set plays rather than zonal, so I had plenty of thoughts about the game on the way home. I spoke on the mobile to both Godders and Dave about what I had seen and how we should prepare ourselves for a tough and physical game. The local south London paper covered my scouting trip with the headlines 'Long-distance Micky is Taylor-made for his role.' I felt proud that the paper had recognised my efforts to do the best I could for the County F.A.

We had another of our training days a week before the game, again using the great facilities at Charterhouse Public School.

The boys were all in great shape and there was that feeling in the camp that it was going to be our year. So, on Friday March 8th 1996, we made the long journey north by luxury coach provided by Safeguard coaches from Guildford. Our F.A. secretary, Peter Adams, found that quite convenient as he was picked up from his front door and dropped back there. Others had to meet at the ground and park cars there for the weekend (pretty safe after all, who's going to nick a car from a police car park!) The roller coaster was certainly travelling fast now as I remember the long journey and the traffic jams but although getting tired, we were all in good spirits and knew we were staying at a class hotel called the Blackwell Grange (indoor pool and spa) just outside Darlington. If ever you had any doubts about how the F.A. spent money, I can tell you now, they only had the best all the time, but of course, we were there to win a game of football and book our place in the final.

We prepared properly, as always; after a good night and a good breakfast, we went across to a rugby club who kindly let us use their ground to have a light training session. After that, it was into the hotel for a briefing session in a private room before going back to our rooms for the management to put their suits on and the players their county dress code of grey trousers, white shirt and F.A. county ties and jackets. There was a nice gesture from the hotel staff as we left the hotel to go to the game, as they stood at the entrance to wave us off. I can remember saying to Dave Martin, "I bet what they really are thinking is hope you get a bloody good hiding, you southerners!" As usual, win or lose when away from home, after the match reception, the boys could go out to enjoy themselves and it was myself and Dave's job to either go with them, or stay in the hotel until the last one was back, but I will tell you later what we decided to do!

On to the game: We arrived at Durham F.C. and their posh new stadium in plenty of time for the game and started our pre-match preparations which always included the team's music blasting out from the dressing room. There was one song in particular, Fairground by Simply Red, which even today when it's played on the radio, still makes me think back to that day in the north-east.

As for the match itself, what a great advert for representative football as both sides were evenly matched and many people said it would have made a great final. We played our 4-4-2, as did they, and in a very tight first half, they drew first blood, catching us too far up the park and breaking clear to fire past our keeper, Danny Burgess (Sutton United), minutes before the break. We had to respond quickly before they got a foothold in the game and the equaliser came, on the stroke of half-time, from the head of prolific goal-scorer, Stephen Hall (Banstead Athletic). With the scores at 1-1, we had our half-time chat and felt no need to change things as we were well into the game even though my fingernails were now bitten down to the quick! We had more of the game in the second half, but again, we were caught on the break as Durham took the lead against the run of play. It is then that, as managers and supporters, you begin to think it's not going to be your day, but we kept searching for that goal to draw level and we found it with the clock running down and extra time getting closer.

Now, on the bench, we felt that we could take care of them if it came to that situation as we had not used any subs and had fresh legs for that period. Then came the kick in the b….cks, or the punch in the mouth; whatever you choose to call it. I can still see it now some 23 years on; we had dealt with the long throws all the game, so when the ball went out of play for a throw-in not far from the corner flag, we had no fear on the bench at all and were waiting for the final whistle and extra time as the ball was launched into our penalty box. It was almost like slow motion as the ball came off the top of one our defenders' head and beyond our now-committed goalkeeper, who had come to take a safe ball. It fell to the far post for a Durham player to soft cushion a header into our net! I still can't describe how I felt as, moments later, the ref brought the game to full time and we were out of the semi-final. The one thought was - all that fucking hard work gone on a poxy throw-in and to think we beat Liverpool in the last round. So, it was back to the losers' dressing room and the group of players that had been so great for us during the season. It was possibly one of the worst moments in the dressing room I had ever experienced. Some of the boys were in tears, knowing that because of their ages, they would never get another chance to play in this competition. I remember there being a knock on the changing room door and I have no doubt that one of the committee members was trying to lighten the mood up by offering a crate of Budweiser which he had in his hands. I politely told him, "No thanks, not at the moment. In my dressing room, I have broken hearts, broken minds, and the management team and staff all in despair. Please could you give us 15-20 minutes to get our heads around things?" It was at this moment that I did give one thought to when I had the Great Britain five-a-side championship snatched from my side in similar circumstances, only that day I had to drive the minibus all the way down the M1 back to London. But I was faced with a worse situation now because, as a management team, we had to pick those boys up to go to the required after-game reception, laid on by our hosts Durham F.C. So, we did allow the crate of Budweiser to come into the dressing room and we set off to the hotel for our after-match reception. I tried to tell the committee that we shouldn't stay longer than required as I needed to let the boys get back to the hotel to get changed and go out for the night to drown their sorrows.

We got back to the hotel and the coach driver was very good and dropped us in Darlington. Myself and Dave decided to join the lads in the pub for a pint and a laugh, and we then went back to the hotel, leaving the boys to try and enjoy the rest of the evening. Needless to say, myself and Dave waited up as the usual watchmen to make sure all boys were home safe and sound, except for one player who informed me he would be exceptionally late but not to worry. So, the following morning, we all came down to breakfast, including the late call player, and were soon ready to get the bus for our long journey home. I remember thinking 'things can't get much fucking worse unless the wife had run off with the milkman'. I did have a player come from the back of the coach to sit with me for a while and explain the late 'phone call. He was a cracking lad and I tried to tell him not to be bothered about the 'phone call, but he would insist on telling me the story which I must admit, brought some humour to the weekend's proceedings.

The player in question said he had met this lady after we had left the pub and they had ended up at her home and they went and did the business. He then informed me that he had given her his name and address because he felt there might be a relationship. He also informed me that her old man was having tea with the queen at a prison somewhere in the northeast. I didn't know whether to laugh or cry but I did see the funny side of it and thought to myself, 'let's hope she destroys your name and address or you may not be playing football much longer!

We did end the season winning the Home Counties championship and Durham went on to win the F.A. County Youth Cup, beating Gloucestershire 1-0 in the final. We did at least have some of the players available for next season and another crack at the County Youth cup. Something did happen to me that season 1995/1996; the Surrey county youth F.A. had been asked to supply the ball boys for the F.A. Vase final at Wembley between Brigg Town and Clitheroe and I felt very honoured that I was asked was going to be in charge of them that day as part of my services to the F.A. It was a memorable day for me and anyone who thinks looking after ball boys is easy in an F.A. final at Wembley, then you had best think again. In the two hours before the kick-off, they were all given their kit which was the F.A. tracksuit, and we were taken round the pitch and on the pitch and shown the exact positions they must take up behind the advertising boards and to keep crouched down all the time until retrieving the ball. A big job was selecting the nine players from Surrey to carry out this task. I picked from our under 16s squad rather than the under 18s. What was good was that they were allowed to have the ball on the surface for 10-15 minutes to have a little loosen up. It was just then that I heard this voice in the distance and you can imagine the scene. There I am, in the middle of the old Wembley stadium, taking it all in and suddenly I hear someone shouting "Micky Taylor!" In the distance I see someone walking towards me. It was none other than my good friend, Steve Clark, secretary of my old club, Reedham Park who was now in charge of all F.A. competitions. He asked me what I was doing there and he said, "Great; when you have come up the tunnel with the two teams and the ball boys when they will know what they have got to do, come round and see me by the substitutes' benches." I met Steve there and he said that we were to sit together and watch the game from the benches and at half-time he would take me into the hospitality area and introduce me to the mayor and mayoress of both teams. Did I feel like Billy big spuds? You can bet yourself I did. I thought the bloody roller coaster was coming off the rails, or was all this a dream? The most important thing was it was true non-league football, and by the way, Brigg Town won 3-0 and the Brigg goalkeeper, Carlo Nash, went on to play for Crystal Palace.

The season ended on a high for me so 1995/1996 season wasn't so bad after all, but as I have said before, in management, as soon as the season is over and the last game played, the new season begins. So now we move on to the 1996/1997 season and a new crop of under 16s and a virtual new under 18s squad. I have to say now, without sounding in any way offensive, the under 16s squad looked stronger, but our under 18s did not seem to have the same quality as the previous season's side which lost narrowly in a semi-final against Durham F.C. so, my thinking was, okay, if we've not got the quality, although we always tried to turn our squad of players into team players and not individuals, we're going to turn this lot into a non-league crazy gang just like Wimbledon. Keep the formations simple, play direct, defend to clear our lines, and be a typical non-league side. We trained again at Charterhouse, but the proof of the pudding is always in the eating and we would be judged on our results. When we had our management meeting and finally named the squad, we raised a few eyebrows among the committee members as to the type of player we were choosing and to some extent, the club they were playing for, although we did have a forward in Gavin Holligan, who would cause trouble in an empty house, he was that good. I will say at this point that when I finish this chapter of the book on county F.A. non-league youth football, I will tell you some of the names that have come through our ranks and made it as professional footballers and well-paid non-league footballers.

I would just like to mention a bit of coincidence, in as much as Dave Martin's son, Matt Martin, also played at one stage for the county as a goalkeeper, as did my son, Danny Taylor. The only thing was that Matt carried on playing and had a good non-league career, whereas my son had started an apprenticeship with British Rail and produced a lovely granddaughter called Lauren. I am sure if this had not happened, he too would have had a good career in non-league.

Right, so back again and to the F.A County Youth cup and we had a trip to Dorset in the 1st round on 22nd September 1996, and the game was to be played at Wimborne Town F.C. There was no overnight stay as the distance did not qualify for that. Needless to say, the management team were a bit nervous, or at least I was, because the last thing we needed was to go out of the competition early. Well, that never happened and we won the game and the team bus was a happy one on the way home. I must say that I do not mention much about our under 16s squad as they were in no knockout cups and played all their games in the Home Counties championship, which they normally won or at least came second.

In the next round, we were drawn away to face Hertfordshire at St. Albans City F.C. on 16th November, so in preparation, we had another training day at Charterhouse Public School (thanks to Godders) and also a warm-up game against a Wimbledon youth team on the Wednesday evening before the game. I did think at the time that maybe we might have overdone it a bit with our preparation and this proved to be so as we struggled against Hertfordshire on a great playing surface. However, we managed to hang on in there to force extra time and a replay. As I said when we made our squad known, it was going to be based on hard-working players who could dig in if they had to and that's exactly what they did to get that replay. We told the players no club football and a complete rest that week and to be ready for them the following Saturday at home at Woking F.C. The rest for the boys worked a treat and whenever we played at Woking F.C. we were always hard to beat as Hertfordshire were going to find out. We expected a tough game in the first encounter and we should have put away some of our chances and gave little away at the back. So, the game was level at full time and into extra time we went. It was then that we really displayed some fantastic football and wrapped the game up with 4 goals in extra time. Gavin Holligan again was showing his class as he netted a couple. Job done and the boys now were excited, waiting for news of the third-round draw.

Out of the hat came Norfolk County F.C., and it was going to be a two-night stopover. The game was going to be played at Fakenham Town F.C., on 11 January 1997. We were to leave on the Friday as usual for a weekend stay and we stayed in a very posh hotel, the Barnham Broom Hotel near Norwich. When there was excitement apart from the game, it normally involved myself and Dave Martin, so you can imagine on Friday evening when we arrived at the hotel and were shown our room, we fell about laughing because they had given us the honeymoon suite. Obviously, there was a double bed in there, a four-poster with all lace surroundings and another single bed made up in the room. I am sure we spun the coin and Dave got the four-poster. We had absolutely hilarious scenes at dinner when the players found out.

Something else was to happen that night which was very amusing as well. For some unknown reason, one of our players who will remain anonymous, missed the coach at Met Police and 'phoned me to say he was on his way by train, so I told him, when he got to Norwich, to get a cab to the hotel and I would get one of the committee to pay the cab and settle the train fare. The player concerned eventually arrived at the hotel and the staff were very good in preparing him a meal, and also the committee in paying the cab fare. What myself and Dave found amusing was that he convinced our secretary Wally Howard that he had lost his train ticket but it had cost him £30 single. Wally always carried what we called the slush fund and duly paid the player out. So, next, myself and Dave Martin were sitting at the bar having a drink and again called the player over, as we knew him quite well, and asked him if he had had the Surrey F.A. over by not getting a ticket at all and I can see the big smile on his face when he said, "How did you know that I had bunked the train?" We gave him quite a simple answer; "Because we know every one of you players and your characters, and only you could have done such a thing."

I sat drinking with Dave, talking about the game, while the rest of the staff and the players had gone to bed as was becoming a bit of a ritual now on away trips. About 2 am, we returned to our room ready for the following day's action. I can remember at breakfast it was still a laughable matter for the boys and to a degree, the committee, when they asked how we had got on in the honeymoon suite, but I saw this all as good fun and after one of Godders' walks around the hotel grounds and our usual team briefing, we set off to play Norfolk. It was a tough game but again our confidence was growing, along with our grit and determination, and we got past them without too much trouble and back to a reception as normal, only this time there was no going out for the boys in the evening after the reception as there was nowhere for them to go and Norwich was too far. We still had some good fun and as usual, myself and Dave had another late night.

Now we were in the quarter-final and you would never believe the draw in a million years. We were drawn away to Durham County F.A. What more could you have asked for than to get a chance to get revenge on last season's horrendous exit from the county trophy in such a cruel fashion? As I have said before, we may not have had the quality we had last season, but Durham would have to worry about us and there was no need for me to have to make a long trip to see them. The quarter-final would be played on 8th February 1997. In preparation for the game, we arranged a training session at Chipstead F.C. and had the use of their floodlights and their fine playing surface. It was great preparation for the game on the following Saturday and so on the Friday, we set off for our weekend away, staying in the same hotel as we had done the year before, the Blackwell Grange in Darlington. We decided that we would keep everything the same and again use the rugby club across the way from the hotel for a little morning warm-up prior to a team briefing. It was funny when the coach arrived to take us to the ground as there were no staff this time to bid us farewell, which I felt was a bit of an omen that things might go badly for us that day.

It was almost déjà vu when we arrived at the ground. Everything was the same; nothing had changed about the place; it was just we had a different team and they had a different team. As normal, we had our dressing room music, but unlike the year before, it was a different type of music that I couldn't get my head around, but the boys enjoyed it. They say that revenge is always sweet but I had to wait as the game went into extra time, or as we call it now, 'squeaky bum time', but we did get that all-important goal and won the game 1-0 in that extra time. I can tell you now, when that final whistle blew and we had knocked Durham out of the cup, I felt like I had been given the crown jewels. It meant so much to me and the rest of the management team. This time, after the game, the dressing room was full of happiness as the boys had their crate of Budweiser. As normal, we had to attend the reception by our hosts, but this time the dinner went down quite easy and we could not wait to get back to the hotel, change up and go into Darlington for a celebration party. We gave the players time to get changed and the coach driver was kind enough to take us into Darlington.

All the management team went with the players to a recommended pub in the town. It was then that the fun started and another story emerged. As I have said, the team was full of a lot of characters; none more so than our goalkeeper, Stewart Vaughan. As is the norm, whenever you have a character, players will always make a beeline for them, and so it was that we decided, at Dave Martin's suggestion, to have a pickled egg-eating competition and of course, Stuart was up for it and so were a couple of the other boys as the management team bought all the eggs. I don't know how Stuart managed it, but he downed six pickled eggs in as many minutes to win the competition. You will hear more about Stuart later in the book as he was to become my goalkeeper at club level.

The boys had decided that they would go to a nightclub, which again was recommended as not being a troublesome place. Godders and the rest of the management team went back to the hotel and myself and Dave Martin decided to accompany the boys to the nightclub. I asked one of the bouncers on the door if it was okay if we both came in to make sure the boys behaved themselves, and he agreed and did not take any payment from us. There we were, in the nightclub, me and Dave booted and suited and still with our county ties on, and the boys all dressed in their snazzy gear. Just for once, I forgot my duties and decided to have a few drinks and not worry about the boys too much. There's an old saying in football management, 'never drop your guard with your players because they will take full advantage'. So, it was on that night and I don't mind admitting I did drop my guard. The next thing I knew, I was breakdancing in the middle of the floor with all the players round me cheering and shouting. I must admit I had had a few too many and after this little episode, both myself and Dave Martin decided to take a cab back to the hotel. Funny enough, on this occasion I can remember I had had a bit of a tummy bug during the week and had asked for a single room for obvious reasons. Now, all I can remember was going into my room, crashing out on the bed with all my clothes on and even my shoes, only to be awakened by a loud bang on the door and Wally Howard, our secretary, shouting, "Micky, you've missed your breakfast and the coach leaves in 15 minutes". I had such a hangover, and what more could you want to overcome such a thing than a 7-hour coach ride back to London?! Needless to say, it was no work for me on the Monday morning and of course, I was to be the talk of the team for the next couple of games. What was funny was I had got a bollocking for the Liverpool game the year before, but I never even got told off this time for not looking after the players. Even the F.A. were laughing about a side of me they had never seen before.

It was that time again as we waited for the draw for the semi-final of the F.A. County Youth cup and we were given a home draw against Lancashire F.A. This time it was Godders who went to have a look at them, as his mother lived in Liverpool and he combined watching Lancashire with a visit to his mum's. We had our normal training sessions and we also had the notes on Lancashire and their formation and Godders was quite confident we could beat them. The game was arranged for Saturday 1 March 1997 at our favourite ground, Woking F.C.

Then something happened which was truly remarkable and many Woking fans reading this book will remember quite well; suddenly, holes started to appear in their playing surface overnight. When I had the 'phone call to say that Woking would not be available and the game was to be switched to Walton and Hersham, I had a gut feeling that this was going to have an enormous effect on the game. The boys were clearly upset not to be playing at Woking. No disrespect to Walton and Hersham, but their surface was not comparable to Woking's and neither was the atmosphere of the ground. I still think we should have waited to play this game, but they chose to play it at Walton. To be fair to them, they were kind enough to stage the game because it is always difficult to get grounds.

The management team decided to meet early on the day of the semi-final and have a light lunch in a pub by the river at Cobham. I was uneasy about the fixture change, and I think, if the truth be known, so were the rest of the staff. I am a believer in omens and it proved to be. Lancashire were not a good side but the bone-hard playing surface suited them because they were more physical and we had now got a team that loved to pass the ball about. They were always going to be a threat on corners, and despite our goalkeeper making some timely catches, it was from the head of one of the Lancashire defenders up for a corner that they took the lead. As I have said many times, we did have a side that would not lay down and, within minutes, we were back in the game on level terms before half-time. The second half was all about us but we could just not find the back of the net and that feeling would not go away. They scored the winner with minutes to go and we were to be the bridesmaids at the wedding again. There was the same feeling in that dressing room - so near, yet so far away and of players never able to play in that competition again because of that age rule. Where was I on the rollercoaster then? I was at the bottom and nearly jumped off the fucking thing I was so disappointed, but as they say, you live to fight another day. I kept thinking to myself perhaps I will give it another shot next season if appointed. Surely, we must win this cup sometime? We were all given the vote of confidence as again the Home Counties championships went fine and we did well as always.

So now, it's on to the 1997/1998 season and the F.A. County Youth cup again. Little did I know, but this would be my chance to win the bloody thing and also the last involvement with the Surrey F.A. Again, we had a bye in the first round and were drawn at home in the second round to Dorset F.A. to be played at Woking F.C., provided that this time they had no holes on the pitch. We had kept a few of the players who were still underage, and after a few training sessions at Charterhouse School, we had what on paper looked a decent-looking side, and could this be the team to win this trophy. We had no problem in beating Dorset and then went on to play the Royal Navy in the Home Counties championship at Portsmouth with another good result. Then we had to meet Worcestershire in the 3rd round of the F.A. County Youth cup away at Kidderminster Harriers F.C. They had the very impressive Aggborough stadium but unfortunately, we were not allowed an overnight stay which was a shame as I believe it did go some way to help bond the side and of course, give the team a lie-in on the Saturday morning instead of the early start.

There is a bit of a story to this trip which involved the so-called F.A. breakfast allowance made for non-overnight stays. We had decided to stop on the M40 near Oxford on the way to the game at those rather overpriced service stations that you must all know about, when I was summoned by Whally Howard, our county secretary, to organise the spending amount, which I think was somewhere in the region of £200.00 pounds to cover 18 players and 7 staff. So, I said to the lads in the squad not to go mad, but be sensible and have a light breakfast. I had also invited some of the parents to join us, so everyone went through the till with their eats and drinks, leaving me last in line holding the F.A. money to pay. Well, the bill came to nearly £300.00 and I shouted to Whally to get some more money up here fast! The look on his face was a picture, to say the least, and he whispered in my ear that there was no need to buy everybody in the service station a fucking breakfast, and how was he going to explain the extra money that had been used to the F.A.? My immediate reaction was, "What do you think they should have had, a fucking boiled egg each? And anyway, what about the game? Is that not the most important issue of the day, not a breakfast?"

During this heated debate, Godders had taken the lads on a short walk to have some fresh air and loosen up a bit before we carried on to Kidderminster so as to arrive in plenty of time, as was always our aim. The feeling in the dressing room was good, the warm up was always professional as normal, and I remember looking down the pitch and seeing the way that Worcestershire were warming up. They had quite a big side and as always at this level, there would be no question about their fitness. There was an unusually good crowd in that day, as Kidderminster were well-represented.

We had our normal chat with the boys before the game, played our usual system and set about winning the game, but you get that feeling sometimes that even from the start, the team were not firing on all cylinders. We soon found ourselves 2 goals down and struggling to create anything. I must say that at half-time, after Godders had had his say, myself and Dave Martin ripped into them. It is the first time that I had really lost my temper with representative players, but I did not mince my words and told them that they were a disgrace to their club and to their county and more importantly, to the management team. We made some changes and then we did have some improvement in our performance in the second half. We did have a ray of hope when we scored, only to be caught again, flat-footed, and Worcestershire scored a third and it was game, set, and match.

It was probably the first time during my five years that I never put my arm around a player at the end as I was thoroughly disgusted and upset. On the team bus on the way home, I remember thinking, 'do I really need all of this, what with my club commitments'? Also, there was some feeling between myself and Mike Godfrey that our opinions were beginning to wear thin, so after deep thought, I declared that I would stand down on the management side at the end of the season 1997/8. Along with the other duties at my club, Croydon Athletic, including reserve and youth team, I was to oversee/manage no fewer than 78 games in that one season, which is some hell of a lot of football.

The County F.A. were very good with me and gave me an inscribed tankard for my services and also a commemorative, gilt-edged blazer badge, which takes place of pride in my football awards collection. There is just one thing that I need to say as I close this chapter; I had some great moments and managed some very gifted young players who went on to have successful careers as pros or good non-league players. Sometimes I am asked who was the best player during my time with the county F.A. that I had the most pleasure working with? For me, it was Kevin Betsy (Woking F.C.) This lad was sheer class. He had so much vision, control, ability to pass the ball, and above all this, he was a true professional in his approach to the game and I took great pride in following his professional career. Now, he is manager of the England under 16 squad and he will learn how hard rep football is. Of course, there were many who came very close to him and I did have some very useful 'phone numbers in my book and many of the players went on to play for me in my non-league club career.

You make many friends in non-league football, none more so than my good friend, Dave Martin, who attended my 60th, 65th, and 70th birthday parties. We still talk about those times we had together. But what experience I had gained from those years with the County F.A. and also the games against the Army F.A.

and the military stadium at Aldershot, and I would be a liar if I said I did not like all of that VIP treatment; the team bus being waved in by armed guards and the playing surface was as good as Wembley. The reception after the game was second to none, as proper chefs prepared our meal and we, the management team had free drinks vouchers. We felt like royalty!

But it was not all about these special treats that sometimes happen in non-league football. It was also about trying to teach young footballers to have respect and make a good and decent life for themselves. It is sad that the Surrey F.A. no longer run a county youth side at any level, and why, I don't know. Maybe in the future hopefully. As for Mike Godfrey, he did manage to reach the final in 1999 but lost to Birmingham F.C. 2-1, and still no trophy!

2016 CALENDAR

Happy Days. Great memories

My 70th birthday. A great line up at Whyteleafe

F.A. Vase final at Wembley 1996. Me with some of my Surrey County Youth players

Receiving another trophy this time from the great Dave Mackay and Crystal Palace legend John Jackson with skipper Martin Whant

Aged 50. Just warming up the Surrey County Youth players

Top – My great friend Bernie Donnelly

Bottom – Me and my good friend Crystal Palace legend Steve Kember

Thornton Heath United 1978. Simply the best

Addiscombe Social 1972/73 – better than the best. In a class of their own

Grandson George (the best) Taylor. The future

Me, my son, and my grandson on my 70th birthday. A very proud moment

Top – Addiscombe Boys' Club. Six of the best 5-a-side runners up in Great Britain 1995

Bottom – Surrey County Youth F.A. at Walton and Hersham

Dad front row second from right St. Andrew's Old Boys. Dad liked trophies too

Top – My Surrey Premier Rep side unbeaten in 5 years in South East Counties Leagues Cup. Me front row first left and Robin 'Merlin' Denman front row first right

Bottom – Fergie, you're not the only team to win the treble. The great Croydon F.C. 2000

Reedham Park. Not bad for my first year in management

The Surrey County F.A. management and staff showing off our new suits!

Just to show off. I love a trophy

I said I liked a bit of racing. One of my fans the great AP

Croydon Athletic promoted to the Ryman League. First season winning the fair play trophy 1997/98

▲ NEW management team Andy Thomson and Micky Taylor point the way forward at The Firs on Saturday.   H15706

ST LEONARDS are looking forward to a successful season in the Eastern Division of the Dr Martens League. H32536a

Sports Argus, Saturday, March 22-Thursday, March 27, 2008

PARK LIFE

Tom Gurney with the best news and laughs from the local football scene

Taylor makes final appearance at 60

Colourful ex-Saints boss pulls on his boots one last time

LEGENDS of Sussex non-league football will be taking a trip down memory lane in honour of one of county's most colourful characters.

Former St Leonards and Three Bridges manager Micky Taylor is celebrating his 60th birthday by holding an exhibition game today (Sunday).

He is set to play his last ever game at Whyteleafe Football Club alongside friends, former players and ex-teammates he has known during his 45 years in football.

Among those playing will be former Albion defender John Crumplin, Dave Garland, who is the father of former Crawley midfielder Peter, and one-time St Leonards winger Des Boetang.

Watching from the sidelines will be former Crawley boss Billy Smith, Taylor's old rival at Hastings George Wakeling and ex-Crystal Palace manager Steve Kember, while Everton legend Neville Southall may also turn up.

Taylor was St Leonards manager when the Hastings-based club were one of the leading teams in the county.

They played in the Southern League eastern division before money problems caused them to fold four years ago.

Taylor went on to manage Haywards Heath and Three Bridges and has been helping out scouting for a number of clubs, including Hastings, in recent years.

Taylor, who lives in Bexhill, said: "It is going to be one big reunion and I'm quite nervous to be honest. I haven't seen some of these people for years so it will be a real blast from the past.

"I am going to play and have been doing a bit of training and then afterwards the boots are going in the dustbin.

"A few of the other players will be coming out of retirement and when you add up the ages of everyone who is taking part it comes to more than 1,000.

"It will be great to see everyone and it's the perfect way to celebrate my 60th birthday."

Taylor singles out his St Leonards days as the best of his football career but says he has enjoyed all aspects of his long time in the game.

He said: "St Leonards was probably my happiest time. I brought in Crumps (Crumplin) which was the big sign-

BIRTHDAY: Micky Taylor

HOPING: Neville Southall

PAL: Billy Smith

RIVAL: George Wakeling

by TOM GURNEY

ing at the time because he was a legend.

"We had some good players like (former Albion forward) Simon Fox but you have to remember that I was competing with George (Wakeling) over at Hastings when he won the league at the time.

"Those were good days and it was a shame what eventually happened to St Leonards. The thing I've enjoyed most about my time in the game is the social side. You meet so many people and down the years I have got to know just about every one."

Taylor is interested in getting back into football if the right job comes along.

He said: "I would consider anything. Obviously I have a lot of experience and believe I can help out clubs so if they want to get hold of me to talk then I will always listen."

Any clubs wanting to contact Taylor can email him at micky_taylor@windows.com.

How wrong they were. I scored a hat trick on my 65th birthday

Mum and Dad – the perfect match

Liverpool training on our lovely surface. Us non-league clubs do have some use

15 Years Old - 1963 - 64
First Cup Final Woodside Albion and Winners Medal

We were not allowed to play any football other than for the school until aged 15

Great memories, sad picture. St Leonards F.C. no longer

Is it a rollercoaster now or a ghost train? My appointment as manager and life with Croydon Athletic 1995/99 and beyond my departure, a circus.

I am going back in time now to May 1995 when I received a 'phone call to give me my first chance at senior non-league club level. That club was none other than Croydon Athletic. It came from their director of football, Ken Fisher, who wanted me to leave Carshalton Athletic youth set up and come over to run the reserve side in the suburban league, with the view to one day becoming involved with their first team who played in the London Spartan League. I remember thinking this might be my big chance to prove myself and work my way up the ladder of a local senior club side which I knew was going to be a hell of a difference than working with the F.A. County rep side, but I still needed some time for thought before I gave them the yes or no. I was happy at Carshalton Athletic and had a good football relationship with John Franks and our first team manager Billy Smith, so it was no easy call to make back to Ken Fisher to tell him that I would join his beloved Croydon Athletic. If only I had known how things would turn out, I would not have touched the club with a barge pole. To think I would end up hating a certain person, even to this day at the ripe old age of 71, would be unthinkable but despite all this, I did have some very happy and successful times there.

So here we go, then, on the senior non-league managerial slog. Nothing can prepare you for a reserve team manager's role at this level and some twenty years ago, when things were a whole lot different than today with academies and under 21 sides, the club had to find a first-team manager after the sudden departure of Martin Caller. He had left the club because, having won the Spartan League championship, he was not allowed to take his team into the Ryman Isthmian league because of the ground not being up to the standard required for that step up. I do not blame him for that, as it must have been so frustrating to have worked so hard and not be able to achieve your goal, but he did in a funny way by becoming manager of Dorking F.C., who were in the Ryman league. Not only was Martin hurt but of course, the club were hurt as well. So, you can imagine, the place was really in a depressed state but they had to carry on despite losing some players to Dorking.

I knew the chairman, Keith Tuckey, and vice-chairman, Clive Thompson quite well from days gone by, and for some mad reason, I thought I might be elevated into first-team management quicker than I thought. I was soon to realise that they had got their man to take the club forward; his name was Ray Purvis, and he had been a player at Epsom and Ewell, Barnet, and also manager at Redhill F.C. and was going to bring some new faces to the club and start the rebuilding process. I could see from the first pre-season training sessions that this was going to be a disaster and if it had not been for Johnny Bellinger, his assistant manager, he would not have lasted as long as he did. Johnny brought in some players and the chairman tried hard with his wallet to entice players back from Dorking F.C. I was even more determined to get some players to the club to play in the reserves and move them on to the first team, as I saw that as my sole purpose of managing the reserves and of course I had to call in staff to help me. I was lucky enough to know two great football characters who decided to come in with me for the bumpy ride that is reserve team football. Their names are Dave Finch and Chick Bain, and they were willing to do almost anything for the club and myself. Dave was a rather a quiet man really, but would take on any duties including kit man and doing the team sheet for the referee, but Chick was more hands-on with the coaching side along with myself. We agreed that the reserve side would be run for the club and not for our own benefit and also the discipline that I had inbuilt in myself over the years would be transferred to the team and the club. I got on with Ray Purvis quite well and we had a good understanding of how things were going to pan out regarding all teams to play the same formation as best we could, which was great. Also, the youth team were to be part of my reserve team plans, so we waited for the pre-season games to come and on this note, I had my first experience of the actions of our vice-chairman Clive Thompson.

When both first and reserve teams were to travel on the same team coach to play Cornard United near Sudbury in Suffolk, the kick-off for the 1st team was 1 pm and the reserves, 3 pm, and there was to be a barbeque and disco to follow the games. So, there we were at our ground waiting for this coach to arrive at 9.30 am when we were told the fucking thing had broken down and another would not be arriving until at least 11.30 am. So, quick plans were made for first-team players to use their cars and get going and the reserves to wait for the coach as we were the later kick-off. We boarded the coach around 12 noon to arrive at Cornard just before our 3 pm kick-off. Now, picture the scene - the first team have played and won their game, stayed to watch some of our game, had a drink and food and then all pissed off home in their cars. We won our game and played quite well, but the time was getting on now and they started this barbeque and disco and Clive Thompson and Paul Timms expected the reserve team to stay on. This was the first of many confrontations with Clive, as I stood my ground and said, "These players have travelled all this way; it is now 6.15 pm, we have a three-hour coach trip back to the club, and you expect me to tell the players to stay for a fucking disco on a boiling hot July Saturday evening? Well, let me tell you, I want that coach to leave here no later than 6.45 pm or you can fucking get another manager!" Needless to say, the players were on the coach at the time I wanted, and although I had let my discipline slip a little, I felt I had made the right decision for the players and they respected that their manager stood by them. That was just Clive Thompson all over - he loved a drink, and nothing was going to stand in his way as I learnt over my years at the club.

Now it was time to get the 1995/6 season underway in my new role. I wondered how I would cope with the different class of player than I had been used to with the county F.A. and to be fair, I was quite surprised at the quality of player at my disposal and how well they understood and respected my thoughts on the way they should play and conduct themselves. It was also quite ironic that one of the reserve teams we had to face in the suburban league was Whyteleafe F.C., which was managed by my great friend and my son Danny's godfather, Bernie Donnelly. They were a very good side but I knew I would take some time to produce a team like he had, but more importantly players who would go on and play first-team football. We had a very bad start, losing our first game to Bromley 4-0 and then Banstead Athletic, but if you remember earlier in the book, I did say that I would take some of the county players' phone numbers just in case I was to go into club management, so out came my book and I made some 'phone calls which added a couple of very good players onto the club's books and into the reserve side.

For the first time, results were not the most important thing to take from a game; it was more that certain players, who I knew had a good chance to progress, were coached properly and given that chance one day. The first team, under Ray Purvis, were doing alright, but of course, first-team football is all about results and the honeymoon period was coming to the end and he was losing games. At this time, it led to a kind of falling out with him over a certain player who he insisted I should play in the reserves as he had been on the bench for the first team. I will always do the best for the club at all times, but in this instance, I felt this player was worse than I had in the reserves, so why should I take a better player out of the side? His name was Mr Steve King and most people in non-league would have heard of him, as he has managed more clubs than I have had hot dinners. To be fair, he has had some very good success and good media coverage, albeit sometimes for not the right reasons, as chairmen and fans of many clubs will know. Again, it comes down to my opinion, as I do not think Steve King can manage any football club unless there is a massive budget. I thought it was worth a bit of a mention as lots of non-league fans think that some of these well-paid managers have been top-class players in their time, but this is not always the case.

Anyway, let's go back to Croydon Athletic and the unfortunate departure of Ray Purvis after just over two months in charge of the first team. I remember the evening well. I was taking the reserves in a coaching session on the training ground and Ray came over to say goodbye. I thought, at first, he was going on holiday, but then realised he was leaving the club. It will always remain a mystery to me whether he left of his own accord, or whether he was sacked. I will never know, but after a run of poor results, I guess it must have been the tin tack. The club quickly appointed my good friend, Johnny Bellinger, as first-team manager and first-team captain, Leon Maxwell, as assistant manager and in total amazement to me, one of my old representative players and a good friend, Kevin (Sibbo) Simpson as coach.

There were a couple of games that stood out for me in the reserves. One was in the London Intermediate cup, where we were drawn away to Cray Valley P.M. who we beat 2-1. To think that Cray would, 24 years later (2019), take the pitch at Wembley in the F.A. Vase final v. Chertsey Town which cray lost, just goes to show it's a funny old game, football. The next game involved my great friend, Bernie Donnelly, and his Whyteleafe reserves, who we faced away in the league shield and I must say the coaching from Chick, myself, and Dave was beginning to pay off as some of the younger players matured and were beginning to knock on the first team door. This particular day, 25 November 1995, I will remember for the way that we played. It was almost like watching Real Madrid as we beat Whyteleafe 5-2, and a certain player by the name of Tony Brown emerged as someone special for me. Despite that win, things cannot always be perfect. As I was walking to the dressing room, my son was standing waiting to tell me that he had reversed my Ford Escort into a post and that his nan was to blame!

Bernie Donnelly was to have his last say when, in both league games, we were well-beaten and Whyteleafe became worthy suburban league champions. But even now, 24 years on, he is still my greatest friend and we still have a bit of banter about that day. There were a couple of players that I must mention who played in the reserves as well as the first team. The first one was one of my Surrey youth players, Kojo Ohene. Kojo considered himself a real hard nut in youth football, but on this day in question, he had his first taste of real men's football away at Molesey. He was tackled very hard by a player and went sprawling to the ground. He was about to get up to square up to the player that put him on his arse, but he thought better of it as the player said, "Come on then, son, if you fancy it!" Kojo was to learn from these things that hard work would see him become part of my first-team plans and a future at the club. Great times.

That was also the game where my next player got sent off, (thanks Darren) but he got a rocket from me when the game ended. This was a player called Darren Powell, who was in and out of the first team and reserves. Darren would always need a Saturday morning call to make sure he was out of bed and then I would pay his travel money out of my own pocket to get him to a game. After Darren left our club, he went on to have a professional football career, making over 250 appearances in total with clubs like Crystal Palace, Brentford, Southampton, Derby County, and MK Dons, and I feel that some of my input into his discipline taught him to treat his football more seriously if he wanted to be a decent player because he had that ability to be more than just that.

Back to the first team now and the three amigos. Johnny, Max, and Sibbo were doing the best they could and I loved the three of them to pieces as Johnny always had a smile on his face, but again, I do not think he was really wanted to carry on after the end of the season. They finished quite well in a respectable position, but Johnny decided to call it a day. I thought to myself that this might be my big chance to become a non-league senior first team manager, and it proved to be, as I was offered the first-team job. I saw it as my biggest challenge yet in football, but one that I would relish as I wanted to get this club into its rightful position in the icis Isthmian Football league. It was made clear to me by Chick and Dave that they wanted to stay as reserve team managers and therefore I appointed Leon Maxwell as my assistant manager and coach. Also, Ken Fisher was there to give me advice when I required it and also helped on the training ground and on some match days, although he had other business working for Arsenal as a scout. For obvious reasons, I had a talk with the chairman, Keith Tuckey, about a playing budget to which he replied, "I will deal with some of the players and the others will play for expenses". That suited me fine, as I needed to get used to being involved in the responsibility of the money side of the game which, in my opinion, in some cases now in non-league football, has gone crazy, and I am glad I never got involved in that circus.

It was also decided that I would take on the role of youth team manager as well and do not forget I was still working for the County F.A., so quite a lot of football was to come my way in 1996/97 season. I also now had to deal with the local press and it was mainly the Croydon Advertiser and their sports columnist, David Groves, who was okay, I thought. However, I soon found out that he was typical - when he could get the knife in your back, he would. To be fair to him, though, he gave me big headlines when I took the job (Taylor-made for the Athletic).

It was a long pre-season with having to see which players I wanted to stay and which players were going to come in and give the club a good fighting chance of getting promoted to the Ryman league. So, out came my little book and I managed to 'phone and convince certain players to sign forms to complete my side. I managed to get Crawley Town down to our ground for a Sunday pre-season friendly, thanks to my good friend, Billy Smith, their manager, and we got beaten by a very good side. Still, I learnt enough to know that I had a good chance of success with my players, as they put up a good show of passing, tackling, and competing in all areas.

Terry Gale, brother of West Ham United's Tony Gale, was going to be my captain and what a very good defender he was. He led by example on the field, but off the field, Terry was a handful in his reluctance to train which led to the chairman giving him a fine out of his wages on quite a few occasions. He did make me laugh sometimes with his antics. We had a big dressing room with a toilet in it but the partition did not go up to the ceiling for ventilation reasons or so the players thought. It will come as no surprise that I had dressing room rules including no smoking in the toilet, so you can imagine the look on my face when Terry Gale used the toilet and a puff of smoke came up over the top of the cubicle. Then there was another puff; the players fell about laughing but I knew I had to stand firm and give him a right bollocking for breaking my rules. As you know, in my first season, the chairman would look after some players and the rest just got expenses, so I told him to fine Terry, which he did.

We were now preparing for our first game when I realised this Spartan league was not going to be just about football, but travel as well, as we were the only club south of the water as Corinthian Casuals had opted for the combined Counties league instead, I must say at this time that I had the best physio around in Micky Reed. If he told me a player was not fit to play, then that was the end of the story, no matter who the player was and Micky was to be with me for the whole of my stay with the Athletic. However, if Mick had one fault it would be that he would voice his opinion sometimes a little too much, but he was a great fellow and we all have our faults, don't we?

In football, you are always judged on results and good performances, and in the club's aim and mine to win promotion, two league games into the season and one point on the board was not a good start. Now, I must say that the London Spartan was a very hard league to compete in, as all of the teams were north of the river Thames and because of the traffic, they were hard places to get to on a Saturday afternoon. Although the club provided a minibus for the travel, what was not told to me before I took the first team job was that our vice-chairman, Clive Thompson liked his early Saturday morning pint or two and needed more toilet stops on the way to the games, so even the minibus driver knew exactly where to stop. All of this was not very good preparation for the game, as we often arrived late, giving us no time at all; just a short warm-up, instructions and out we went. So, can you imagine what it must have been like on the way home; win or lose, when he had consumed all the beer he could after arriving at the ground until we left to come home. Despite this, his heart was in the right place and he would do anything for the club.

There would be many first times for me during my managerial role with the Athletic and one was coming up now when it was my first game as manager in the F.A. Cup and we had been drawn at home to Lewes from the Icis league division three, a club I held in high regard and still do to this day. Now, what about the roller coaster? It was heading for a high or a low because clearly, we were the underdogs. There were two reasons why I wanted to do so well in this game; first, I wanted to gauge ourselves against a side from a league we hoped we would be playing in next season, and second, we wanted to progress to the next round of this famous old competition and play a higher-rated side.

The day arrived; a nice summer's afternoon, Saturday 31st August 1996. There was a good crowd as Lewes had brought their supporters on their team bus, and what a great result! A 2-0 win! Now we were the only Spartan League club left in the F.A. cup, which I was proud of. The roller coaster was on a high despite having to make changes with my top striker, Johnny Fowler, who was unable to play, and a change of formation. But the group of young players I had brought to the club all showed that they were ready for first-team football. Again, the Surrey County F.A. players' phone numbers came in handy!

What a draw we were given in the next round a trip to Icis league premier side, Hendon, who had a great history with many honours to their name and also, at the time, a well-respected manager, Neil Price, but before that, we had a game in the F.A. Vase away at Redhill. There is a little story to this game and it involved our vice-chairman, myself and a player I had wanted to sign after some impressive pre-season games. He was a French player by the name of Yaker Belkacem. We needed clearance from the French F.A. for Yaker to start the season with us, so Clive Thompson, whose heart was definitely in the club, got the Eurostar from Waterloo to Paris to get his clearance in time, although he could not play in the Lewes game. So, against Redhill, I left him out and put him on the bench, as I felt the lads deserved to keep their places. Well,

I must say there was an outburst from Clive and his words to me were heard all round the ground when the teams took to the field. He shouted, "Micky, I went all the way to fucking Paris to sign Yaker and you have put him on the fucking bench! That is not okay!" We lost to Redhill and me and Clive had words afterwards, but little did I know that the following week he would be involved again in our F.A. cup game at Hendon, only this time in using his language in a proper manner. The local paper was all over us regarding the game and our chances, but again we were the underdogs and myself and my team felt under no pressure at all. We had all the trimmings this time - a proper team coach and not that fucking awful minibus that I knew could, if I let it, send me mad. Hendon's ground, Claremont Road, had a slope end to end, but a decent playing surface and also, they had just signed a player Curtis Warmington, who was going to have a big say in the outcome of the game. We started poorly and my young keeper, Danny Burgess, was picking the ball out of the net after just two minutes. We managed to steady the ship and put them on the back foot for long periods of the first half, and even had a goal disallowed when John Fowler scored. It seemed to me a perfect goal but then I saw the lino with his flag up for offside.

So, we finished the half 1- 0 down and were prepared to give it a right go in the second half, but I had one problem as the teams left the pitch and made their way to the dressing room. How was I going to get the information to my French lad, Yaker, as I wanted him to do a man to man marking job in the second half on one of their midfield players, who for my liking, was having too much of the ball and stop him doing so. It was now my turn to shout at Clive Thompson, as I needed him to come to the dressing room to explain to Yaker what I wanted him to do. Well, you can imagine the scene; Clive marched him into the shower area to speak with him, while I tried to give the team their orders for the second half and lift their game even a higher level. I could see the boys beginning to laugh as Clive began to raise his voice in frustration so as to get the message across.

We came out for the second half, but all of our hard work seemed to go to pot when a Hendon player clearly handled our defender Paul Muir's clearance. His hand was high above his head in what may have been an instinctive reaction, but it propelled the ball into his path, then he crossed it for Michael Banton to put us two down. We carried on playing our football and were still in the game until another incident on 70 minutes when Johnny Fowler and Curtis Warmington exchanged some words. They were not to the liking of the referee, who promptly gave John his second yellow card and sent him off. I remember thinking, 'fucking hell, what on earth have we got to do to get anywhere in this game,' but despite having ten men, we still pushed forward, searching for a way back into the game. This was not to be and we, therefore, lost the tie. I must say I was very proud of the boys, especially our younger players, but obviously, it was the result that counted. I'm not a great one for the saying you were as good as us; unlucky. I would sooner have played shit and won the game.

One thing that did happen which was encouraging though, was their chairman spoke to me after the game and said, "For the money I'm paying for my team and the very small budget you are on, I would sooner be chairman of your club any day," which to me was a very rewarding comment. So it was now back to the league and we followed that game with a 5-1 victory at Woodford Town in the league, and just as I thought we had turned the corner, we got the biggest kick in the bollocks I have ever had in a football match the following week when we travelled to play Cockfosters in the London senior cup. We lost the game 7-0! I have never lost a game of any kind of football by a 7-goal margin, ever, and would not dare to dream that it could happen. I went absolutely berserk, to say the least, and took things upon my own back, ringing the press myself on the

Monday morning to say how disgusted I was with my team and their lack of commitment and there were to be some big changes. As this was reported in the paper as headlines, I was pulled in to the boardroom and told no way must I, as first-team manager, go directly to the papers and slaughter my football club without first speaking to the committee. I took that on board and realised that I had made a mistake by doing that and learnt from that error of judgement.

I was to be tested again against higher opposition when on Tuesday 29th October 1996, we made the short trip to play Icis division one side Whyteleafe in the Surrey Senior Cup, 1st round. Only a year earlier, I was reserve team manager when we played their reserves and funnily enough, my great friend, Bernie Donnelly. was manager. He had also been promoted to the first team as big Lee Richardson's assistant. They were not doing that well in the league at that time and I thought we could take a scalp, but I have to admit, they were far better than us on the night and we got turned over 4-1, but we gained some more experience with our young side and anyway, it was a top-three league finish we were after.

There was another incident that took place towards the end of 1996; the date was 21st December and we were away at Brimsdown Rovers. There was very little in the way of festive spirit being shown by both teams as a crunching tackle on my young full-back, Colin Ducasse, led to Colin retaliating and then both sides deciding to join in the fracas. The referee had no control at this point and waited for both managers to calm things down before he started to show his authority. He gave Colin Ducasse a red card and another of my players, David Emery, also got a red card. He also proceeded to send two of the Brimsdown players off. Now the fun began, as we were in control of the game. If you are good at maths you will know that it should have been nine-a-side, but instead, Brimsdown continued to play with ten men and forced a 2 all draw. I was livid at the time, not so much with my players, though, because if one of the team gets taken out, we should all pull together. After the game, I went to the referee's room and insisted on knowing why, after sending two Brimsdown players off, they played the remainder of the game with ten men and not nine. He promptly replied, "I have no answer to that; it will be in my report, as I thought both players had left the field." I must say I have never heard so much bollocks in all my life and when our very efficient secretary, Dean Fisher, took it up with the F.A., he was told that the referee's report was inconclusive. To make matters worse, both of our players were suspended and fined and only one of theirs. Are referees entitled to make such a mistake as that? I don't think so. I think he should have been struck off the referee's list. I have always been understanding of a referee's hard job and mistakes, but not to that degree.

So back now with our progress in trying to make a top-four finish to help with our push to join the Icis league. Also, being a master joiner and having friends who were carpenters in the building trade, we were helping to get the ground ready to help achieve our goal. I had to get rid of the French player as the language situation was driving me mad and it was also interfering with pre-match preparations, half-time team talks and tactics. I think it proved to be the right decision as by March 2017, we were fourth from top in the table and going very well.

I must pick out one game during this period when we played at home to Waltham Abbey and beat them 1-0. It was reported that I had fielded Croydon Athletics' youngest team ever. No fewer than seven teenagers were included in that fourteen-man squad, which I think was very pleasing for my chairman, Keith Tuckey. My job was to encourage young players and a lot of that was down to the hard work of my good friends, Chick and Dave in the reserves, and Dave Martin, who was running the youth team. We were nearing the end of the season now. Our secretary, Dean Fisher, was working hard behind the scenes on Nick Robinson of the Icis league, trying to get our ground grading accepted. I duly obliged by doing my bit on the football pitch and we finished third in the table and it was fucking goodbye to that bloody minibus and Clive Thompson's weak bladder! We then awaited the day that Mr Robinson was going to come down and make his inspection. Everyone at the club on the committee and work parties had done their bit, including myself and my family, and even on the day of our inspection, the afternoon was spent sweeping the terraces and putting on the last lick of paint. Even my good friend, Micky Southwick, was putting handles on toilet doors and of course, the boardroom sandwiches were laid out as though it was royalty arriving. I remember clearly when Mr Robinson turned up in his flash car and started his walk around the ground with Dean and Keith Tuckey and others, everyone held their breath, thinking we would have our answer, but we had to wait until a few meetings with the league and the F.A. had taken place. Finally, we were able to open the champagne bottles at a reception at the club, as we had gained our rightful spot in the Icis Isthmian League division three.

So, another first for me was being the first manager at Croydon Athletic to lead a side out in that league. Before I could do that there was plenty of work for me to get on with in respect of recruiting new players and of course a restructuring of my management team. I felt that I would need an experienced coach and I mean no disrespect to Leon Maxwell who I felt was much more needed on the pitch using his experience. So, I brought in a good friend of mine, Des McCarthy. He was not the best communicator, but certainly one of the best coaches around. Des had been a player at Crystal Palace, Portsmouth, F.C. Bruges, and a coach at Sutton United, not forgetting being an England schoolboy international. Chick had decided to leave the reserves and I appointed Carl Gibbs as assistant to Dave Finch in the reserves. Dave Martin was to remain as youth team manager and Ken Fisher as director of football.

My next duty before pre-season training was to speak to my chairman about a proposed budget, as we were now in with the big boys and unfortunately money did talk. I was quite open and frank with the board of directors and they felt the same way, that as long as I kept them in the division that we had strived so long to be in, they would be quite happy with that and therefore the proposal put to me was you can either have a decent coach to travel in for away games and they would pay a couple of the players, or there was a very small budget on the table of around £200 per week.

However, before our big day arrived there are some stories to tell in pre-season and as all non-league fans will know, our game is all about surprises which you don't get much of in the football league or championship and premiership. The first one came when I turned up for training early one night, only to see this black lad waiting outside the club gates. I asked him what he was doing here and he replied, "I would like a trial and to play for your team". I asked him some questions about where he had been playing and he told me a few clubs that I didn't recognise and then out of the blue, he informs me that he is the brother of the Leeds United player, Tony Yeboah, who had been a top-class professional at clubs abroad as well. With that, I asked him to wait on our small training ground while I went into the clubhouse and got some balls out to give him some basic ball drills, but before I did that, I rang the chairman and said, "Keith have you any pro contracts to hand, and if so, when you come to the club tonight can you bring one with you, as I have Tony Yeboah's brother here at the club". My chairman got so excited he said he would bring it down as soon as possible. In the meantime, out I went with this lad, threw him a couple of balls to his head, then a couple of little cushion volleys with his right foot and then the drama unfolded. I threw him a couple on his left foot. The ball went everywhere except back into my hands. To be fair, I thought this might be nerves and continued with some more with the ball. Things only got worse and to put it bluntly, he was fucking useless. This proved to me beyond doubt that football doesn't always run in the family. I quickly 'phoned my chairman again to tell him not to rush his tea and not to bring a contract down, which made him laugh. To be fair, he was a nice lad and I told him there and then that he wouldn't fit into our side. He reached inside his kit bag and he gave me a signed picture of his brother, Tony, which I still have today, and he went on his way, leaving me thinking, you lose some and you win some.

There was also another drama to unfold when two lads turned up for training one night out of the blue. One was Richard Lawrie and the other Tristan Wood. Richard had been around a few clubs and seemed a good prospect and Tristan had moved up from Cornwall having played for Torquay United and Truro City. To say that in the future the pair of them were going to be a right pain up my arse was an understatement, Tristan Wood more so than Richard Lawrie. Tristan had a great sense of humour in as much as he thought it funny to ring me on my home 'phone at 11.30 pm or sometimes midnight or later, pretending that he was an agent from a big club requiring my services, which was a bit over the top for me. He also overplayed this type of foolishness which would see him in trouble.

They say save the best till last and so it was a week before our first game, Friday 8th August 1997 when I had a 'phone call from my secretary, Dean Fisher, to say that Roy Evans, the Liverpool manager at that time, had rung him as Liverpool would like to use our pitch to train on that afternoon as they were staying at the Croydon Park hotel. They were playing Wimbledon on the Saturday at Selhurst Park. I must say I thought this was a wind-up and rang Dean back a couple of times until I realised this was for real. I was there to help let them into the ground along with some of the committee, and I took the picture of them, all 50 million pounds worth of talent training beneath the stand, which clearly identifies Croydon Athletic Football Club. (Twenty years on and you couldn't buy one top player for that amount, let alone a whole team!) What was ironic about this training session that I was witnessing and also in the picture, was that there were players, Paul Ince, Danny Murphy and Karl Heinz Riedle, who were going to make their first-team debuts for Liverpool on the Saturday 9th august and there they were on our pitch, training along with other famous names such as John Barnes, Razor Ruddock, Michael Owen, and Steve McManaman among others. As you can imagine, it was a great surprise, an everlasting memory and a picture to keep of a day I will never forget as they also left some souvenirs for the club. It was also the last ground where John Barnes was seen playing in a Liverpool shirt in the premiership. They complimented us on our playing surface as well.

It seemed like it was a very busy pre-season, because now there was going to be another first for me; my first appearance on TV on a Monday night live non-league football show. Okay, it wasn't the BBC or ITV, it was cable TV, which was a big thing in those days and had quite a big audience in south London, so to say I was nervous is an understatement. I made sure that I had a nice clean white shirt on with my club tie and blazer. Before I arrived at the studio, I went across to my neighbour, Bob, who had cable TV and gave him a blank video cassette and asked him if he would tape the show and I would pick it up from later when I returned from the studio. Little did Bob know then he was going to have three years of this unless I was going to subscribe to cable, but he was a lovely chap and didn't mind at all. I still have the tapes to this day.

We were now at the studio and I was sitting there watching the first half of the show in the guest suite, knowing full well that when the adverts came on ending the first half of the show, I was to be rushed down the corridor to the studio, wired up and the countdown to the start of the show would begin. I remember vividly being told only to look at the interviewer and the other panellists – do not look up at the monitors. I also remember there was a glass of water put in front of me. During the show, I tried to take a sip, but my shaking hand wouldn't let me lift the glass. What was even more dramatic was that it was a live 'phone-in as well, so you had to be prepared for almost anything. Also on the show was my good friend, Jimmy Thompson, a good player in his time, and he used to do a slot called Jimmy-cam where he used to go out and interview the likes of myself before a game and do some Sunday league park football, I must admit, they used to send a film crew to some of our games and they were obviously very professional and I would be a liar if I was to say I didn't like it because I loved every minute of it. Now, because of that experience, I sit and watch the TV at these sporting events and laugh at these overpaid pundits who sit there and waffle on and are paid thousands to tell you what you have already seen. I am envious because it's a job I could do with my eyes shut, so anyone in Sky, BT, or the BBC who wants a non-league guy to join their circus, then do not hesitate to contact me.

I think it is now time to get back to the football and the season ahead. The big day arrived after our pre-season games and training and it would be a game and an experience that I would never forget. We were away on 16th august 1997 to Tring Town in our first ever icis league game. We had already had the signs done to put in the front and back of the team bus, which read 'Croydon Athletic F.C. Team Coach' with our emblem, a ram's head, by the side of the writing. I now felt we were in the big time and could you imagine putting that on the fucking minibus?). I made sure the players had drinks and fruit on board the bus as would be proper, and so with great expectations, off we went to Tring. I remember so well it was a glorious sunny day and I kept saying to Des, as we chatted about tactics, "I wonder what their stadium is like and their playing surface," because you all know the work that we had put in to get into this league and quite rightly so, our expectations of other clubs' facilities should be equal if not better. You can imagine the look on our faces when the coach pulled in to Tring F.C.'s ground. The pitch looked more like a ploughed field than a football playing surface and then I was completely bowled over when our dressing room door was not even on its hinges. During our team talk, Des had to put the door into the hole and lean against it. There was no bench for Micky Reed, our physio., to work on and you had no room to swing a cat round, let alone fourteen players. When you think about it all, it was quite a slap in the face really, after all the work that had been done by Dean and the club members to get our ground grading. I would have liked to have asked Nick Robinson or Alan Turvey what all the fuss was about, but this was our first game and things could only get better, or so we thought. We managed, despite the surface, to get a draw out of the game when my new pre-season signing, John Kennedy (ex. Swindon town), came off the bench to get our equaliser.

I must mention at this stage that during the latter part of our Spartan league campaign, I managed to sign a prolific striker in Lee May, who knew exactly where the net was but I was wondering how we would handle this class of football as Lee had a bit of a fiery temperament about him. A new goalkeeper was also on the scene, his name being Glynn Shimell, who I also signed during the latter part of our Spartan league. I felt the side was balanced but the road to success is always under construction, and therefore our first season at this level was going to be a revolving door where players were concerned.

Our next game was a midweek trip to Ware Town, and talk about sublime to ridiculous, we arrived at their very impressive Wodson Park stadium. There was a perfect surface, although an end to end slope, but it felt that the league did have an air of importance about it after our disappointing encounter at Tring, as there was not a ground anywhere near this standard in the

Spartan League. We lost the game 1-0 but myself and Des felt that we had at least something to build on.

Another first for me was going to happen in our first ever icis league home game against Hornchurch as we had our first home game in the league and we won 2-1 with goals from Mr Smooth Simon Rollinson and my new signing, Tristan Wood. We then went on a four-game unbeaten run, including an F.A. cup win and beating Ware in the Guardian league cup after a replay, our third meeting with them in our first seven games. The replay at Ware was a bit special because, to the delight of the players, the chairman and board and myself and Des, we now faced a daunting but exciting trip in the next round to the big boys, Aldershot Town, at their famous old ground in front of what would be a big crowd, and to our chairman's delight, a share of the gate receipts. I remember our chairman, Keith Tuckey, giving me £50 to get the boys a drink with. He was so elated, but of course, we had a long journey home, so we put it in the pot for the next home game.

Before we played Aldershot and our victory at Ware, we had an F.A. Vase game against Hailsham Town to contend with. Although they were a Sussex County League side, they were still no pushover, but what happened that day down at Hailsham again was another situation where I had a player to deal with. The player in question was Richard Lawrie, and despite his five goals up until that game, I decided to leave him on the bench. The player created merry hell, for what reason I don't know, but again, a football team in those days was made up of fourteen players, but he didn't see it like that and sulked, which made myself and Des very angry. He was to play in the replay after a 1-1 draw which we lost 2-1 and his days were numbered really because I would not and did not have players upsetting the rest of the side and not respecting the club.

So now we had the disappointment of losing to a Sussex league club, but went on a three-game unbeaten run, including a 7-1 victory at Dorking, when Lee May scored five of the goals, which gave us some confidence facing Aldershot town. But all the fun stops there as, just our bad luck, Aldershot had appointed the well-voiced, big-time manager, George Borg only weeks before we played them. Despite his reputation, I knew his sides were always on good budgets and he accepted nothing short of a win in whatever game his side played in. With that in mind, I approached the game with a more defensive formation which was alien to the players, but I felt might prove to be the right move, to pack the midfield out and play one upfront. That was to be our striker, Lee May, who had scored 10 goals in 17 games. I remember saying to Lee, "Son, you will have to feed off the scraps tonight and then maybe you might just get a chance when we can get the ball to you, and of course you will have to work harder". I could see he was not happy with this role, but in the first half, it nearly paid off as he scored what looked like a perfect goal to me, only to be flagged offside. I thought straight away of the Hendon game and how we were robbed there, but in this game again we kept our shape and came in at half-time 1-0 down and still very much in the game with a comeback in the second half still possible. But sometimes what you think you had in your side will come back and smack you straight in the teeth and that was what happened with Lee May. He never stopped moaning all the way through the half-time team talk, not caring at all about his teammates, and also forgetting that this same group of players had provided him with the openings to score five goals against Dorking in a recent league game. I said to myself, "You are on the fucking way out of this club, sunshine, as I want players who play for the club and me and your team." As I said, we were still in it 1-0 down and went pushing on for the equaliser, leaving gaps and tired legs which saw us collapse and concede three goals in the last ten minutes. George Borg did speak to me after the game and said, "You can be proud of your boys tonight, as this is only your first time you have met this type of company." Thanks then, George, but little did I know, we would meet on different terms some three years later when we had some differences of opinion in a couple of games.

After the Aldershot game, it was going to be another four games of narrow defeats before we got our first win again, but we were playing some sexy football and feeling our way in our first season and certainly never flirted with relegation. But again, I had another problem with a referee, only this time in a league game on the Saturday after Aldershot. To be fair I was beginning to worry about the standard of the officials in what was considered a very good league. We went through a period of narrow defeats, but in the home game against high-flying Ford United on 25th October 1997, which we lost 1-0, I felt that I needed to knock on the official's door and have words, so this ref asked me what my problem was and I made it quite clear that he had been bullied by Ford the whole game and that, we had a clear penalty turned down and he gave them one that clearly was not, which cost us the game. I also informed him that in my opinion, perhaps he should referee at a lower level to which he replied, and I will never forget it, "Okay then, I will retire from the league and football altogether." How weak is that! I shared my comments with Ford United manager, Dennis Elliot and he laughed as I told him what I had said, but it showed me that at least other teams would not have to put up with that type of performance. After all, there were six Essex sides in the league and they would always give you a game and more. (That still applies today, as I am sure managers south of the water know what's coming, when you cross that Dartford bridge or under the Blackwall Tunnel, you're in for a tough afternoon or evening.)

So back to life with Lee May in the team and I explained to him that I was not prepared to have players in my team thinking only of themselves, so when I had a phone call from my good friend, Lee Richardson, the manager of Whyteleafe F.C., enquiring about Mr may as he had heard that I was wanting him out of the club and they would like to sign him, I replied that he was under contract and I wanted a fee for him. I remember the conversation well when he said, "You want a fee but you don't want him?" to which I replied, "You are correct, but you do, so the fee is £500." He came back and said £300 and I agreed to let him go for that making me, I believe, the first Croydon Athletic manager to ever sell a player to another club.

I had good support from the board and chairman, and also the club as a whole was doing okay and certainly on the social nights, most members, players, and staff were present, which was good for club spirit. I can tell you now that the karaoke nights were very special events at the club; special for one reason and that was none other than Mr Clive (Frank Sinatra) Thompson, our vice-chairman when he used to do his famous impersonation of the great man singing 'New York, New York', It wasn't just a case of Clive going up to the microphone; it was the preparation. He would disappear into the toilets which led off from the bar and the DJ would have to wait until he got the signal to put on this song. Suddenly, Clive would appear from the toilet doorway, as though he was coming on the stage to a rousing reception from all present, and he would finish his little act with 'My Way'. Normally after that, he would collapse into a corner pissed as normal.

We did have a bit of comedy which did make national headlines for all the wrong reasons and to my despair. As I mentioned earlier, I had a very good player by the name of Tristan Wood, who was under contract but did not realise the conformities of a professional footballer's contract although they were quite clear for him to read. This one incident was the straw that broke the camel's back. I remember receiving a 'phone call from my secretary, Dean Fisher, one Sunday evening, asking me if I had seen any of the Sunday papers. I politely replied, "No, I don't get time for that." said he then said, "Well you best believe this story now because Tristan Wood has gone and won the national lottery and has become a millionaire." I replied, "You must be fucking joking; it means he could buy the club and sack me; I just can't believe it." Dean replied, "Well, it's all in the papers, pictures of him in an expensive car, waving to the camera." To say the least, I went to bed feeling if anything a bit envious but still could not get my head round it. Monday morning came and Dean was on the 'phone again. Woodsy had been charged with deception or something like that and therefore he has not won the lottery. Because the club was involved in national headlines and he was one of our players, I asked Dean if I was able to terminate his contract. Dean gave me the all-clear and I called Woodsy in on training on Tuesday evening and terminated his contract as he had breached the terms. Sadly, it was the end of a good player's stay at the club.

There was also another amusing story during this first season, when, after our encounter at Aldershot Town in October we had to face Woking in the Surrey Senior Cup at their Kingfield stadium. I mentioned quite a while back that our loss in the Spartan league to Cockfosters 7-0 would never happen at this football club again. That time I blamed the players, but what was to happen at Woking I totally blame myself for. In this instance, my heart ruled my head and I paid dearly for it. Our regular goalkeeper, Glyn Shimell, was available for this big game but had missed the last two games and our reserve goalkeeper, Tony Prime had done very well in his absence. So, I decided to give Tony a big game at Woking, not even putting Shimell on the bench (as in those days you only had three subs). Again, there was to be a big crowd and again, we would share the gate receipts which our chairman was very happy with. We had our normal team bus to take us to the game and arrived in plenty of time before kick-off.

Then something happened in the dressing room corridor that will also live in my memory for the rest of my life. If you have ever seen the film 'I Believe in Miracles' you will remember a particular Nottingham Forest player/captain who had won back-to-back European Cups with a certain Mr Brian Clough. His name is John McGovern, and at the time, he was Woking's manager. He called me into the laundry room and explained to me, "Micky, we've had a couple of disappointing results losing to Yeovil Town and a poxy draw at home to Halifax Town on Saturday. The crowd tonight will want to see a response from those results, so I have had to put the full first team out tonight, which included one of your Surrey County F.A. boys, Kevin Betsy who was beginning to make his mark in the non-league game. I'm sorry to have to do that". To which I replied, "Well, what do you want me to do, John, go in and tell my players to get on the fucking team bus and let's go home because we've been threatened with a defeat? You must be joking". He looked at me and smiled as he said "Do you know what, Micky? That's exactly what my old boss would have said, Brian Clough. Thank you very much and best of luck tonight". (I wish to fuck we had of got on that team bus and gone home).

So on to the game itself, and behind one of their goals was their fantastic new stand. As we went out for our warm-up, I could see a nervous look in Tony's eyes as the ground was filling up, and would you believe it, Woking won the toss which meant Tony was in goal in front of that big stand full of people. I have never seen such a goalkeeping display in a long time. Poor old Tony threw three in his own net in the first twelve minutes. I felt for him because I had put him in this position and for the first time ever, I had let my players and my club down in making the wrong choice. We went on to lose 7-0 as Woking were relentless, but to be fair to the boys, we still tried to play football on a perfect surface but obviously, we were very disappointed to have been beaten by such a score line. John McGovern did come to see me at the end of the game and said to me, "I bet you wish you had got on that team bus now, Micky". I remember saying to him, "Fuck off and go and get me a pint, because I know your old boss would never let his heart rule his head when it came to selecting the team. The best team available always plays". He laughed and I went into his office and had a pint with him. What a great person and footballer. I was very proud to have met him and he came across as a very humble man, especially when you think of the legend he became and still is at Notts Forest.

Away from that game, we carried on and finished our league programme with a game away at the Dripping Pan, Lewes, which even today is always one of my little trips out to watch a game. I must have been doing something right at the club because during the March of 1998, it was my 50th birthday and I had a big party on a Sunday afternoon at my local, The Cricketers pub in old town Croydon. I invited quite a few of the players and also the chairman, then suddenly, with the party in full swing, the local paper turned up with their photographer and took a group photo with my family and the chairman. I must admit that I never took much notice until the following Friday when there, on the back page of the local paper, was a full-page colour picture of the event which I still have to this day in one of my scrapbooks and I do remember thinking I must be a local celeb now. While writing this book, I had a phone call from my old Sunday league team secretary, who still lives in Croydon, to tell me that the local paper were running some article on the past in photos of Croydon and its well-renowned people, and lo and behold, the picture from some twenty years ago was in the middle pages, although not in colour. That was this year, 2019. I thought to myself, I am still remembered after all this time.

There was going to be even more icing on the cake, as not only had we completed our first season and finished in quite a respectable position, but we were awarded the prestigious trophy of the fair play award and that set the foundation that we were a footballing side and had been recognised as such and also outlined the discipline of my players on the field and towards the referee. So, it was another first for me being the first manager to put an Isthmian Icis league trophy in the cabinet. Not a bad season's work then and with even more ground improvements, the stadium was looking quite nice.

The league was also renamed the Ryman football league for the season 1998/1999. It meant all new kit and bench wear for the first team, which had to be provided by Vandanel. It showed our club logo, two rams' heads back to back, and on the back, our chairman Mr Keith Tuckey's company, TCS Media (which you will read more about later). The playing kit had to have Ryman league on the sleeves. I managed to get my great friend and a very kind-hearted man, Billy Small, the roofer, who sadly is no longer with us, to buy the club a brand-new away kit, such was his nature. I also managed to get a sponsor, local builder Dunwoody, to buy space in the programme. So, I was doing my bit on and off the pitch. I had also made some changes to our managerial staff in appointing the manager of a team called Wallington Youth as joint reserve team manager. They had used our pitch for their Youth floodlight league. I can tell you now it was a move that I regretted from the moment he took the job! His name does not matter now, but it will crop up later. I also had a new youth team manager in Jeff Ray and chief scout Robin (Merlin) Denman. So now with all my staff in place for the 1998/9 season and my coaches Des McCarthy and Leon Maxwell preparing the team for the start of the season, my next meeting would be with chairman Keith Tuckey, to discuss the playing budget that would make us at least in with some chance of finishing higher than last season. I knew this was possible with the new signings I had made, and this was going to be the first-ever manager-controlled budget at the club. It also meant that our treasurer, Alan McSweeney, would have to have the wage packets with him on a Saturday after our game, home or away. There would be fines in place for non-training and lateness which I had to set after training on a Thursday night. To be fair to Keith, this was new ground for him I think, so he asked me what I needed and to include myself and Des. I also wanted our physio, Micky Reed to be paid for the first time, but with my old mate, Dave Finch quite happy to be match day assistant for a pint at the bar, I was now ready to hear what Keith was going to propose to me to cover 14 players plus the staff I mentioned. The amount was £415.00 a week + £30 for myself and the same for Des and £20 for Micky Reed - a grand total of £495.00p. I could never work out why Terry Gale, my skipper, was always looked after by the chairman and the same for Leon Maxwell.

Anyway, with all that settled, it was time to take stock, get my telephone book out (good old Surrey F.A.) and build my squad and agree with players their wage and in some cases, contracts. I had got the services of the best young goalkeeper around in Stewart Vaughan, and also some good young players in Damian Ray, Simon Ray, and Martin Beard and I had kept most of the squad from last season. As we progressed into the season, I was to add a few more players and of course another ride on the roller coaster, but this time there was the ghost train as well. There was also going to be cable TV, not only doing the Monday night show, where by now I was almost part of the furniture, they were going to be doing some of the games live and I was just hoping that they would pick the right one when it came to us.

So, with the pre-season over, I felt really good for the season ahead and our first Ryman league game away at Lewes. Over my two seasons in charge, I had done very well against them, but Lewes had made changes and they were not in the mood to be the whipping boys again. We fought out a well-earned draw 1-1, with John Kennedy scoring for us and we went on from that to lose only one game out of six.

Included in that was a hard-fought 2-2 draw at home in the league cup against Eddie McClusky and his talented Harlow Town side, who we would now have to meet in a replay, but before that, we were sent crashing out of the F.A. Cup at the first time of asking, away at Kent league side Hythe United, which was very disappointing as we had played most of the game as usual but conceded two sloppy goals in our 2-1 defeat.

So we made the long trip up to Harlow for our league cup replay which had to finish on the night, which meant the dreaded penalty shootout if need be, so what I decided to do before the game was to pick my five penalty takers so that if it came to it, we would be ready. I also picked the reserve takers should a first-choice penalty taker not be on the pitch at the end. Well, I can tell you I was bang on, as the game did go to penalties and calmly, I watched Eddie trying to sort his players out. We both stood on the halfway line together and exchanged our feelings about bloody penalty shootouts, but my pre-match preparation was spot on, as we won the tie 5-4 to the players' delight and they knew that myself, Des and Max were a well-organised management team.

However, we could be Mr Nasty as well, as they were to find out a couple of games later away at Ford United, where we got beat 4-1 thanks to their prolific striker Jeff Wood, who bagged a hat trick. It was not the result as much it was some of the players' attitudes before the game, moaning about the underground, the traffic, the trains and they did not get their football heads on until it was too late. They wished they had done so after the game, as Des jumped in before me and called them all the names he could think of before throwing the plate of sandwiches against the wall and tipping the drinks tray on the floor and stamping on the plastic cups. I remember quite clearly what I said to him after his act of rage, "Des, but I wanted a cup of fucking tea and a sandwich as did Leon Maxwell". I was not best pleased and told him I didn't want that in my dressing room again, as it proves nothing to the players, only that you have no self-control. However, I am afraid to say Des was too far gone to save, despite him being a great coach.

After that incident, it was time to make some moves for some more players, so I managed to sign Johnny Fowler back to the club again and got Simon Mitchell from Molesey to form a strike force that were to be nicknamed the EastEnders (Mitchell and Fowler). They did light us up no end in their goal-scoring ability as we had been creating the chances but not putting the ball in the back of the net. We started to put a decent run of league games together, including a good result away, a 1-1 draw at Egham town who had the experienced Eric Young, the ex-Chelsea/Crystal Palace player.

It wasn't just the game that came into mind that day but it was a question of the wage packets which our treasurer, Alan McSweeny always had ready. I had given him the wage sheet on the Thursday after training and left it at that, so it was just as well that I always had a wage sheet copy in my kit bag just in case there was a problem because there certainly was that day as Alan had not drawn the wages until the Saturday morning and of course, they were not in the brown wage packets. So, plan B was put into place and we went into the boiler room along with Dave Finch and started to count the money out and put it into the envelopes to give to the players waiting in the changing room. Can you imagine that with Man United? They would be there all day just doing one player!

There was also going to be another incident during our climb up the table and that was away to Wingate and Finchley, managed by the ex-Chelsea player, Colin Pates. Also included in their line-up was a young player by the name of Ben Strevens, (who had a good pro career with Barnet, among others and is now manager of Eastleigh in the national league (small world, our non-league), but the game will be remembered for one player and one player alone, my young goalkeeper, Stewart Vaughan, who on the night, saved three penalties of which one was a retake and then as much to say thanks Stuart for that, Simon Mitchell popped up and got the winner right at the end to secure a 1-0 win and that was done without Johnny Fowler who got caught up in traffic. These were the games which took us up the table to sixth from top and only five points behind leaders Cheshunt on the day we made Ryman club history.

It was the 12th December 1998 at home to Tring town and a game I would have expected us to win, but never would I have dreamt how it unfolded. We had the added bonus of our Christmas team party to look forward to that night at a local pub, the Hare and Hounds on the Purley Way, Croydon, but more about that later. So, to the game itself and the 9-1 home win which at this level of football is some kind of achievement, to say the least, and I think was the club's goal-scoring record, but anyway, if that was not the case then most certainly, the first ever was the fact that three players scored hat tricks! Even more remarkable was that one of those players, young Alan Hazell came off the bench with 15 mins left in the game to score his hat trick. All I said to Alan was, "Go on, son, enjoy yourself on your first-team debut!" As you might have guessed, the EastEnders got into the act with Fowler and Mitchell both getting hat tricks.

It was national headlines in the Mail on Sunday, and we had the Daily Telegraph rushing for the non-league history books as they were the only Sunday paper that had some non-league news (thank God for the non-league paper!) I wish it had been as popular then as now. Fans asked me if I felt sorry for Tring and their manager, and I remember saying, "Fucking hell, you have got short memories! You must remember Cockfosters and Woking when we got beat 7-0? No one felt sorry for me or my team then". I must say I did milk the achievement a bit. Our local paper wanted to be part of it, coming down to the club to take pictures of the goal scorers with me in the goalmouth, but unfortunately, I could not get all three players there but myself and Simon Mitchell would have to do.

It was our Christmas party after the game and were we in high spirits, but I again was going to become a victim during the night's events. All the players and staff and committee were sitting down to dinner when the door burst open and there was this woman clad in leather shorts and boots with a top to match, standing there with a whip in her hand! I thought, 'Great; the players are having some fun. I wonder who is going to cop it?' and sure enough, she made her way over to me, put her leg on the table and began to wrap this whip-round my neck. Then she got me on all fours, leading me along the floor to the roars of laughter from all present. I shouted out, "You fucking bastards, I will fine you all for this next week!" and at the same time I tried to tell this shapely young lady, "Look luv, I need a hip replacement and I need to stand up or I will never get up again!" She replied, "I am being paid a lot of money to do this, so just a few more minutes and I will let you go!" I thought, what would the wife say, let alone me mum and dad and of course my son if they ever found out! Then, of course, there was the local paper, the cable TV show that I appeared on most Monday nights and also the supporters. I still don't know to this day who organised it all, but my guess would be Richard Powell and Stewart Vaughan who were both the dressing room jokers! I will talk about them later in the book with great sadness; I wish the costly night would have been the end of it, but there was to be another twist by the little bastards (I did love them all really)!

The EastEnders were up to their old tricks again, this time away at Dorking, Mitchell with a hat trick and Mr Fowler with another two in a 5-1 win. So now on to the Lewes game, our last of the year in 1998. There was another prank, only this time by the club. This was fun for the club, but for me, in such a game as this, it was to make me livid.

As always, at least six of the matchday programmes were left in our home dressing room for the players and myself to read. As usual, I was in the dressing room at least two hours before kick-off, putting the team and set play positions up on the whiteboard and the players were beginning to arrive. I heard a couple of the players start laughing their heads off as they showed the programme to some of the other players and of course I wanted to know what the laughter was all about. Stewart Vaughan said, "You are not going to like this, boss. Have a look at this!" Well, I can tell you, I was not happy to see a picture of me in the programme with this scantily dressed woman with a whip around my neck! The wording over the top of the picture read, 'So this is what our first team manager got up to at the team's Christmas party recently - shame on him!' What made this worse was that I had invited my near neighbour, Mr Alan Smith, to the game and was thinking what must he think of me let alone the supporters?

Meanwhile, I had to keep a calm head as I had a team to prepare for a massive game and would sort this out after the game, and so I did by bursting into the boardroom and asking, "What the fuck is this all about?" holding the programme in one hand. They should not have done this without my permission, but the boardroom was in hysterics to see my face and anger as they informed me that there were only six of these programmes issued with me in the picture and they were all put in the home dressing room! I stood there and laughed my head off but that was not to be the end of the matter as on most Sundays, I used to pop round Mum and Dad's for a cup of tea and give Dad the programme from the game, home or away, so now he opens the thing and sure enough, I had put the wrong one in my kit bag and Dad is looking at his only son there with this woman!

In that game, if we took all three points, we would be second or at worse third from top in the table. I felt this was a great achievement given our playing budget, and also all credit to the players, Des, Max, Dave, the directors, and not least of all, myself. Well, we managed to beat Lewes with a weakened side, but sometimes when you create a good squad, having players missing gives other players a chance to prove themselves and they did me proud that day. The only goal came from Simon Mitchell, but also that win gave me the Ryman league William Hill Manager of the Month for December and a free £100.00

bet for myself, which I donated to the club. I was also the first manager in Croydon Athletic's history to receive this great honour and I have kept the plaque to this day in my non-league football trophy museum. This was possibly one of our best performances in 1998, as Lewes had a very strong side and were going for promotion, just like ourselves (or I thought we were).

1999 was upon us now and little did I know it was about to become one of the worst years of my life. With the roller coaster now at its height, it was going to have its bumpiest ride ever in 1999 and at one point, I wished it had come off the fucking rails and that would have been the end of it. Suddenly, we had a ghost train as well as the roller coaster. I had had my doubts about my reserve team manager for some while; not in his ability to run the reserves, but why he constantly visited my site hut in south Norwood and used to ask me for advice, opinions and knowledge. I felt it was not a problem, just a young lad here wanting to do well and maybe one day he may be the man to follow on when I had taken the club to where I felt it needed to go. Rumours began to fly about and it was very distracting for myself, the team, and the staff. Being a person who doesn't beat about the bush, I decided to go and ask the board for a managerial contract for two years, not for financial reasons, but to safeguard the hard work that I had put into the club and to allow me to see my mission through to the end.

Also, at that meeting, I knew we required another two class players and I knew that these players would have got us promoted to division two. I was willing to cut two of my players' wages and it was a quite simple equation that the board/chairman would have to make up the balance. When I say this, we are not talking a lot of money here; £80 per week at most. The chairman, Keith Tuckey, and vice-chairman Clive Thompson told me they would see me with the rest of the board in a week's time to give me their decision. But you see, I was a bit of an old fox and was ahead of the game because I was testing the water because I thought

I had done enough to convince them that I was fully committed and confident about the future. I mean whether you were or are a manager, a player, a chairman, or supporter, would you not want this man, Micky Taylor, who had sweated and toiled for his beloved club for four years, starting at the bottom with the reserves and youth team while at the same time getting the club promoted, who had also won their first trophy in the icis league in the first season out of the Spartan League and was now sitting in the top three of the Ryman league?

Sadly though, I knew the answer before I even attended the board meeting because I knew the rumours that were being circulated inside and outside of the club as being well-founded and that I was being stabbed in the back. I knew this because I had two great guys in Peter Eaton and Dick Clayton and also my old mate, Paul Courtman who knew what was going on behind the scenes. So, I attended the board meeting and true to the rumours and my thinking, back came the answer "We have no money for the extra players and we have no contract for you, as it is the club's policy only to award players contracts and not managers." I thought to myself the gunpowder plot was nothing compared to the board at Croydon Athletic and I really felt that I was starting to deal with nothing more than the nearest thing to the Flowerpot Men and these people were men I considered to be friends as well.

Needless to say, I tried very hard to keep my feelings to myself and not let it get to the team which was very difficult for me to do as I still had my pride to think of. I must say that despite all of this, there is a funny story that concerns one of the players that was going to come to the club and help us get that promotion. That certain player was John Egan and he was playing for Banstead Athletic at the time, under manager, Bob Langford. It was a known fact in non-league football semi-pro that you never put a 7-day notice on a player from another club unless you have spoken to him and he has agreed to come. That is what makes the 7-day notice rather silly in a way, but protocol must be upheld to give a club a chance to keep their best players before being informed that they are wanted elsewhere. I made a few 'phone calls and got hold of John Egan's 'phone number. The 'phone rang and it went to answerphone saying just to leave a message. So, I left a message saying, 'John, I would like you to come to Croydon Athletic and help us get promoted from division three'. 'I will also give you more money in your wage packet and would also like you to be my captain'. My final words were that 'this would be a good move for you, John'. I left my home 'phone number and awaited John's reply. Sure enough, the phone call did come that Sunday night, but it was not at all what I expected. When I answered, a voice said, "It is Bob Langford here, manager of Banstead Athletic." I said, "Okay Bob, what can I do for you?" He replied, "What can you do for me, Micky? You must be some kind of fucking prick as you have left a message on my answerphone thinking I was John Egan, giving a load of bullshit about come to my club and stuff like that. I could throw the book at you for that, but I won't because you have made yourself look a right asshole. I will have fun telling people about this phone call and by the way, John Egan does not want to play for Croydon Athletic!" I knew that not to be true as I had been informed he did want to play for us when given what I thought was his number by a reliable name. However, I would not have been able to sign him anyway after the board's decision not to allow me the extra money.

I must say the roller coaster did not like that and shot very quickly to the bottom track, but football life had to go on and there were to be some more surprises to come my way. Although not happy with the situation that was brewing, I still found time to enjoy what was certainly going to be my last season at the Athletic and one story will amuse you. We, as a club and first team, had been chosen by G.M.TV to try some beauty products and were visited by the TV breakfast show star Kate Shapland.

This was in the local paper along with the picture in the dressing room with Kate. So, the lads and myself duly obliged and were filmed using the products and the take was going out on the daily Lorraine live show. I did worry that some of the other teams might have seen this and called us a load of old softies, but how wrong they would be as we were soon to find out.

The roller coaster started to run well again and was soon heading for another high point. There were two games in question that come to mind, the first one being Ford United at home and in front of the cable live TV cameras for Match of the Day and there was also a large crowd. We wanted revenge for that 4-1 hammering we took over at their place on 13th October 1998, but this was now 20th February 1999 and we were a lot stronger and still, despite the gossip around the club, we put on a display that I can only describe as complete football.

I had made one of my 'take a chance' signings two weeks before the game. His name was Steve Sacco a midfield attacking player, and I remember that I had to go to Victoria station in London to sign him on. He had scored in his first game with Corinthian Casuals, but it was against Ford United where he became the talk of the town. He scored two great goals and was a real thorn in their side and of course, the EastEnders also got in on the act with another hat trick from Mitchell and Fowler completing a great 6-2 win against the would-be champions. Also, two other players made their debuts, Elliot Dell and Graham Harper. 'Harps' as I call him was to play a big part in the future of my life in football and we speak on the phone even now after 20 years of first meeting him. Here I have to thank his dad, George, for a lovely son and John Crumplin for letting me have him on board my team. Sadly, George passed away at a young age and is sadly missed.

Back to the Ford game and Dennis Elliott, their manager was shell-shocked so much, it was six o'clock before they emerged from the dressing room. I tell you now this was no fluke as I knew someone was going to get a good hiding one day, but I have to be honest in saying that I never thought it would be Ford United! I am glad I kept the recording of the game, as I have done with all my TV appearances.

There are a couple of games to talk about now, and how proud they made me feel of the work I had done at the club. One was away at Southall and I quote from their programme dated Wednesday 24th March 1999: 'Welcome to Croydon Athletic for tonight's game and I hope we do better tonight. We played each other three weeks ago and basically got a good hiding 5-1. They played some fine football and scored good goals, and it is a surprise to me that they are not in the top three. They are, without doubt, the best team we have played.' That totally made my day!

There is one last thing on the playing front - it was to be my last away Ryman league game at Aveley on the 10th April 1999 and as usual, I picked up the minibus from Thomas More School, picked up the team and drove around the M25 to the game, with Dave Finch sitting upfront with me. I had a few reserve players in the squad and made it known to Dave, very clearly, what I thought of the reserve team manager and how he was trying to take my job behind my back. I didn't know for sure and had no proof, but I think it involved money being given into the club, but that was only my belief. As it happens, we beat Aveley 1-0 and home we went. I always used to go home and go up to my local and have a chat with the regulars unless the club had a function on for the staff and players which I would attend. Not this particular night though, no football talk until my mobile phone went off and vice-chairman Clive Thompson came on shouting that I had been slagging off the reserve team manager. I replied, "Yes, and you know why, and I will see you all Tuesday as Max can take training. Make sure all the board are there and the chairman". (I must add at this point, it is not my policy to speak ill of the dead, but things have to be said in my defence). Also, there was some old crap about me taking a seat on the board and staying on until the end of the season and then stepping down as first-team manager. My good friend and coach Des McCarthy must have known what was on the cards when he left to join Whyteleafe, and so I decided to not bother with the meeting on the Tuesday and instead ring Clive Thompson and tell him straight that I didn't want a fucking seat on the board. He replied in a voice cold as ice, "Does that mean that you are handing in your resignation as 1st team manager?" I replied, "No, you have sacked me! So, you tell me why you have done this when we were sitting in a promotion place and you would not give me a contract and a small amount on my playing budget to see me over the line to promotion? I am sure we would have been promoted as we only fell away because we did not have those two players I needed for the midfield? Well, I will tell you why, because that fucking reserve team manager has been stabbing me in the back for months now, along with his band of Wallington youth players. Again, I ask, why would you want rid of me for someone who has never played the game, has never managed senior players, only kids? He must be giving you something in return!". So, any chairmen, players, supporters who have had dealings with this man may now understand my anger at being asked to step down for him to take over the 1st team. This man's name is Hayden Bird and to think I helped him with my knowledge of the game but they say a leopard never changes his spots and he took my job away from me at the club most dear to me. I am a gentleman in football and would never stoop to his level. In fact, during his reign at Croydon Athletic, I gave him some good reviews as a sports writer in my local Guardian paper Ryman league column, but I was a bit amazed to find in the year that he won the Ryman league division three, he did so by slinging money at it when I felt the budget would have been best saved for a very difficult time in the newly formed Ryman division one south, as six or seven teams were to be promoted that year. One thing that did become clear was that he certainly did not have the managerial capacity to compete at that level. According to my Ryman league review on February 12 2003, Croydon Athletic were lying 8th from bottom after what I believe was an unwanted club record of seven defeats in a row, which clearly proved my point.

At the end of the season 2003, I think he either left or was sacked, I have no record of that. One thing is certain though, he did get the sack from Bromley and Carshalton Athletic, so he knows how it feels and I wish well the clubs that he ever manages because I have no wish for those clubs to fail in any way, but the fact is I hate this man and if anyone can arrange for us to put the gloves on for one round under rules, even at my age, then tell him I am ready. You see, I come from fairground stock and that is the way for me to at least pay him back. Perhaps he will or perhaps he won't, who can tell? You could say, you know where he is, so go for him, but why should I have a charge of assault thrown at me? After all, I believe he has already had one good hiding from the Croydon Athletic reserve team manager, John Connell after he bad-mouthed him in public at The Plough pub in Beddington. To be fair, he has tried to patch things up with me. but I can't see that happening. At the time I also lay blame on all the board at Croydon Athletic, except Ken Fisher as he had a job looking after the chairman, and I know he would have wanted me kept on. I also blame David Groves, who worked for the Croydon Advertiser, with his bad press. Maybe that's a journalist's prerogative, to raise you up and then drag you down, but that was never my practice as a sports columnist. To make that statement in the paper suggesting that my future was in doubt was untrue and no official on the board ever said that to me.

Mind you, no one realised what was about to happen there in the future and how the lovely little club could become national headlines for all the wrong reasons. I know Keith Tuckey would turn over in his grave if he knew. I only really found out the truth when I was in a hospital waiting room and picked up a copy of Esquire magazine, quite by chance. I must say the club was going along okay until chairman Keith Tuckey passed away in March 2006. I was at his funeral, along with many other people from the world of non-league football, at Croydon Parish Church. I remember well there being a big marquee on the pitch with catering laid on and drinks. While I was with the club, I was led to believe that if anything was to happen to Keith, there would be money left for the football club in his will. This was only hearsay and apparently, there wasn't and so having had the ghost train with Hayden Bird, we now have the circus which was to be the finish of the club.

I find the events that finally led to the ending of the club a damning insult to committee members, also Dick Clayton, and three players whose names were Paul Muir, a long-serving player, a super young goalkeeper Stewart Vaughan, and Richard Powell, who was loyal to the club. I cannot help but have a tear in my eye every time I think that those three boys were going to lose their lives before the age of 40 years. I will always keep one of these programmes with me just to remind me of how lucky I am to have reached the ripe old age of 71 and have had all those years of non-league football to reflect on. I feel these players were insulted, and if you read on, you will learn why.

I must just add one thing here; it must be obvious to all that I kept most of the programmes of Croydon Athletic and to some extent other clubs I had managed, otherwise, I would not have been able to write this book. Now, all of our home programmes had a player profile, where the players are asked what they like/dislike, favourite food/music etc. When I read from Stewart Vaughan's profile, he had written, 'To have as much hair on my back as Micky, (Captain Caveman) Taylor, my manager', and under the heading Likes and Dislikes, in the Likes column, he had written, 'Playing under the great Micky Taylor again'. I saw this as a great tribute from an outstanding young goalkeeper. He used the word 'again' as Stewart had played for me in the county F.A. side before I finally got him signed from Banstead Athletic.

So now back to the magazine and the circus. The whole situation started with the death of chairman Keith Tuckey and the fact that the club did not get the money they thought he would leave it in his will, so Dean Fisher decided to take the money from the chairman's business, T.C.S. Media in which Dean was employed. The amount was around £500,000 and it was reported that he ploughed £250,000 of that money into saving the club, but also, he kept up a lavish lifestyle and he got found out. It was quite a shock to me to think he could be so foolish, but he got nearly three years in prison for that; you do the crime, you must expect to do the time.

Some of the headlines from the magazine which hurt me read -Football in the Gutter, The Match-Fixing, Suicide, and the Curse of the Sugar Daddy. Then came the words, "But the real villain was a chap by the name of Mazhar Majeed, known by many simply as Maz." He was to pile money into the club and also appoint the former pro from Gillingham F.C., Tim O'Shea as the full-time first team manager, and with a big playing budget, he was able to win the Ryman division one south and take Croydon Athletic into the Ryman premier for the first time. I saw some of their games and they used to turn up to away games in the official England team bus, which got up the nose of the opposition straight away. Then another chap turned up on the scene by the name of David le Cluse, who by all accounts had a pest-control business and had made friends with Majeed. After Dean Fisher stepped down as chairman, Mr le Cluse took over, Mr Majeed, as you probably saw at the time, was found guilty of cricket test match-fixing and was later sent to jail, but funnily enough, he had put some kind of bond up which enabled the club to continue in the Ryman league. So why, then, did Mr David le Cluse decide to take his own life? In my opinion, that was criminal, seeing as those three players in my team, Stewart Vaughan, aged 28, died 2007, Paul Muir, aged 35, died 2000 and Richard Powell, aged 39, died 2016, had everything to live for in life and they were taken away and yet a man goes and does that and leaves his family to suffer.

There was some talk of a Danish consortium taking over the club, but I don't know if that happened. All I do know is the club came to an end and the fans suffered too, but to give them full marks, they started a phoenix side called A.F.C. Croydon Athletic, and after a long fight with Croydon Council, were able to return to the Keith Tuckey Stadium to take their place back in senior football (good old non-league football fans) and now play, 2019, in the Southern Counties East League premier division. I will see them play this season again, only this time, I will introduce myself as one of the former managers of my beloved Athletic! Have a good season, boys, and hope you get promotion and to see a side back in the Isthmian league with honest people involved.

I felt fucking insulted and disgusted myself and was glad I was not part of it although, at the end, I did help my old mate, Dave Garland, on the playing side, to try and keep the club alive by finding players who would play for nothing. God bless Dave for trying to do the best he could as, like myself, he loves his football. But there is just one last thing on this whole affair and that concerns a football colleague of mine who I have known for years and he is the current manager of Folkestone Invicta F.C., Neil Cugley. In the year when Tim O'Shea took Croydon Athletic to the premiership of the Ryman league, Folkestone had to settle for the play-offs because they had 10 points deducted for putting their hands up and going into administration. It is greatly felt by the Folkestone fans and the club and by myself that, had the affairs of Croydon Athletic been known earlier, then Cugers, as I call him, would have had his title. Croydon Athletic had no right to that title because it has been reported that they were using money sought from other means, and therefore they would have been investigated and had points deducted which would have given Folkestone the championship. So, my feeling is, and this is my last word on the subject, Croydon Athletic's title as division one south winners should be expunged from the records and Folkestone should be awarded the title.

I know one thing - it doesn't matter how much money the Athletic had at one stage, they could not have created the forward partnership I brought to the club that I called the EastEnders - Johnny Fowler and Simon Mitchell. At least something came out of all the mess! Then I managed to get Simon Mitchell to sign for my new club and play at a higher level for the 1999-2000 season, although, to my credit, I achieved the same thing again with two other strikers that you will read about later. I think it was a lot to do with me being quite a good right / left winger in my playing days and knowing what the two strikers wanted from each other in their play. I also knew how the team were going to get the best out of them, in from the flanks or on the deck into channels to use their speed and find the back of the net, which they did with great effect. Johnny Fowler stayed on at the club and then moved onto Whyteleafe F.C., where he eventually became manager and steered the club back into the Ryman league after gaining promotion from the Kent league. He made a good manager so I must have had some influence on that, but I think I would be blowing my own trumpet a bit hard to expect John to agree to that!

CHAPTER ELEVEN

1999 - 2000 - Life after Croydon Pathetic and the rollercoaster does come off the track but then hits an all-time high as history is made in non-league football.

1999 was proving pathetic, certainly in football terms and Croydon Athletic had left a rather bad taste in my mouth. However, there was only one thing that would hurt me more than any football club or any defeat could do; in July, I lost the most wonderful lady that had ever been in my life, my dear old mum (Doll) at the young age of 72. It was the lowest point of my life as I am an only child, and she meant the world to me and more. Again, our non-league football family came to the rescue as I needed something to concentrate on. I had a 'phone call from one of my dearest friends, a certain Mr Colin Turner who asked me to go over and meet someone who was to become another great friend, Ken Jarvey, the chairman of Croydon F.C. They asked me if I would take up the position of director of football, which I accepted, and also to carry on representing the club on the cable TV show on a Monday night and my newspaper column in the south London Guardian.

I can remember them both putting their arms around me and saying, "Micky, we know about the death of your mum. Go home and ask your family if you can go on pre-season to Scotland to take your mind off things". It was going to be a weekend trip and it took my mind off the funeral which was a week later. I must admit I thought that fucking back-stabber had done me a favour because with Ken being chairman and 1st manager, he wanted the best in staff /players and a total professional feeling round the club. The only thing that was a bugbear to him was the stadium (Croydon arena), but he even improved that with covered terracing on the other side to the main stand. I also felt, as soon as we met, I liked this bloke. He seems to know what he wants and that was promotion into the Ryman premiership 1999/2000, but he got more than that as you will read later.

So on to the pre-season trip to Scotland and of course, me not knowing what to expect going away with a new club. I had done this so many times with the County F.A., but would it be of the same class that I had been used to? I did have a chance to meet the players and staff in training the week leading up to the trip and I knew most of them anyway, so as I arrived at the ground on the Friday morning about 7 am in my new blazer and with club badge on breast pocket and club tie. I waited with the rest of the team for the coach to arrive to take us to Euston station in London to catch the train to Motherwell. Talk about feeling important, as this luxury coach arrived and we all helped the kit man Arthur West and the two physios, Ian Fairs and Stuart Wilbrey load their gear onto the coach. I also put our club name in the front and back window, just to let people know who we were (Ken and Colin were quite impressed with that little bit of class). I could not help thinking though, how on earth are we going to get this lot off the coach in the station forecourt and march it to the train? After all, Euston is quite a big train station. With rush hour in full swing, the coach was also starting to run late with all the traffic and we were booked on a certain train, but Ken had organised everything to perfection because, lo and behold, we were delivered onto the platform right by our train coach, which had been reserved for Croydon F.C. I kept thinking, am I dreaming? This, after the way I had been treated at Croydon Pathetic as I now called them? This was top-drawer stuff and I was going to love every bit of this set up with a chairman/ manager, which Ken was. Mind you, you were soon told to fuck off if you didn't toe the line and I liked it like that with no one trying to creep up and nick your job.

The journey up to Motherwell was a laugh, as Colin Turner got involved in a card game with a few of the players. Being soon rid of a few bob, he came and sat with me and Ken, but he didn't realise that the sods could see his hand in the reflection of the train window and so he got turned over! But, as always, he had that big smile as he bonded so well with the team. Of course, it was okay having this train journey, but we did have a game to play that Friday night away at Stranraer and we would not have a lot of time to spare. When we arrived at Motherwell station, there was another luxury coach to meet us and take us to the Bothwell Bridge Hotel to check in and then to take us on the long trip down the west coast of Scotland to the Stair Park stadium, the home of Stranraer F.C., managed at that time by Billy McLaren. I must say I don't know how the boys ever played! Even I was getting tired, but they had 90mins of football to play yet against a very strong side! We played very well, despite the travelling, and won the game.

A few things stood out for me that night, which still live with me to this day and not all concerned with the match itself. I could tell, even then, that we had the makings of a very good squad and would be in the shake-up come the end of the season. I also saw a display from a very promising 16-year-old youth team player who shone out like a bright light with what I can only describe as a display which seemed like he had been playing top-level, non-league football for years and I will never know why he never went on to a football league club. His name was Craig Dundas. He went on to have a great career with Sutton United and still plays now for Hampton and Richmond borough.

So, away from the team, I found myself in the boardroom at half-time and being offered a scotch pie with gravy. It was the best pie I had tasted for many a long time and I could not wait for another after the game. With Mum passing away, my dad was soon going to be tasting a lot of these for some time! As I said, we won the game and we then had to go into the town centre, where Stranraer had a pub, as you could not drink in the stadium. We all stayed for a while before the long journey back to the hotel. I was sharing a room with physio, Stewart Wilbrey, who was a nice bloke. Upon arriving at the hotel, he decided to go to the room as it had gone well past midnight, but the players were given a 'no rules' weekend by Ken, as it was a bonding trip as well as playing, and to be fair, the lads never abused that freedom as they knew they had to be up on the Saturday to board the coach to Cowdenbeath, so most went to their rooms, leaving the staff and a couple of players to have a chat and a laugh.

However, there was one thing missing - the bar was shut! I saw Ken, in all his glory, go to the bar and demand drinks from the night porter, but he said he could not work the pumps as they had been shut down by the barman. The reply from Ken was, "Right, okay, we will have every bottle you have behind the bar and find some ice." He put them all in a bottle skip and wheeled it round to the lounge area where we were all sitting. We all put into a whip and gave the fellow about £100, or even more, to cover the cost, so a session was on and it was now a case of last man standing. I must have got my head down about 3 am, only to be woken up by Stewart about 5 am to tell me I was fucking snoring! Then he promptly fell asleep and started to snore himself. With that, I got the right fucking hump and told him at breakfast, but all was okay, as some of the players were laughing their heads about what had gone on and of course, myself and Stewart were seeing the funny side of it all by then as well.

It would soon be time for the coach to arrive and take us over the Forth Bridge and on to Cowdenbeath F.C. for the game on Saturday afternoon. Some of the players were tired and some had knocks from the night before at Stranraer, so we were really down to the bare bones. We had a pleasant journey there and were quite taken back when we arrived at the Central Park stadium, as it had some massive stand and like a race track around the pitch! Cowdenbeath, who were managed by Craig Levein, also had the nickname the Blue Brazil, and I think it must be something to do with their kit.

They looked a million miles away from playing like Brazil, but they were still good enough to force a draw against us and it was more scotch pies for me as well! During the game, I noticed that loads of people were beginning to arrive at the stadium and loads of cars, nearly blocking the team bus in. Then it dawned on me what the track round the pitch was for: stock car racing! For obvious reasons, this seemed to be more popular than the football at the time.

After the game, it was back on the team bus and to the hotel for a quiet Saturday night and also a surprise in store for the staff, as the players were allowed to go into Hamilton for their night out. God knows what they found to do in Hamilton on a Saturday night! Anyway, as I said, there was a surprise for those who stayed in the lounge of the hotel that night, as who should walk in but Alex McLeish, the Hibernian F.C. manager, who chatted with us for most of the evening. But you are never off duty as a football manager, whether non-league or full-time pro; he wanted to know about football down in the south of England and he needed a southern scout. I felt quite interested, but I felt I had only just joined the club and it would be very disloyal to put myself forward for the job. However, one of the travelling party, a man named John Broughton, who was a great bloke and knew his football inside out, was in a position to take up the offer and did so, taking in his first game for the Hibs going to watch a player at Bournemouth and as far as I know, went on doing the job all the time McLeish was at Hibernian. So, for

John, it turned out to be a great trip as I think he had only come up to see some of his family for the weekend!

I must say now that there was no snoring from myself or Stewart that Saturday night and we were all up for breakfast on the Sunday morning, having a laugh about the hectic weekend. We were looking forward to getting back home, but not forgetting how well-received we were by our friends across the border. The coach turned up for the short trip to Motherwell station, where we were told that the line was closed and we would have to go to Carlisle to get the train back to London, but there was also a nice little story to this diversion and Ken still talks about it to this day. The coach driver, upon his entry to Carlisle, did not have a clue where the railway station was, so I said to Ken that I would direct him and proceeded to the front of the coach. I started with, "Chuck a left here mate, then a right and go round the roundabout, take the second exit and down the hill to the station." Ken didn't know that I had been there earlier in the year with mum and dad on a day trip and knew the place, and you should have seen the look on his face as he said to me, "Do you know every fucking thing?"

The train journey home was one for reflection on the players and how well we had done, and so myself, Colin Turner and Ken expressed our thoughts of the season that was lying ahead and the expectation of promotion as champions. Mind you, I was only thinking of Mum and her funeral really, as normality started to kick in and I wondered how I was going to cope with it all as the train fast approached London Euston to board the team bus back to Croydon. I needn't have worried, though, as I knew the non-league football world and my family would help me through this difficult time, which they did. It was soon back to football, but not till after the funeral and a short family holiday to recharge our batteries.

I remember we had a staff meeting before the season got underway and the message from Ken Jarvie still echoes in my ears as he said, "You all know your jobs at this club, so get on and do them and I don't want any more fucking meetings, because if you have a problem with each other or me, then get it sorted out in private!" Oh, how I wish it could have been like this at the Athletic instead of the back-stabbing from certain people, and I'm sure we would have had a much longer time together.

I was still furious with it all, and I remember Ken pulling me to one side and giving it to me straight about his views. He said, "Micky, you blame Hayden Bird and you are right. He did ponce your knowledge and then stab you in the back, but the chairman, Keith Tuckey is the man to blame for it all, as he let it happen, and who knows, took the help with the budget and fucked you off, because if he had said 'no, Micky is staying and for at least another couple of years', there is nothing the board could have done as he was putting all the money in and he had the final word. So now, let that be the end of it and get on with your job here and I don't want to hear no more of it!"

That is what I needed to help me get over the situation and so I went and took one of my strikers Simon Mitchell from Croydon Athletic, and also Graham Harper. They fitted in just great as I knew they would. I have a little story about Harps and how I tried to help him improve his game as he played wide right whether overlapping full-back or in midfield. Ken asked me to go onto Harps' side of the pitch and work with him when he was on the opposite to the dugout and being a wide player myself in my playing days, I believed I did help him, but there was one game in particular that I can remember well. We were away to Wealdstone who at the time were ground-sharing with Edgeware at their White Lion ground and it was a tight ground but cosy and a great atmosphere. In the first half, it was my job to go and stand in amongst the Wealdstone fans to give Harps some instructions on when to deliver the ball as his crossing of the ball was a lethal weapon. to say I was greeted with hostile reaction was putting it mildly, but all of us were in it together and what the guvnor wanted, you just did, no problem. We won the game 2-1.

This non-league football is a strange place to be sometimes, as during that game, a lad walked into the ground to the cheers of the crowd. He was former player, Rocky Baptiste, and it was to be 11 years later that I would have dealings with him as one of my Club players.

It was the start of the new season now and we had a good playing budget, but by no means the best in the league. It was more a case of getting the right players in. And so, it proved with our first league game, a local derby away at Whyteleafe, which we won 2-1 with Eben Allen getting both goals and we were up and running. Sadly though, despite my feelings of how good we were, we made an unexpected exit from the F.A. Cup first qualifying round away to Egham Town F.C. Disappointing as this was, the league was to remain our priority, and with some good wins to follow, we slowly climbed up the table. One outstanding result I remember was when we beat Dagenham and Redbridge, who were a premier division side in the Ryman full members' league cup 5-0, leaving them shell-shocked as most of their squad had semi-pro England caps. Manager, Garry Hill, tore into them for about an hour in the dressing room after the game.

We carried on with our league performances and Ken's theory, which he instilled into my head, 20 pts from 10 games keeps us on course to be fighting it out in the last couple of games to decide the champions. I still believe that his maths was correct and if you were to look at the non-league tables in football, you would find this to be true.

Away from the league again, and this time the F.A. trophy first qualifying round at home to premier side Margate. There is a story to this game which has caused many a laugh over the years. As director of football, I could make a choice as to what I did every Saturday or midweek, so I decided, with Ken's blessing and expenses, to travel down to Taunton Town F.C., to watch Margate in the F.A. cup the week before we played them. I knew Chris Kinnear from previous experiences and knew of his side, but wanted to see them play so that we had good information. (20 years ago, we had no video footage on Ryman websites or anything like that). I arrived at Taunton in plenty of time to watch Margate warm up and obviously, Chris noticed I was there. There was one player I was mainly interested in, and a prolific goal-scorer, his name was Paul Sykes, as many a non-league follower will know. Margate were far superior in every department, and with about 15 minutes to go, I had seen enough to give Ken the information he needed and I got the early train home. I 'phoned Ken on the train to see how we had got on and we had won 3-0, which was good. We decided to discuss Margate on the Tuesday evening. During this discussion, Ken informed me that the papers were saying that Paul Sykes took a bad knock in the last 10 minutes of the game against Taunton and was unlikely to play against Croydon. My reaction was that it was a load of bollocks and that we should prepare the side to starve Sykes of the ball. Ken, Colin and John Finch made their plans according to my report. The day arrived and Margate turned up at the arena. We had a very entertaining game and Paul Sykes never had a sniff. Our game plan had worked a treat. We could have taken a good scalp, but Andy Fisher and Ben Judge missed glorious chances in the final minutes of the game.

We were therefore set for a replay at Margate on the following Tuesday. We were in the boardroom after the game when their manager, Chris Kinnear, came over to me and said, "Micky, how did you know that Paul Sykes would play today? You must have seen the way he went down at Taunton and there was never a way he would be fit". To which I replied, "Nice try, Chris, but I was already on the fucking train home. I had seen enough and therefore had not seen him rolling around to your instructions on the ground. So as far as I was concerned, nothing had happened". This brought a roar of laughter in the boardroom, but I must say, I was apprehensive because just like Jaws in the film, I knew Sykes would come hunting again on Tuesday night's replay and you only get one shot at stopping a prolific goal scorer.

Ken decided we would have training on Tuesday evening and I would do my normal spot on the cable TV non-league show on the Monday evening, as the players were in for light training. Another amusing story to come out of this Margate game was that we had a very good winger in Lionel Best, who had been sub against Margate. I was in the TV studios on the Monday evening and was asked about the game against Margate and was quite explanatory as to the fact that we had a game plan and we should have won the game as we missed two late great chances. I said we were very professional in our approach to all games, having done our homework, and that the side were fully prepared for the replay on Tuesday. What I did not know was that, in the first half of the show, there was Jimmy (The Cam) Thompson showing his Sunday morning park video, which clearly showed Lionel Best playing although we had an important replay on the Tuesday! And there was me waffling on about how professional we were and how we prepared for our games. (I thought, this tv can be good, but you could also get in a lot of trouble. From then on, I watched the first half of the programme (and Jimmy's cam in every detail).

As for the replay against Margate, we did not turn up but Paul Sykes did. As I said earlier, you only get one shot at winning the game against higher opposition. To say we were outplayed was an understatement. We were absolutely awful and I will never know, with such a good side as we had that season, how we could draw 0-0 with a side and then go and get thumped 5-0 in the replay. So now it really did mean the league cup and the Surrey senior cup was our season.

This bloody roller coaster was now getting on my nerves a bit, but I had a feeling with a few new additions to the side and a couple of our younger players coming through and all of the staffs' commitment, that the roller coaster was going to climb to the summit. Also on the roller coaster, we had some women, and they were called Croydon Women F.C. They were on their way to the summit as well. They were top of their league and doing very well in the Women's F.A. cup, sponsored by Axa. I always thought that they were a thorn in Ken's side and were more trouble than they were worth, but of course, that is only my opinion, and you are allowed that from time to time, but for some it's all the time. They never stop poking their nose in, that is why I am not a great lover of all this Twitter and fans forum where all people do is make comments and hide behind the computer.

Anyway, on we marched in the Ryman league and I knew once we reached the summit there was going to be no side to stop us as that formula of 20pts every ten games was going to form. We were still in the full members league cup and this time, again from the premier division, we faced a very strong Graham Westley side in Farnborough Town. The game was played on Tuesday 16th November 1999, and you might think why should I be so reminded of this date? Well, the fact was, the following day I was going into Mayday Hospital for a total hip replacement but what I did not know was that I was to have company on that day from the events of the Farnborough Town game. We won the game 3-0, but it will always be for me and others not about the score, but the terrible injury to our striker, Simon Mitchell, who had his knee smashed up in what I can only describe as the worst injury I have ever seen in a non-league game. The ambulance was called and Ken asked me to go with Simon to the hospital as I was going to be there in the morning anyway (thanks a lot, Ken!) I was already nervous as it was, but what they did to Simon when we reached hospital was completely gob-smacking, as one of the doctors smashed his knee back into place prior to him facing a big operation to put it back together again. I informed his family and got a taxi back to the ground to collect my car and congratulate Ken and Colin and the boys after another great cup win. We would now have to face Oxford City in the quarter-finals.

On to the following day now, and my hip operation on the same day as our player, Simon, had his operation. Needless to say, apart from our families, the place was full of Croydon F.C. visiting us both and I can remember Tony Reid pushing me in a wheelchair round to see Simon in another ward. He was not going to play again that season and Farnborough Town did make a fine gesture by having a collection for him to help out. So, like with everything, you have to move on and Ken had Simon Liddle signed on to play upfront with Eben Allen. There were also youth players coming through, like Nick McDonnell, and Craig Dundas, who were on the verge of first-team football and ready to take their chance. Their time would come, but the roller coaster was about to hit the highest point again when we beat Staines Town away 6-2, after being 2-0 down at half-time with Graham Harper bagging a hat trick. We were strutting our stuff now, sending a big message out as winning was starting to be a habit and losing was just the odd curse. This happened at Barton Rovers, who we lost to at home and away. Mind you, their pitch was awful. I remember looking out from the team bus as we pulled into the ground and seeing children playing in the goalmouth, thinking we have to play on that pitch soon! What a state it was in and at this level, how can that be allowed? I made my feelings known to the referee and asked him to do something about it, which he did, but someone had laid the Barton Rovers curse on us because they beat us that day and did the double over us towards the end of the season.

The reserves, managed by my good friend and great player, Billy Patterson, were going well and were heading for the title in the suburban league, and we were still leading the pack in the league, as well as progressing to the Surrey Senior cup final against Woking. We also went on to beat yet another premier league team, Gravesend and Northfleet in the semi-final of the full members' cup. Then we played another premier league side, Purfleet, on their own ground, Ship Lane in the final, but little did I know that history was knocking on our club's door, just waiting to be let in and I was going to be part of something that will never ever happen in non-league football again.

It started on the 1st of May, a bank holiday Monday in 2000 and we were away to Oxford City in a fixture to decide if we would be league champions. Also, on that day, our women were playing in the Women's F.A. cup final against Doncaster Belles at Sheffield United's ground, Bramall Lane. Things could have gone wrong, but not a chance; this was Croydon F.C. and we beat Oxford to win the title with two games to spare. But we would not open the bubbly until the result came in from Sheffield. Ken's mobile rang and he was told the women had won the F.A .cup 2-1 to complete a league and cup double, so only then did we start to celebrate in the changing rooms, on the team bus and back at the club, but the history was still waiting at the door and it was another week before we could let it in and keep it forever.

We had another league game on the Thursday, away at Maidenhead United, in front of a big crowd where we were presented with the Champion's trophy, but although we lost, which meant Maidenhead had secured promotion, you could not dampen our spirits as the trophy made its way back to Croydon and the clubhouse for another late-night celebration. I will say one thing about Ken and Colin; they could keep you there all night with their thoughts and sense of humour as the players slowly gave back to the club some of their wages.

There was not even time to breathe, as on the Saturday, we were away for our last league game at already-promoted Grays Athletic, at their old ground, The New Rec Bridge Road, but it was to be a special day for one young lad, Nick McDonnell, who bagged himself a hat trick as we won 5-2 and put himself in the frame for, would you believe it, two cup finals! One was on the Monday night and then again on the Tuesday, both on the opponent's ground!

Having worked for the County F.A. for some years, I always knew Woking were in favour and this proved to be the case with the Surrey Senior cup final.

We were due to play that at Sutton United's ground two weeks earlier as an evening game, but the game was called off because of the state of the pitch and I found that strange as Ken had gone over to look at the pitch and there was nothing wrong with it. Also, Woking were involved in a Vauxhall Conference league bottom-half battle at the time and were not wanting to risk too many first-team players, so we all believed they did not fancy it as they wanted to be safe before they played the final. They were allowed to get away with that type of thing and they even talked about playing the final at the start of the next season. Meanwhile, we were being asked to play six games in 10 days but we just had to do it as we had a lot at stake as well.

So back to the final now, on the Monday night at Woking's Kingfield Stadium, and we had no choice but to play our best side and see what happened regarding the players for the league cup final the following night. We played very well and were more than a match for manager, Brian McDermott, and his team. That was until tragedy struck us when we lost Jamie Ndah, the brother of top pro footballer, George Ndah, with a bad shoulder injury. He was causing Woking big problems and I remember thinking, 'fuck me, not again! Another cup game and another big player injury', so once again those instructions came, "Get Micky to the dugout!" Ken greeted me with, "Can you get Jamie back to Croydon now, as we do not want to leave him at a Woking hospital, miles from home?" I thought it was just my luck, but my thoughts were for Jamie. I had travelled on the team bus, so I had to be quick and asked one of the supporters if they would take me and Jamie to Mayday Hospital in Croydon.

By the time we arrived at the hospital, Jamie's family were there and of course, I was in touch with the club to see how we got on. Unfortunately, Woking scored the only goal of the game and we were defeated 1-0. I feel sure, had Jamie stayed on the pitch, things would have been different.

I must admit I persuaded Ken that the staff should all have the club colours in carnations as buttonholes for the two cup finals, which made us look very professional and I remember getting home that night and putting mine in a little jar and thinking maybe tomorrow night we may have good cause for celebration.

Now on to the second final away to premier division Purfleet on their home ground in the Ryman league full members' cup final. I can remember boarding the team bus at the arena and very surprisingly, as they must have been very tired, the boys seemed very up for the game. I remember sitting with Ken at the front of the bus and Colin was his usual self, in amongst the players, having a laugh and a joke, when I suggested that we should play the young lad, Nick McDonnell. But as always, the last word came from the governor and I left it at that. We also had another plan because Purfleet had a midfield player by the name of Jon Keeling and we knew that we had to take him out of the game, so we played a formation to do exactly that. Well, whatever thoughts Ken had about my advice, he decided to play Nick McDonnell and it paid off when he scored the first goal just before half-time. He was also responsible for Croydon's second goal when making a run in the penalty area, only to be brought down and Eben Allen stepped up and put us two up. We came under a lot of pressure in the second half but we stuck to our task and won the game and lifted the trophy among jubilant scenes.

Now we come to the history that will never ever be repeated by any non-league club again in England. The senior men's side of the football club had won the league and cup double and our women had won the F.A. cup and premier women's league double. For good measure, the reserves had also won the Suburban league. I just could not believe sitting in front of the team bus with the cup in my lap, thinking also about the loss of my mum. My light and dark blue carnation buttonhole would be at the cemetery the following day as I knew she would have been proud of what we had won and what history we had made. It was only when deciding to write this book that it dawned on me what a great achievement this was. It can also be said that we were the first team to win the cup and Ryman first division in the 21st century, and I was also given a jacket by Ken that the women had to wear on the day of their cup final, which was sponsored by Axa and the badge shows the F.A. cup trophy with the Axa logo. When I wore it, you would not believe the number of people that stopped me to ask where I had got that from. That jacket is still with me today, hanging up alongside all my non-league football trophies and memorabilia.

We finished the season off in style at the Hilton Hotel in London with the Ryman league millennium presentation. We arrived on a double-decker bus which did not go down very well with the hotel doormen, and we were asked to remove the bus as soon as possible as it was not appropriate for the hotel's reputation. Little did they know that walking through their door was a club that had just made such history. It was also a special night for myself as, while I was sitting at the table, Croydon Athletic's Hayden Bird came over to my table to offer his congratulations and asked if I would like a drink. It took a lot of thought but I felt at least I would have a drink from him and we would see where we go from there. We were out in the bar area and he was trying his very hardest to explain what went on and how he was not to blame for my departure from Croydon Athletic. It was then, after such a pathetic speech, I knew what had happened and what I believed in was the truth. So, as he went to shake my hand, I put my fist towards him as a gesture. He thought I was going to hit him but I said to him I wouldn't waste my time and they were the last words we ever spoke. Of course, you would have read also that I still seek my satisfaction and my conditions of doing that.

Despite that little episode, we collected our trophies and medals and enjoyed the rest of the evening, including a wonderful performance from stand-up comedian, Frank Carson (it's the way I tell 'em). We were back on our unpopular double-decker bus to take us back to the club for a champagne reception. I don't think the first player left the club before 5 am and it showed just what a great team spirit had carried us through the season. There was to be another recognition of our achievements and that was by Croydon Council with the cabinet member for culture and leisure inviting us to a civic reception at the Arnhem Gallery, Fairfield Halls, on Friday, 9th June 2000.

I must add that although the season was great, we did have a rather unwanted tag in that, despite us having all the success, we had the worst home attendance figures in all the league division one. I could never work that out, what with Croydon having such a huge population and our premiership /championship friends Crystal Palace always enjoying good crowds, win or lose. Perhaps, as Ken said, it was just the bloody Croydon arena and its cold feeling and that running track round the pitch putting the fans so far away from the action. At least the two sets of players and the dugouts could not hear some unwanted words from the fans, which I am sure were spoken or shouted.

Despite this, the work never stops though and we had to prepare for the following season at the arena and life in the premiership.

On one of my many scouting missions, Ken asked me if I would go and have a look at a team from our league called Barton Rovers. Well, what a mission that turned out to be! First of all, I had to find the bloody place which was located in a village called Barton-le-Clay in Bedfordshire, so on the train, I went direct from Croydon to a station called Harlington and from there I thought I could get a bus to the ground. No chance of that, so then I went into the local pub, The Carpenters Arms, to see if I could get a cab, only to be told that both cab drivers were over the limit and could not drive. So, some kind bloke offered to take me there when he had finished his pint! I got to the game just in time for the kick-off against Bromley and made my usual notes, and then I had the problem of getting home again.

But before that, I rang Ken to see how they got on, as the first team were away to Harlow Town, and also to tell him that I was going to have to get a taxi to Luton station, as I was well fed up and could not face another episode at this place. As you might remember, we got beaten there in December and it had curses all over the place. I shouted to Ken that I needed to spend £25 to get back to Luton, and he said that was okay. I finally did get home that Saturday evening about 8.30-9.00 pm. It wasn't even worth it, as Barton Rovers came down to the arena on 8th of April 2000 and beat us. If anything, it did prove to me that the league was very strong and no game was taken for granted. End of story.

The next escapade Ken sent me on was after the loss of Simon Mitchell through injury. We felt that although we had signed Simon Liddle, there was a lad at Thame United called Wayne Court, a striker. His brother Carl was playing at Newcastle United at the time, so I approached Wayne after the game at Thame United, gave him my card and asked him if he would be interested in making a move. He said he would call me the next day and let me know. The following day, my mobile rang and instead of Wayne Court, I had his brother Carl on the 'phone. The conversation was quite funny as he said to me, "I understand you want to sign my brother?" I was quite blunt about the situation and said, "What's that got to do with you? I need to negotiate with your brother and not you." He then asked, "Do you know who I play for?" I said I hadn't a clue, but of course I knew he played for Newcastle United; I was just playing him up. I also added, "If I can't speak to your brother and negotiate, then there's no deal." So, we left it at that, awaiting a 'phone call back. We didn't have to wait long, because when I told the governor, Ken, he promptly said don't want him. "If he can't speak up for himself, he won't fit into our side." But to be fair to the player, he did go on to make his mark in non-league football and his brother did have a very successful professional career. But when I needed to stand my ground that's exactly what I did.

Also, not so much a story, but a great accolade after the dramas at the Pathetic was when we had our own celebration night at the club marking the historical events of the season 1999-2000. Ken, in his speech to the players, staff and friends, made a comment which made me very proud of being part of that great season when he said, 'my director of football and chief scout, Micky Taylor, has been responsible for at least 15 pts this season with his correct information on our opposition, and his general presence around the club with all the sides'. He also awarded me a small plaque in appreciation by way of a keepsake as well as the Ryman league championship medal and cup winners medal.

CHAPTER TWELVE

2000-2001 Ryman premier league, here we come, but I find myself getting involved at a non-league club by the sea, which seems appropriate for my roller coaster.

During the summer break, Ken took the boys to Spain for a rest and I spent time down at my beloved caravan at Hastings which I did not know was going to play a big part in my football life over the next two years. This started with me asking St. Leonards F.C., who had just been relegated from the Dr. Marten's premier division, if I could bring Croydon down for a pre-season friendly on Saturday the 5th August 2000 which we won. More important was that I made a good contact and a friend in their manager, Andy (Thomo) Thompson, and towards the middle to end of that season, the football relationship became stronger.

Also, I decided to carry on writing my weekly Ryman league column in the South London Guardian, but my appearances on the non-league cable tv show was slowly dying a death as Sky and other tv companies took over. Also, we had none of this website stuff and videos and of course the great non-league paper we now have all grown to love. All we had was the Ryman weekly news bulletin for the weekly non-league news desk and for Team Talk, the non-league monthly. They were a great read as they listed players who were up for transfer and also results, fixtures, league tables and form guide and top goal scorers, as well as news from around the pyramid, but that was 19 years or more ago and how things have changed.

So now on to life in the Ryman premiership and Billy Patterson had moved up to first-team coach and I had another job, having persuaded Ken to have a side in the Capital league which was far better than the Suburban league. Although all games were midweek and we had a lot more travelling to do, it was a far better test for our reserve players and up and coming younger players too, so now for our baptism and our first game away at Hendon F.C. Of course, I had been there as manager at Croydon Athletic in the F.A. Cup, but not with the class of players we had on parade that day. I remember looking in the stands, never mind on the bench, and thinking, 'Fuck knows how much that is costing for those squad players just to watch and have no chance of playing at all in today's game. Have we arrived or not?' was all that kept going round my head, but I was soon to be brought down to earth as we got spanked 4-0.

To make things a whole lot worse, we didn't have a win until our 8th game into this new season and that was a bloody league cup game at Harrow Borough when we needed the points more. Ken's 10 game-20pts rule had truly gone out of the window for the moment, despite the hard work that Ken, Colin Turner and myself were putting in to turn our fortunes around. I must add that Ken, even by his own admission, will say that he made what I call a bad move in signing the former Aldershot Town player, Jimmy Sugrue, who was a big name at The Rec and Ken must have seen him as a good advantage, although Colin and I did not. I could not work it out though, because Ken never got much wrong. He didn't ask or my opinion or I would have told him to forget it, and even now, he regrets his mistake. Mr Sugrue didn't come cheap, I can assure you; he was a top-paid player and with Croydon, he was just in it for that reason. When we played his old club, Aldershot Town away, he had the number 11 on his shirt but was nowhere to be seen on the pitch as we got beaten 4-0.

I had been to watch Aldershot on the Tuesday night at Slough Town, where they won 1-0 and could see we were in for a tough time. They had a forward, Gary Abbott, who in my opinion, was the best forward I had seen for many a year in non-league football and it was the supply to him we had to stop or we would be in trouble. But there was also another problem, and that was their manager, George Borg, who would not leave the officials alone all night, and I feared that Ken, Colin and myself and the rest of the bench would not stand for any of his old nonsense should he behave like that on the Saturday. As I have said earlier, I had taken Croydon Athletic to Aldershot Town in the league cup the season before when he first took over, but he had not been there long enough to create his bolshy manner that the fans, believe it or not, actually liked as he slowly built up his image of Mr Nasty. So, with all this in mind, on the Saturday we travelled down to Aldershot with Mr non-existent Jimmy Sugrue. We did have a player in the side, a big centre forward, called Chuck Agudosi, who we felt might cause them a lot of problems as he was a big lump; not great pace, but he was brave in front of the goal.

The game itself was not one that you would want to remember from our football point of view because all that I had feared came to fruition. I'm not complaining about the way that Aldershot went about their football and Gary Abbott was again on top form and with no answer. So that all being fair and square, it was the unnecessary actions of Mr Borg when Chuck Agudosi went for a cross and collided with one of their players in an attempt to get to the ball. Outrage followed and Mr Borg was shouting and yelling at the linesman, calling for a deliberate elbow and asking and begging for Chuck to be sent off when he knew full well that there was nothing malicious in what he had done at all. This then led to uproar on our bench. First of all, I wanted to have words with Mr Borg and called him everything, only to be sent to the stands by the referee. I was then followed by Ken, who could not hold back his feelings and if Colin could have got to him, he might have killed him. However, he got his comeuppance when at Harrow Borough the following season, he was assaulted by one of his former players and put in hospital. They say what goes around comes around; not that I condone that behaviour because there is one other person I would sooner it had been....

I must just end the Jimmy Sugrue situation and an amusing little story about Jimmy. As I said, he did nothing for Croydon at all really, but there was one occasion away to Sutton United when I was watching the side warm up and noticed that Mr Sugrue left the warm-up and proceeded down the tunnel to the dressing room. Colin, Billy, and Finchy were busy doing the warm-up and Ken was talking to some of the players, so no-one was aware of the situation. I decided to go to the dressing room and there was Jimmy, lying on the physio's table and our physio, Ian Fairs, was working on Jimmy's legs with a massage. I remember saying to Ian, "What's wrong with him, then?" at which Jimmy lifted his head and said, "I'm stiff". I must admit, I replied with a smirk on my face, "The only thing stiff with you, Jimmy, is your fucking prick. So, get your fucking ass off the table and go and join the rest of the lads in the warm-up, because I know you don't fancy it today against Sutton. We are near the bottom of the league and you need to work your bollocks off for this team." Despite my rage, he did manage to persuade other members of our staff that he was not fit and we had to make a quick change to the team sheet. I think he lasted maybe four or five more games before Ken had had enough and said goodbye to him. So that was beginning to sum our season up really.

In my opinion, we had players on good money, some of whom were not earning it and we were finding life hard in the premiership. Even in the F.A. Cup, we managed to get to the third qualifying round, only to be bashed up away at Gravesend and Northfleet 4-1. That was quickly followed by a quick exit from the F.A. trophy away again to Havant and Waterlooville, only this time we at least gave a brave account of ourselves, as they were top of the Dr Marten's League premier division.

It was then that the roller coaster was in for another big change and I'll explain the reason why. When I was at my caravan down in Hastings, sometimes during the midweek I would go and watch either Hastings Town F.C. or St. Leonards F.C., despite already having played St. Leonards in a pre-season game. It was one night when I went to watch a struggling St. Leonards team that a thought came to me that they might just need some help. It would be a good idea not only to help with the wage bill but also give some of the players first-team football at a decent level. With that, after the game, I approached their manager, Andy Thompson who I already knew, to see whether he would be interested in taking some players on loan. Well, he nearly bit my hand off and said, "How many can you give me?" I replied to him, "I haven't even spoken to the guvnor yet, but I'm sure he will see this as a positive move". So, the following day, I 'phoned Ken up and asked what he thought of the idea. He agreed that it would help and the pre-season game was the beginning of my relationship with St. Leonards F.C.

My club, Croydon, was still finding life difficult, but keeping their head above the relegation zone and some of the younger players like Nick McDonnell, Craig Dundas, and Omari Coleman were beginning to shine out and all three were destined for a brighter future in non-league football. Craig Dundas, in particular, has had a most wonderful non-league career with Sutton United, which I think I have mentioned.

But there were still some stories to tell, as there always are in our beloved non-league, and this certain day on 25th November 2000, was when I knew that Ken was a good manager and knew his football, and despite that bad signing that he had made earlier in the season, he was to show his business head. We were at home to Heybridge Swifts and the game was in doubt with the arena being under water. Heybridge needed an early pitch inspection with the distance they needed to travel, but Ken, in his wisdom and with his business sense, persuaded the powers that be to have a pitch inspection again, prior to kick-off, and by this time, they were well on their way to the club. I remember quite clearly that they arrived at the club at about 1.30 pm to be promptly told the game was off. Ken had already got the training ground dressing rooms were already warmed up and the boiler on for the showers and he convinced the Heybridge manager, Liam Cutbush, seeing as they were at the ground already, to join us on the training ground and have a few beers and some food which had already been laid on for afterwards. They accepted Ken's invite and decided to stay. What was ironic about it was that they enjoyed themselves so much that their team bus never left our club until about 7 pm that evening. After all, both sets of players were going to have to be paid whatever, so why not try and cover the costs?

The next story, which I really found hilarious but also embarrassing, was our away game at Chesham United and it concerned the playing kit and our kit manager, Barry Bates who to be fair did like a sherbet from time to time, even when he was washing the kit in our laundry room. It struck me as strange this day was that there were no towels in the kit basket. Our physio, Ian, used to take some from the hotels he stayed at during his business trips, or so I was told!) All I know is that it was a good job that the players were out on the pitch getting some fresh air and checking footwear as normal, because when Arthur, our kit man, started to put the kit up, I thought, 'they look a bit small to me the shorts and shirts and socks'. As you know, we had a women's team and Barry had packed the fucking women's kit instead of the men's! Talk about red-faced when I had to go and ask Chesham if they had a spare kit that we could use and the reason why! Their staff were falling about laughing and informed me that they had never won in that kit!

Despite that, we then had to explain to our own players what had gone on and why. It certainly made us relax a bit more, but it was a problem for the management team to keep a straight face when it came to the tactics board and addressing the team to fire them up to go out and win the game. Well, a win was not to be. You have a shit start and everything goes downhill from there, which was reflected in the result. We lost 4-1 and the curse on that Chesham kit was not lifted.

The next incident had been brewing up from our first encounter with Aldershot Town and Mr Borg, who was not having things his own way in the league, despite his big budget and neighbours Farnborough Town, also with big money, running away with the league on their way to the nationwide conference. The game at the arena on the 17th of February 2001 was incident-packed, starting at the turnstiles, where Ken asked me if I would help out with a big crowd expected and also put up the entrance fee so we could make a bit of extra money. I must say this did not go down well with the Aldershot fans as I faced the onslaught of abuse. They said that no matter where they went, all the clubs charge more and not only at the gate, but also in the bar and at the burger stand. With that over, I took my place with the management on the bench and you could have cut the atmosphere with a knife as we were all up for revenge and to shut Mr Borg up. It was not long before the players and benches were at each other, with verbal abuse flying about all over the place, and it was a good thing that we had that damned running track round the pitch, or the fans would have got involved, making the situation even worse.

I must say at this time, our small band of loyal fans, led by big Andy, had a song for me whenever they saw me; Hey Micky, your so fine, your so fine you blow our mind, hey Micky! I used to give them a wave and a big smile. Good old Andy; I still see him at the horse races now and again and he still mentions that song.

So, back to the game, and the goings-on on the pitch and the pace and high tempo was such a great advert for the Ryman league and non-league football in general, to see two sides battle it out as though life depended on it. Our scorers that day were Eben Allen and our ever-popular youngster, Nick McDonnell, with the latter scoring right at the end to give us a deserved well-earned point, but unfortunately, Mr Borg was clearly not happy and made gestures to our bench, which was a mistake, as Colin Turner decided to go after him. If he had got hold of him, he surely would have landed a right hook on his chin, and I can tell you now, I would not have liked to be on the end of that, but in the end the referee had control and both sides left the pitch without any more trouble. Our fans were so totally ecstatic with the result and the events of the day that the clubhouse was nearly drunk dry.

Like it or not, George did get results under great pressure at a big non-league club, and he had his own way on match days and had legend status. I'll never understand his behaviour, and still, 15 years on when he was manager at Enfield Town, he still had plenty to say, which just goes to show some managers never learn. They seem to think they are bigger than the club they manage, which of course no one is, not even a chairman/manager which Ken was. Ken hardly ever lost control and always had respect for the officials who, despite not always being happy at taking control of a game at the uninspiring arena, always found the boardroom a special place where Sally, Ken's wife would lay on the best of all spreads after the game, with hot food and the best Marks and Spencer had to offer in the way of sandwiches. She would have won best boardroom hospitality award if there was ever such award created.

So back to the football and we had acquired the services of the gifted Peter Garland, who was the son of my good friend

Dave Garland, but Peter was a bit overweight after his playing days at Spurs, Newcastle United, Charlton Athletic, Wycombe Wanderers, Leyton Orient and England youth level, but what class he had. However, if you wanted him to run his socks off for you, he was not your man, but put the ball at his feet and he would make the bloody thing talk as he sprayed passes around all over the place, always one step ahead of the next move. His free-kicks were special. What made him so special to me was when he had the ball, the opposing fans would always chant who ate all the pies then. Peter would always laugh and most times he would have the last laugh, and unlike today, would brush it off as banter.

I remember one game in particular when we were away at Dulwich Hamlet on Boxing Day 2000 in front of a decent crowd when the Dulwich crowd started the chants towards him. By God, they wished defeat upon their team as Peter controlled the midfield and was the main man as we bashed them 4-1! Once again came the proof that sticks and stones may break my bones but your name-calling won't hurt me, so deal with it like Peter! So, with Croydon still keeping their head above the relegation zone, I remember I started to loan some players out on a permanent basis to St. Leonards with Ken's agreement, although they had been having players from us all season even for one-off games. As the season went, on St. Leonards were having a bad time so we gave them Danny Moody, Dominic Barclay and Ross Venables, and I also made some enquiries about some of the other players I knew from other clubs, and they included a young talent called Des Boateng who decided to join and boost the squad for a difficult run in to avoid the drop back into Sussex County football. With all this going on, I then had what I thought at the time was a strange 'phone call from Lewes F.C., and their manager, Jimmy Quinn, and his sidekick Bill Nixon. They were also after players on loan to boost their squad, but for a different purpose, as they were hoping for promotion in the Ryman league and it was ironic that Ken's son, Sean Jarvie, was also sent on loan to them and played a part in Lewes winning the Sussex Senior Cup, a game at which I was present as they beat Bognor Regis Town 2-1. I had Ken on the mobile 'phone asking me how Sean was doing and it was with great delight that I rang him and told him that they had won the cup! I felt like a football agent more than director and chief scout at Croydon. Then came the bolt out of the blue when the manager of St. Leonards, Andy Thompson, asked me if I would join him for the rest of the season as his assistant with immediate effect. To say I was flabbergasted was an understatement, but deep down I saw a challenge in a very tough league and so I approached Ken, my chairman, and asked for his permission to leave the club and take up the post offered as I could not carry out my work with the Capital league side. I remember him saying to me with a grin on his face, "Thanks very much, Micky. Leaving a fucking sinking ship, are you?" He then said, "You go and test yourself, as I know you love to manage and thanks for all you have done at this club". I remember being quite saddened, thinking of all the fun that I had had with Colin Turner and Ken and the players, and also our kit man Arthur West and his son Dave West, who sadly, have both now passed away, Dave in particularly tragic circumstances. I felt I was making the right decision and so picked the 'phone up and told Andy Thompson I would be joining St. Leonards for the remainder of the season. I remember meeting the chairman, John Cornelius, and he came across as quite a decent chap and welcomed me with open arms.

So now Croydon had gone and the next thing was to be introduced to the players and I did so, prior to the game on 31st March 2001 in the dressing room at Corby town's Triangle stadium. They were managed by ex-Crystal Palace favourite, Eddie McGoldrick. I had never travelled that far except with the County, but I was excited about going up to the Midlands for what was to be not only a football challenge but also a long journey. We needed points on the board and we were fast running out of games, so a win or a draw was vital. Unfortunately, we did not get either as full-time approached in a very tight game. I was certain we were going to get a draw, but our full back, Micky O'Callaghan, gave the ball away and Corby fired in the winner right at the death. So, now it was my first time in the dressing room after a game with St. Leonards and Andy Thompson, the manager, asked me to address the team and give them my thoughts and I remember going straight for Micky O'Callaghan's throat, telling him in no uncertain terms that he let us down and cost us a valuable point. The managerial adrenaline came flooding back and we had a right fucking tear up and I made it clear to him that I was the assistant manager at this football club and we weren't going to get relegated.

The problem that I did find hard to deal with was that I still faced a three to four-hour journey home having been beaten in the way we were, but it was something I was going to have to get used to. I remember Thomo saying to me, "You were spot on, Mick," and he felt that Micky was just testing the water. On the Sunday morning after the game, Thomo proved to be right as my 'phone rang and Micky O'Callaghan apologised for his behaviour and accepted his responsibility and my part in trying to save the football club, so I knew that I could control the dressing room. In situations where you are in trouble, you need to have that as no. 1 priority. Micky turned out to be a great asset to the club, despite his fiery nature. So now with Croydon F.C. clearly behind me, I looked forward to our last few remaining games as the biggest challenge I had yet to face in non-league football, but through it all, I always had Croydon in my heart and would phone Ken after every game to see how they got on and give him the report on our players. I stayed at St. Leonards for the last ten league games, of which we won 3, drew 1 and lost 6, but despite that not being a great record, we were fighting for our lives and those 10 points saw us escape relegation to the joy of the club, fans, staff, and players. It was a near-impossible task to do when I joined the club, but Andy Thompson and myself could reflect on those games and be proud of the players we had. I was also pleased for Ken and Colin at Croydon, who also steered clear of relegation and also had reached the Ryman league cup final, only to be beaten by Heybridge Swifts 3-0.

But back to St. Leonards and our great escape! I feel I must mention some of the games that helped us achieve, and some of the wins. One of these was away to Bashley, who was managed by the former Reading prolific striker, Trevor Senior. First, we had to find the bloody place, deep in the New Forest and then to take the 3 points was great. We had home wins against Burnham and more importantly was a 4-1 home win against Rothwell Town. I could not believe for one moment how they beat St. Leonards 10-2 at their place back in October 2000. What a revenge party that was!

Then came the home derby game against Hastings Town, which we lost 1-0 on Easter Monday. I am sure we had the nearest senior club grounds to each other. Suffice to say that a well-driven ball over the crossbar at the Hastings end would end up in their penalty area and I also believe there was some wording in the F.A. cup competition handbook law that, because of the close proximity of the clubs, if both teams were drawn at home, Hastings Town would play on the Saturday and St. Leonards would play either Friday night or Sunday afternoon!

Before we were safe, I remember myself and Andy Thompson going over to watch Sittingbourne play Grantham Town at their very impressive central park, Eurolink stadium, in a game that we wanted Grantham to win and, on this occasion, they truly obliged which made our position easier. It also showed me the strength of the league when a side can make that long trip south in midweek and be positive to go out and win the game.

The other situation we found ourselves in was that we were going to get involved in the outcome of who would be league champions. Because of all the bad weather we had endured and with so many games called off and teams playing catchup because the league would not have what we called doubleheaders, we found ourselves going to champions-elect Chelmsford City on a Saturday, and also at home to the other champions-elect, Newport I.O.W, 24 hours later on Sunday afternoon. We went to Chelmsford City and gave them a great game, losing 2-1 right at the death. For all our hard work and good football, it felt like we were robbed of at least a point, so after the game, their assistant manager, Paul Parker, (ex-Man United and England) came into our dressing room and said, "If you can play like that tomorrow against Newport and get a win, we would be most grateful!" to which I replied, "Paul, the boys have given everything today, but we are at bare bones and it is the league making us play 2 days in a row that might cost you, not our boys." Well, we tried our best but we were tired and Newport had the better energy levels, but we gave our best, and despite the 3-0 score line it was a bit of a close game, but considering that was our 3rd tough game in 6 days, we showed some character. That made me and Thomo think positive for the season 2001/2002.

However, like a bolt out of the blue, Thomo said he was calling it a day and had put my name forward for first-team manager and asked if I would like to go and meet the chairman on Saturday and discuss the position and give him a yes or a no before he let the job go to outside for applications. I got the feeling that they wanted me there to carry on building a team. I gave it some thought, all 20 seconds I think, before I made a phone call to Ken at Croydon F.C. for some of his thoughts on the matter. He just said, "Micky, go for it, and if it doesn't work out, come back to us. You have nothing to lose and plenty to gain, and in a very tough league among the best in the non-league game. That will test you, as a manager, and your character and you are good in both!" to which I said, "Thank you for those kind words!" and promptly phoned chairman John Cornelius and told him I would meet him on the Saturday to accept the job. I also wanted to discuss the playing budget and inform him of my intentions for taking the club forward and announce my assistant/coach. I had no one at that point to take the job, but one phone call to my old mate and my coach at Croydon Athletic, Des McCarthy asking him to join me, was all that was needed as he jumped at the chance to coach in that league and team up again. There was also a nice article in the Croydon local magazine, whose headlines were 'Seaside Rendezvous' and the first line said that one of Croydon's most famous football sons was starting a new era managing St. Leonards F.C. in east Sussex and they had done a complete page. I felt it was very nice to be thought of in that way.

CHAPTER THIRTEEN

2001-2002 the rollercoaster, good old Sussex by the sea, sunshine all the time, or so I thought.

So, with the meeting arranged for the Saturday, I made my way down to St. Leonards, taking the train from East Croydon and on arriving, walked to the ground that was simply called The Firs. I got there early, as was usual for all my football appointments and games, and I remember thinking, 'this is now all mine; back to the limelight again'. Instead of the tv on Monday, it would now be the local radio station which was then called Arrow FM and the weekly calls from the BBC Teletext information and the ITV equivalent and of course a wider exposure with the newspapers. This was all going to be right up my street. I met with the chairman and the board and outlined my expectations for the season and the players that I would like to bring to the club, and of course, some of last season's squad that would have to go as they were surplus to requirements. I found John Cornelius a very understanding chap and very supportive in what ideas I had to try and bring this club back to where it should be, and that was competing for promotion, not trying to escape relegation. What was ironic for me was that, at the same time as I was having my interview, my good friend, George Wakeling, was taking up the first team manager's job at Hastings Town! So now I have not only got the added pressure of Hastings Town but their manager as well. George was like any other manager; he wanted the best for his side and if I could have had somewhere I could have locked my players away, then I would have done it, because before I could count to ten, he came in for, and took, the boy who would have been my captain, Adam Flanagan, which made me obviously angry. But I was also going to go robbing players from other clubs as well. Another manager I had to contend with and also someone I consider a friend and a great manager, was Gary Wilson, manager of Eastbourne Borough F.C.

As I have said, John was very understanding and offered me the best budget the club could afford, which was £1,380.00 a week, including all management, staff and the physio. I respected that and although some managers I dare to mention put their own money in to not only keep their jobs but to boost the quality of players, I was in no position financially or morally to enter into that and of course, I wanted my club to be stable financially for the foreseeable future. I must admit that I did tinker around with some of the players' fines and myself and Des used to take money out of our own wage packet and pay their fines to keep a happy ship. There was one player in particular I needed to raise private funds from supporters for, with the help of Andy Thompson, to secure his signature. I put my feelers out and, with the help of those supporters, I managed to sign the Brighton and Hove Albion legend, John Crumplin, who was going to come to the club as club captain/player/coach. Talk about the big time! I could not believe it when the Friday edition of the Hastings and St. Leonards Observer came out and there, on every newsagents' headline board, was the heading 'Taylor signs Brighton legend Crumplin for St. Leonards'. My first reaction was, beat that, George and Gary! I am sure they were not worried about that in the least, as they too were preparing very good sides.

So now you have the three amigos, all wanting a bit of the action. Also, at the interview, when we had finalised all my requests and the club's requirements of me, John knew that I frequented the old town quite often as I had my caravan in Hastings, so he even suggested what pubs would be better to drink in to avoid confrontation with Hastings Town supporters. I remember thinking and actually saying to him, "Fuck me, this is almost as bad as Rangers and Celtic!" So, what did I do? I went and had a drink in exactly the pubs he told me to avoid and I found everybody to be not so much pleasant, but not in any way hostile to me being the manager of St. Leonards. Of course, with my position cemented, it was time for me to recruit, and organise my pre-season friendlies and I arranged all of the games via my secretary, Peter High. I also arranged to have a meeting with the club chaplain, Rev. Wallace Boulton, at which I asked if we could have a little word now and again on a Sunday morning. He laughed but he was good fun and a good person to have around the club. So, with everything in place, a date was set for pre-season training at a lovely location at a school towards the top of the ridge, where our training ground looked out across the town and the sea. I also required the club to provide fruit and fluids as we would train all day Saturdays from 10 am to 4 pm. I must admit that when the players turned up on that first sunny day and looked out as I did, they certainly must have felt they were at a training camp abroad. Either that or they wished they were on the fucking beach with some bikini-clad girl!

I must admit their attitude to the training was nothing less than 100% and I did feel that the surroundings did help. What's more, I was lucky to only have lost the one player from last year's squad, Adam Flanagan. So, with training underway, we also played some friendly games to get the team and its shape together, and this happened quicker than I expected with no defeats and a very good win 2-0 away at Carshalton Athletic, managed by Frank Murphy. Also, we played a team at The Firs from New York (Fairleigh Dickinson University) and beat them 1-0, which was a very impressive display as they had players from all over the world and were as fit as any side we would face in the future. I saw that my club liked things done in the right manner as they had brought and flown the American flag for the game, but what was strange about that game and the flag was that we were to fly it again only at half-mast just over a month later, for a reason that no one that day would ever have believed, when the twin towers in New York were struck by terrorists.

Back to our last pre-season game now and Ken and Colin accepted my invitation to bring Croydon F.C. down to play us on Saturday 11th August as I still had strong connections with Croydon F.C. and the town. I had lived there for 55 years and it was with that in mind that I decided to still carry on writing my Ryman league round-up in the South London Guardian. It seemed strange managing a team against my old club, and in a way, it was to be my first and only game where I would not care too much if we had lost, because of the way that club had treated me with utmost respect and given me their blessing to go and make a go of it again in management on the south coast. Well, it will come as no surprise, but we beat them with Ken making his usual comment, tongue in cheek; "First you leave me, then you fucking nick some of my players and finally, put a nail in the coffin as you go and beat us!" but it meant that our unbeaten record pre-season was intact and we were ready for the first league game.

That was not to happen before we had a few photoshoots with our sponsors, one of which was fast-food giant McDonald's, which our business rep, Dale Seymour had secured. So here we go - first during the week the Hastings Observer, then the Sussex Argus, and on Friday afternoon, Teletext wanted all the team news for our first game away to Histon as did Arrow FM radio, all of which was okay with me as I had been doing that type of stuff for a few years anyway and the bigger profile I could give the club the better.

So, the rollercoaster is up and running as we make our long journey north to face my first league game in charge of the side.

With Des by my side, we arrive at their ground, Bridge Road, and I met their manager, Steve Fallon, who I found to be okay and just as confident in getting a result as I was, but their home record was impressive, having not lost a league game there for two seasons. I was pleased with the way we played and the way we had to dig deep at times and the performance of my keeper, John Odlum, and my captain, John Crumplin who, during the game, showed the team spirit and leadership that I brought him to the club for. He demonstrated that when defender Danny Moody went down with some kind of injury and Crumps did not want the physio on to look at Moody, which seemed strange at the time, but up got the player and carried on as though nothing had happened. So, at half-time, with the game level 0-0, I asked Crumps in private what had gone on and he simply said, "I told Moody you are not going anywhere. You're not hurt and you'll fucking stay and see this game out or me and you will be at it in the car park after the game!" Well, if that's not leadership, I don't know what is! That is why we spoilt their home record and got off to a flyer, beating them 2-1 with goals from my new signing, Jason Davy and one of last season's squad, Carleton Chatelier. So, we were smiling all the way down the M11!

The only bad moment for me was that in the dugout, there were tip-up seats and after my celebrations for our winning goal and giving instructions out for the remaining 10 minutes of the game, I went to sit down and forgot to put the seat down, and landed on my arse wedged between my substitutes, only to be carried into the dressing room and receive treatment!

It is also worth remembering that on this ground on 30th November 2008, Histon knocked the mighty Leeds United out of the F.A. cup 2nd round 1-0 in front of live B.B.C. cameras to earn a home tie with Swansea City in the third round. I was watching the game at home when all the memories came back of my first league game in charge of St. Leonards and recording a win.

Back to 2001 and the Dr. Marten's league. We won our first three away games for the first time in five years and beat Ashford town away for the first time in five visits. We also played twelve games without conceding a goal there as well and were sitting 6th in the table after 4 games, and 1 point behind leaders Grantham Town, which was not a bad start. I must say that I always had control of the dressing room and also had my ways of dealing with situations and I will let you in on some of them now. I always made sure that I stayed in the dressing room after the game for a while with the players, first was to congratulate them or bollock them, but also to analyse their game and of course have a shower before returning to my office to get changed into manager's dress code - always grey or black trousers, white shirt and club tie.

Also, during all that time, I was gathering my thoughts ready for the press, who were waiting outside to come in and get my thoughts and comments on the game. Sometimes they tried to trap you into saying something you were going to regret when the local paper or the Sussex pink Saturday night sports and Monday morning Argus went to print. Then, after dealing with the press and once all the players had gone to the clubhouse for their food, I used to go back into the changing room and help sweep up, and also help with the kit, but again I used this time to gather my thoughts, because next step at home games was up to the director's lounge and be interviewed live by Arrow FM, and that could be a tricky one. Then I had to report to the chairman for him to have his say, good or bad, and sometimes questioning your choice of play and formation, but I let them have their say and take a pat on the back or one on the chin. That is why away games gave you a bit more freedom and time as you had the long journey home when you could think, and interviews were done on the phone and were briefer.

So now, on to some of my pre-game antics in the dressing room! The players who played for me will remember these, I'm sure, but they were always reminded that what is said or done in our dressing room stays in there and never, never comes outside; this is a rule in non-league football that is written in stone. I remember before one game, I went along to the referee's room and asked if I could have the match ball to which he replied, "No, I'm not happy with that". I found his attitude rather strange as I believed he thought I was going to tamper with the ball in some way. However, he then said, "You can have the ball, but I will be checking it when you return it and you've got 10 minutes". So, into the dressing room I went with the ball. The players were all sitting there in their warm-up kit and I remember throwing the ball to our midfield player, young Des Boateng and telling him to catch it, not to trap it with his feet like he would normally do. So, now you can imagine the scene where 14 players are sat down and Des Boateng has the ball in his hands. I informed him it was the match ball for today's game and to give it a little kiss and embrace it. Well, if you could have seen his face; it was a picture! The rest of the team, including Des McCarthy, my coach, thought I'd gone mad or been down the local and had a few beers and were roaring with laughter, but I was soon to get the point across to them as I said to Desmond, "You see, young man, that ball is going to be like your girlfriend or someone you love for the next 90 minutes, in as much as you must look after it, treat it with respect, do not give the fucking thing away to the opposition, and if and when you get your chance, strike it and put in the back of the net. And lastly, when they have it, get it back". He demanded an explanation, so I simply said, "Would you let your loved one be kidnapped? Would you let your loved one go with a stranger? Would you treat your loved one with respect and care? And if she was kidnapped, you'd fight your hardest to get her back, and as for putting it in the back of the net, I will leave that to your imagination, young man!" Then I asked Des to give it to the next player, and so it went round the dressing room, player to player, and as it was doing so, the message was getting stronger. I can then remember a knock on the dressing room door and Andy Hargreaves, my team attendant, opened it to see the referee standing there and saying, "You've had your 10 minutes. I want the match ball back". I replied, "There you are, ref. There's the ball and it's been hugged and kissed, but I'm sure there's no lipstick on it!" With a smile on his face, he took the ball but didn't have a clue what I was on about. My last comment to the players was, "There you have it. Go and have fun with your loved one for 90 minutes!!

Once, I went to each player and asked them why they played in their chosen positions. They all knew why and what they had to do in their role but a lot of the time I used to say at the end of a game or at half-time, "So, if you know what to do, why the fuck didn't you do it?"

So, on to the season and I had a certain chap who would ring me up and offer me players and good ones at that. He was not a football agent but just wanted to help the club and me. His name was Wally Petty and we still talk about the non-league scene even today. So, I was never without decent players, but it was hard to get local players. One local player was Simon Fox, who I felt was one of the best footballers I had worked with. He had everything except the desire to play the game on a regular basis, and left the club in October, citing that he was not enjoying the game enough, which, to be fair to him, was the truth. It was a shame, but as I have mentioned many times before, no player is bigger than the club and these things happen. As you know, in non-league football it is a revolving door as we do not have transfer windows, so it was just a case of bringing another player in to replace him. I had a good side at St. Leonards and we got off to a real good start in the league. I had got a side together that could adapt to our home ground playing surface and also the physical and football side to this strong Dr Marten's league.

Of course, there were certain players that revelled in this type of atmosphere, one of them being centre forward, Tony

Reid, who would knock brick walls down for you and could find the net well. Tony is still a good friend of mine 18 years later and is, in my opinion, on his way to a very successful managerial career. Also, I had Danny Fletcher on the left-wing, who could beat a player with ease and pace. Also, there was Carleton, Des Boateng, Micky O'Callaghan, and John Crumplin, and of course, our ever-improving goalkeeper, John Odlum. We also had two young players, Tony Cornelius, the chairman's son, and David Henham, who were both local lads. The player that improved more than anyone was my right-sided player, Sean Campbell, who was not only a gentleman on the pitch but also off it.

I must tell you now about our home pitch. It was probably the worst in the league. There was a slope end to end, and it also got very muddy in the central areas with the slightest of rainfall. I even came under some criticism from another manager who made a remark, "They can only play well and win games away from home because of the fucking awful home pitch of theirs which I hate going to". With the squad that I had assembled, we could have played anywhere, but there was some truth in this and it must have reflected in our results because along came the F.A. Cup first qualifying round and a tricky tie away at Herne Bay, managed by the ex-Carshalton athletic player, Johnny Warden, player/manager.

It was going to be a momentous day for many reasons. We had the long journey across the marsh over to the coast of Kent. I remember saying to the Argus that we were thinking of speaking to one of the trawler boys and going round there by boat, which would have been a first for turning up to an F.A. cup tie. Now, Herne Bay were no mugs and in a hard-fought game and with goals from Tony Reid, it saw us through to the next round and also financially pocketed the club a few grand in prize money, giving us a home tie in the next round against B.A.T. Sports from Southampton. Not only did we have a good win at Herne Bay, but there were other events that day, Saturday the 1st September.

England were playing a World Cup qualifying game in Germany, where they beat the Germans 5-0, I came under some criticism, not from my players, but from Herne Bay, as they wanted an early kick-off so that both teams could watch the game in their clubhouse after the cup tie. I was unwilling to do this as I did not feel that my players should have to get up early and travel over there for the sake of a professional game, even though it was my beloved England. So now the day was turning into complete perfection and you know what that means - something's gonna spoil it. We certainly had a pleasant journey back with the players jubilant with our result and also that of England. When we got back to the clubhouse, there was drama because, when the coach driver went to open the side panels of the team bus, he realised our footballs, our physio's bag, and more importantly the kit were missing. Somewhere on the journey home, they had slid out of the coach and were somewhere on Romney Marsh. We did have a call to the club a few days later from someone who had found the kit and the physio's bag, but we never saw the footballs again and even today, 18 years later, whenever I cross the Marsh Road, I still look to see if there are any sheep kicking a football about (good old non-league football)!

We were still doing okay in the league and that win should have set us up for a decent run, but we fell short and suffered two defeats, one against Burnham and the other at Dorchester, which will be remembered for not only a 1-0 defeat when we certainly deserved a draw from the game, but also for two other reasons; One of our players, Patric Ankrah, had decided to make his own way down from London on the train, but for some reason, he had failed to turn up in time for the team sheets to be handed in, so when he did arrive at the ground, I told him he was not even on the bench and he could sit with me in the dugout. That lad accepted the situation and apologised for his lateness, such was the respect he had for me and the club. There wasn't a single moan out of him at all. He was a top minder for all the top celebrities, so he knew how to handle himself and he could have picked me up with one hand and said, "Fuck you!" and gone home, but what commitment he had!

That night, there were far more terrible events that had happened in New York, prior to the game, which was on Tuesday the 11th of September. We were unaware, at the time of kick-off, what had happened in the U.S. and obviously, that game will stay in my memory for reasons other than football and Patric being late.

Now back to the F.A. Cup and a 2nd qualifying round and the visit of B.A.T. Sports, the game played on a Sunday. This was the day that I sent the ball round the dressing room and it seems to have done the trick okay as we beat our visitors 3-0 and picked up another £7,000. So, we waited for the Monday draw for the third qualifying round, hoping for something a bit special and what did we get? A poxy 3rd qualifying round away to Fisher Athletic, who were doing quite well at the time in our league. So, after our F.A. cup win, we followed that with a draw against Rothwell Town at home and then possibly the best performance I have seen from a team that I have managed as we had an away league game against Dartford played on Tuesday evening, the 25th of September at Gravesend and Northfleet's ground which they shared. Now, as any non-league fan will know, you don't go to Dartford and their fans and have an easy time of it, but we absolutely demolished them on a most pristine playing surface which seemed to draw the football out of us. It was a special evening for one of my strikers, Dominic Barclay, as he, having returned to the club, was to score 5 goals that night and Desmond Boateng the other in a 6-2 win. We were in control from the word go and soon silenced the Dartford fans. Dominic had gone four games without scoring a goal, but that night he had one in the back of the net after just a minute on the clock. I have always been proud of the football teams that I have managed, but tonight would go down amongst one of my proudest moments. For some unknown reason, Gravesend and Northfleet's ground was always a good ground for me as, with Croydon, we won the league cup semi-final there.

Again, there is a story as always, and it came when we were awarded a penalty. My penalty-taker was always Dominic Barclay and I was a bit amazed to see that Desmond Boateng was going to put the ball on the spot. I raised the alarm very quickly to the linesman, who flagged the ref. I asked Desmond to come over to the touchline very quickly. He said to me, "What's up boss?" and I simply said to him, "If you take that fucking penalty, you're coming straight off the park and I will fine you a week's wages!" to which he replied, "It would set me up to get a hat trick!" Continuing our heated exchange, which I must admit the linesman found amusing, I said, "Yes, but you wouldn't want to take a fucking penalty when it was 0-0; you'd run a mile, and that's why we have a nominated penalty-taker no matter what the score is. So, fuck off back to the ball, pick it up and give to Dominic Barclay!" This he did and Dominic dispatched the penalty in his usual manner. I was very hot on discipline, winning or losing, and after the game, Desmond apologised to me for taking matters into his own hands. He also got a bollocking from Des, the coach, for the same reason, but Des was probably worse than me at times. Quite rightly, he wanted to know why we had conceded two goals, but I managed to persuade him to let it go, as the team had played really well.

So now, with our fans and Hastings Town stunned by the result and some spies from Fisher Athletic in the ground, we were ready for what was going to be a hard game for us as Fisher had appointed the Millwall legend Keith (Rhino) Stevens as manager. They were also doing well in our league with a big budget and a few top-class non-league players such as Leroy Huggins, John Mighty and Tony Dolby to name a few, but names don't win games and I felt we could go up there and cause some kind of upset with the players I had and the result against Dartford.

Indeed there was an upset, but it was caused by the Almighty and I think our chaplain, Rev. Boulton, because being 2-1 down at the interval put Fisher in the driving seat but as we were in the dressing room, the heavens opened and there was this torrential downpour during a violent thunderstorm that flashed across their Salter Road Surrey Docks Stadium, leaving the playing surface as near to a lake as you would see. I was thinking to myself that there would be fucking ducks on there before long and rowing boats, with someone shouting, "Come in number 6. Your time is up!" So, what chance of finishing a football match? Myself and Rhino were called by the referee to come out onto the pitch where a decision would be made as to whether we could continue or abandon the match. Rhino was insisting that the game should carry on and I said to him, "This is not Millwall and the New Den with ten thousand in the ground; there are 250 fans in here today and all they will do is go to the bar and have a few beers and come back Tuesday". Despite the work of the ground staff, trying as hard as they could to get the water off the playing surface, the ball would just not roll and it was dangerous to the players, so the ref. called a halt to the match and said, "See you all again Tuesday evening" So with that, we told the players and gave them their instructions for the rearranged fixture, had a beer and food and we left for the journey home. It was then that myself and Des McCarthy decided to go and have a beer and talk about the rearranged game to be played on Tuesday, and if we should change anything as I felt we had seen the best of them and knew where their dangers lay. We decided to keep the same starting line-up and formation and have a right go and get a result, as we had done at Dartford.

What was to happen next came like a bolt out of the blue. On the Sunday, I was rushed into hospital as my legs had stopped working and there was no feeling in them. The condition needed urgent diagnosis and tests to see what was wrong. As it turned out, I had a bulging disc and needed bed rest under observation for a week. I had spoken to Andy Thompson on the mobile on the day of the game with Fisher and asked him to ring my mobile with the result and just brief details of the game. So, on that Tuesday evening, lying in my hospital bed, Thomo called me on the 'phone and said, "Sorry mate, bad news. We lost 3-1, but I couldn't understand the changes you'd made". I replied, "What do you mean, changes?" It had been agreed with Des that there would be no changes and we would play the same formation. "I'm not happy about the situation and when I get out of here, I'm going to tell him so." I still believe to this day that had we stayed the same, we would have had a good chance. As for leaving Sean Campbell and Micky O'Callaghan out of the side, this made me even more furious. The next time I got a 'phone call it was from Thomo again, on the Thursday evening, to say that after some questioning of the line-up on Tuesday, Des decided to walk out of the club. I love Des to pieces but the one thing he finds hard to take in the football world is criticism, and that is part of the game, as was proved in those ten days. You can be top dogs one minute, then you get beaten and start to panic if that's how you are. Andy Thompson and John Crumplin took the side until I was out of hospital, unfortunately losing both games to Erith and Belvedere and Chatham Town.

During my recuperation, I made a few calls to a good friend and football colleague with whom I had worked in the past at Carshalton Athletic. His name is Chick Bain and at that time he was managing Dorking F.C. in the Ryman league. I asked him to come over and be my assistant and he jumped at the chance to be involved in the Dr. Marten's league and to work with me and of course, he had a good player contact base. I resumed my duties with Chick as my assistant, but I felt something wasn't quite right at the club. I was immediately asked to cut my wage bill and so I had to work with Chick and decide who I would keep and who would go. I am always a man for admitting, in the football world anyway, mistakes that I had made, but

I decided to offload John Crumplin and his heavy wages and one or two others had to go. I remember feeling sad to have had to do that and felt that maybe this was the beginning of the end, but I did the best I could and took a much-changed side on the long trip up to Spalding. I remember on the way up, my mobile rang and it was Ken, my old chairman and governor from Croydon F.C., who were beginning to have a torrid time of it. I could tell by the tone of his voice that he was right pissed off when he said, "Who motivates the motivator?" My reply to him was, "You do, Ken; you are the man who motivates the motivator". I don't think he ever understood that reply but it cheered him up anyway to talk to somebody. So, we arrived at Spalding and they were their delightful accommodating selves as usual and couldn't do enough to disrupt our preparations by leaving the away dressing room open with no heating on, we couldn't get the gate open for the kit to be taken round, and all that type of stuff. I didn't mind really, because the north versus south was how it was. I had this little motto: One day it's gonna rain on you so when you come to St. Leonards that's what we'll do. Enough said about that then.

As for the game - great going forward, scored three goals away from home which should have at least got you a draw, I did miss Crumps, as without him, we looked a complete and utter shambles at the back, conceding four goals to a team that was just sitting above us in the league. So, on the way back down the M11, as I was driving, I decided to get Chick to ring Crumps and put the loudspeaker on so that I could talk to him. I asked him to come back to the club and players would have to go to compensate his wages, and sweet-talker that I was, he agreed, just as quick as the fucking speed camera that had just flashed me doing over the speed limit. I thought, nice one, 300-mile round trip, lost the game, got my captain back, and instead of taking the three points out of the game, I managed to get them and a fine on the motorway instead! No wonder the scars and wrinkles were beginning to show on my face, let alone the bags under my eyes (good old non-league rollercoaster).

With my captain back after my U-turn, which I was always honest about as I had made a mistake, we played Eastbourne Borough in a Sussex County cup replay. After our full-blooded first game ended 2-2, despite having Crumps back, we lost the game through poor refereeing and finishing by our two strikers. After the game, when I was just about to make my way home, the chairman pulled me aside and told me he had signed a very good player, Steve Smith, and he was to play on Saturday away against Stamford and I was going to pay him £150.00 a week out of my budget which had already been cut. I was gobsmacked and so was Chick, not because Steve was not a good player, but how dare the chairman do that and totally undermine my position as first-team manager? So again, I juggled the budget about and reduced some players' wages.

Then we had another long trip up the A1, only this time we had a very good result, beating them with goals from Boateng, Barclay, and Ankrah, and of course, the chairman and the team were pleased as we made our long trip south again back home. But neither Chick nor I was happy and I saw this as the thin end of the wedge and felt it was just a matter of time before we both parted company with the club. We were not going to show any of our discontent in front of the players, although they knew something was wrong.

It certainly did go wrong the following Saturday, when we travelled up to south London to face Carshalton Athletic and manager, Frank Murphy again as we had done in a pre-season friendly. As soon as he saw me, he reminded me of the score that day and you could see that he wanted revenge, and to be fair, he had built a very good side on a budget which was twice the money I had. But money is not everything, as I had proved by beating some of the best sides. I thought we played well enough, but you can't brush away a 5-1 defeat. We were only a goal down at the break and we equalised early in the second half when our tricky left-winger, Danny Fletcher, scored from a cross-shot and we still had chances, but again, we were denied by the ref. and young Tony Cornelius should have had a penalty, but it was all going Carshalton's way. The score line seemed to show we were bashed up, but we were not and I felt that we did not disgrace ourselves. Even their manager made a point of saying how well we played despite that score line, so I did take something positive away to keep building on.

My first thought was to get revenge on Spalding Utd the following Saturday after our narrow defeat away only a couple of weeks ago at their place. Then the bombshell came on Tuesday the 6th of November, the day after the fireworks. That would have been the best day for the chairman to ring me up and sack me for being a south London man, as he put it, and also stating there were too many London-based players in the side and they would have to go to make way for local players. I found John Cornelius's behaviour towards me an utter disgrace! I mean, you would have thought that his intelligence would at least lead him to have another excuse other than the one he chose. He did not even have the bottle to face me and Chick to give us our final wage packets on the Saturday morning, and all this from the man who wrote to me thanking me for helping Andy Thompson in the relegation escape and getting the 4pts we needed!

We travelled down to Hastings before the Spalding Utd game to collect our P45s, and also some personal bits from my office. In these days of discrimination over almost anything or anybody, I perhaps could have taken him to court, who knows, but what I will say is that he had not minded the London players the season before when along with the London-based boys, I had helped the club to escape relegation and a certain place in County league football. Also, I had the club in a far better situation than when I took over, having a respectful position in the league and £8,500.00 in the F.A. Cup and a budget cut nearly every two weeks.

What a hypocrite the man was, as he said and I quote from the newspaper; 'It is the hardest decision I have made as chairman as Micky has done an excellent job for the club, and I don't think we will ever find anyone more passionate about football'. What a load of bollocks is that, after all, I do know that managers in non-league football do get pushed around a bit by jumped-up big-time chairmen, as most of us have no contracts to settle up. It's just a case of thanks for everything, now piss off, so that is exactly what I did and, me being me, said to the players, "You do not need to go as you have a new manager who will make you even better players and a team, as he quoted in the paper, fitter as well." His name was Terry White and at the time, he was with George at Hastings Town but decided to take my vacant position and climb over the fence from the Pilot Field to The Firs and he must have felt great as the chairman, Mr Cornelius, stated that he had been after Terry for two years to manage St. Leonards. Then it all became clear to me; I was just a gap-filler who had done so well it was just finding a way to get rid of me! Terry White lasted one game, the home game with Spalding Utd, which apart from no more than two players missing from St. Leonards, both teams were at full strength. Surprisingly, the team lost 5-1, Des Boateng got sent off and the new manager resigned after just one game, stating that he had made a mistake and wished to return to Hastings Town with George, which he did, and they became Dr Martens league eastern division winners. With both George and some of the players being London boys, I asked the chairman and supporters if they minded that. Of course, it was none of my business, but I was so sad to see my hard work slipping down the drain hole. It did become my business when another manager by the name of Glyn White took over and accused me in the press of over-spending on the playing budget. Now, any manager in non-league or otherwise will tell you that the chairman sets the budget and also reduces it when he sees fit, which I had to deal with quite a few times, so how on earth could I overspend what is not there? I have no grudge with him as he had to make some excuse for his failure! Glyn left the club and then Gary Bowyer took over, only to see the club slip into county football.

The final nail in the coffin came in 2004 when the club folded completely and I must say now it was not something I gloated over. I just felt sad and I still go over and look at what is left of the old ground and think how great it could have been. After all, I was always blessed with good forwards, Danny Fletcher, Carlton Chatelier, Tony Reid and Dominic Barclay, as those four were enough to scare any defence in the league. Then, of course, I had Crumps at the heart of my defence.

To put things into perspective, something which was far sadder was the fact that two of the footballers in my side passed away before they reached their 40th birthdays. God bless to Steve (Smudger) Smith and Patric (Bunders) Ankrah, who both died in tragic circumstances but are not to be forgotten. That made a total of five of my players in two clubs that I had lost, the others already having been mentioned earlier in the book…

2002/2003 Still in Sussex at Haywards Heath.... Three Bridges or was it a bridge too far?

So, the roller coaster is in for a rest and repair after the goings-on down on the south coast and I was watching quite a few non-league games, keeping my profile up as a manager wanting a job if you like and also still doing my weekly Ryman league round-up column in the paper. I'd also been asked to do a column on entertainment as I loved my music and still do. Word got around, and that's when my good friend, Wally Petty contacted me to see if myself and Chick would be interested in taking the first-team job at Haywards Heath Town. I thought it was a joke as I had only got Haywards Heath down as a train station on the Brighton line! Anyway, I contacted Chick to see if he was interested in taking the job with me and to come and meet with the chairman. I must say, he was a bit apprehensive about it but decided to go and see what it was all about.

And so there followed a meeting at a pub on the crossroads at Turners Hill, West Sussex, with their chairman Roy Hatt, Wally Petty, myself and Chick to find out about the club's ambitions as they were in the Sussex County league division three and it was a big step down for us after the Dr Marten's league, but in a strange way, we both felt that it would be a challenge to take this club to its rightful place in division one. First, the impression the chairman, Mr Hatt, gave us was one of a man that lived only for that football club and truly a non-league man, putting some of his own money into Haywards Heath. He was a perfect gentleman in every sense of the word and a man we felt we could trust. There was not a lot of money regarding a playing budget but there were some expenses which were okay. We then went down to their ground called Hanbury Park stadium and I can tell you I was quite impressed, not so much with the playing surface, which was okay, but with the big old stand that incorporated the dressing rooms and bar, along with the boardroom. All of it was a bit like Hastings United Pilot Field. The stadium was opened in 1952 by Sir Stanley Rouse and the side became members of the Metropolitan league, playing against the 3rd teams of such clubs as Arsenal, Spurs, and West Ham, who had players who played there on their climb up the ladder to play for England in the winning of the 1966 world cup. I remember saying to Chick, "We have got to fill that stand for every home game if we get the job, and then we will be heroes here." We were then summoned to the boardroom to meet the rest of the committee and were offered the job, which we both accepted, and made arrangements for the pre-season training schedule and the equipment we needed. We went back to Saturday all-day pre-season sessions at the ground as we started our recruitment drive, just like I had done at St. Leonards, and players were beginning to sniff around to see the changes that were being made.

Of course, then came the press release on the 23rd of April 2002, under the heading 'Heath will be Taylor-made', but what I was not expecting was the paper to carry on about the good job the previous manager, Ken Swallow, had done. Also, the fans were upset about his sacking, leaving me with the Brian Clough and fucking Don Revie situation. Let me give you an example; I was getting comments like, 'Ken never did things like that,' or 'Ken never fined us for being late,' and so I thought again it's just like Leeds and just like Brian Clough. Remember all that time ago at Woking, when John McGovern likened me to his boss, Clough? So, I called together those players who played under Ken Swallow and stated; "You will now do things Micky fucking Taylor's way, or you can fuck off and get another club!"

Little did I know, I was going to receive a phone call from one of my former St. Leonards players, Brighton legend John Crumplin, asking me if I was interested in taking the job at Three Bridges F.C., who were in division one of the County league, as their manager, Darren Barker, had left the club and they needed a quality replacement and quick, as pre-season training was going to start in two weeks' time. I said to Crumps that I would think about it, but they must ring me and arrange a meeting with myself and Chick, which their secretary, Martin Clarke did, and we both went down to the club to meet with the committee and the chairman Alan Bell. We liked the setup and they seemed to like our ideas for the future, our player contacts and also our tactical knowledge of the game and experience at a higher level. So, with that in mind, they offered us the job and to start a.s.a.p. to prepare for the coming season, which gave us a real big problem as we were still managers at Haywards Heath and had a few training sessions with the club already. But this was the only time I ever let anyone down in non-league; it was myself that used to get let down by the chairman and the back-stabber at Croydon Pathetic.

When I talk about the situation, it was only Roy Hatt, the chairman, that I felt for and not the fans, as they had made it clear that it would take a lot to come onside, but I am sure I would have done that and brought them some glory. At the time of writing this book, they have finally arrived at a good standard and they are mid-table in the Isthmian BetVictor league south-eastern, and Roy would surely have been a proud man had he been alive today.

So now, back to Three Bridges. I had lost a few players but not enough to cause too many problems and pre-season was going well. A surprise turned up on the doorstep as Wally Petty had informed me of two decent players at St. Francis Rangers, a team I had never heard of, so I took Wally's word and got the lads over to train with us. Their names were Andy Turner and Phil Gault and they seemed to be nice lads as well as good players.

At the club, there was also a prolific striker, Pat Massaro, who scored goals for fun and I was lucky to keep him, but he needed a forward partner and it was hard to shop around as the players were on small wages and every player got the same money. Then bang; it hit right away. What we would do is work with Phil Gault on a one to one, so in pre-season, myself and Chick took turns to teach him how to play his position. I also had some of the St. Leonards boys and some County F.A. players and we were beginning to shape up to be a decent side.

We also tried a different formation in practice games, the so-called 'diamond midfield', which was going to allow us to cover all areas of the middle, restricting the opposition to having the ball in that area, but like all formations, if the players can't pass the ball, time tackles, read the game and recover when the ball changes hands, then no formation will compensate for that as I was soon to see.

Still, we only lost by the odd goal to Dulwich Hamlet and Croydon F.C. and had a draw with Tooting and Mitcham in pre-season. I could see that we would have to go back to the tried and trusted 4.4.2, using which we had good wins against local sides before the big kick-off on the 10th of August 2002, at home to the well-fancied Wick F.C. Of course, I had no experience in Sussex top county football and so I asked my good friend, Billy Smith, who was also in charge of neighbours Crawley Town, if he had any tips for me at this level and I remember him saying, "Micky, you done a good job in the Dr Martens league; this will be a lot easier". I remember, when working with Andy Thompson at St. Leonards before I took charge, we played Crawley Town away in the league cup quarter-final at Broadfields. Although we lost, Billy and John Broughton did come in and say we wouldn't get relegated, and he was right then so, let's hope he was now as I had not had a chance to see any teams.

Still, Wally Petty knew enough about the league, but I did know one thing, that our new forward, Phil Gault, had come on leaps and bounds under our coaching and Gault and Massaro were going to be the most feared front two in all the league. I asked the chairman to offer Phil Gault a contract, which he did and it was duly signed by the player. I knew I had also a good midfield but was not so sure about my defence and the young keeper, Alan Mansfield, but the team reminded me of the Croydon Athletic team that I got promoted out of the Spartan league a few seasons back, and surely this league wouldn't be any tougher than that?

Mind you, why should I worry about defending, with the attacking midfield players and two outstanding forwards who we had worked so hard with on the training ground? As a manager, what would you sooner have, a 4-2 win or a 1-0 win? I would always go for scoring goals as I'm sure it pleases the fans and also the players, but it can give managers high blood pressure! At least clean sheets do mean you will at least get a draw, but again I challenge that theory in as much that 1 win, 1 draw, 1 loss, is better than three draws as points on the board matter more. Also, as I discussed before, if you are going to be serious about promotion then you will need 20 pts from each block of 10 games, leaving the last 2 or 4 games to sort out the title or automatic promotion.

So the big day arrives and that home game against Wick and what a start we had with a fine win, 6-2, and some really attractive football, and as promised, Phil Gault and Pat Massaro were in amongst the scoring, Pat with 4 and Phil scoring on his league debut, but of course, you will say that we conceded 2 goals. I feel that no matter how many we concede, we will try to score more and win the game and enjoy it after all. This was a rebuilding process as only three of last season's squad were left, apart from the very promising youth team led by Simon Boddie and Paul Faili, who were doing a great job along with Derek Pyle, the second team manager.

Well, as for the rollercoaster, it was running quite well in its new surroundings, so on we go and another 3 games before we play in the F. A. Cup. We had 3 wins and 1 loss in our first four games, which was a good start, but in the F.A. Cup, we had a tricky extra preliminary round tie away to Greenwich Borough, who had been selected as the F.A. .com team to follow in the cup, which meant that if you beat them, you became the team taking the limelight and so on until you lose and then another team takes over until the final. That was added pressure which I must say I used to our advantage, telling the team how we could go on and make a name for ourselves being followed nationwide, and to some degree, it did the trick as we won a hard-fought game against Greenwich Borough, a physical side.

We were a goal down until I went three at the back and we scored four goals in the last ten minutes to book a home tie against Oxfordshire-based Didcot Town or Alton Town in the preliminary qualifying round, but before that, we had a league cup game at home to a strong Southwick side. This one we lost, but I had rested some players in view of the home F.A. cup game on the Saturday, which would give the club some extra cash. First, there was a replay as Didcot had forced a draw at Alton Town and so I decided, along with Chick and secretary Martin Clarke, who offered to drive us, to make the long trip to Didcot to run my eye over both teams. Didcot managed to win but there was a player with a huge reputation who stood out for me as he had scored a total of 53 goals in the previous season. His name was Ian Concannon and he was going to be a right handful for us on the Saturday. I made my notes and because we had had a game on the Tuesday, we had light training on the Thursday and then a team meeting about the big game on the Saturday. I remember quite clearly that Martin Clarke had gone around the football club frightening the life out of every supporter and the committee about this centre forward. I remember clearly at the team meeting, my first words to the players, "Fuck Ian Concannon, and now I'm going to tell you why. He may have scored 53 goals last season and is already finding the net this season because he is Didcot town football club. So, what I'm going to do on Saturday, I'm going to change the formation to how we finished against Greenwich playing a 3-5-2, and fuck him right up because it doesn't matter how good a centre forward you are, without service you're nothing to worry about. So, what we're going to do is fill the midfield and cut off his supply, because he is the type of player who I am sure will turn his back on the game if he's not having things his own way".

Saturday came and Didcot arrived on their team bus with their players and supporters. We had a good crowd and I just felt very confident in my players' discipline to carry out the plan. And so, it proved to be. We started on the front foot and we never looked back, with Danny Punt, our centre half, getting our first goal after 3 minutes, but despite only leading 1-0 at half-time, we had kept Concannon quiet and I told the lads the body language from Didcot was poor and, "We've got 'em by the bollocks here, boys!" This proved to be right, as a few minutes into the second half, Gareth Gregg scored on his debut. One lapse from us saw Concannon find the back of the net to put Didcot back in the game. I remained quite calm and got instructions out to the players to carry on, get back on the front foot again and let's finish the game off. We had tightened up all over and we weren't going to let them back in again. Our lively forward, Pat Massaro, raced clear to score a third and dump Didcot out of the cup. Myself and Chick hugged each other like we'd won the lottery because again, all non-league followers will know that it's very hard at that level with limited training (especially ours as it was the car park that we had to use unless we could get on the pitch) to have the players disciplined to a game plan for 90 minutes.

So, we were through to the first qualifying round and found out that we were away to Chipstead from the Combined Counties League (and prize money of £7,500 for that game) which was a bit of a local derby for us. Before that game, we had another cup game, this time at home to Burgess Hill Town, who were the top side in the league. We lost that 2-0 and then another cup game, and so now we turned to the F.A. Vase and I have to admit, it was not a competition that I had done well in, so to say I was a bit nervous about our trip to Guildford and Godalming was a bit of an understatement. We played very well on the day despite missing key players. Five of our better players were not available through injury. Despite that, we were guilty of missing many chances which should have seen us at least 3 goals to the good by half-time. We had a very poor referee who was a bit whistle-happy and sometimes he must have felt he was left out of the game. The reason why he gave out 5 trivial yellow cards in the space of 10 minutes was beyond me, but then he set a standard of poor refereeing for the remainder of the game and awarded the home side a penalty that never was, which was adjudged to have come off one of my defender's arms. Even the player who hit the ball, Godalming's Simon Ray, one of my former players, admitted that it never touched my player's arm. I said to him after the game, "So why did you put the ball on the penalty spot and put the fucking thing in the net, if you knew it never touched the player?" (joke).

We missed further chances to equalise but we ran out of time and lost the game. I must admit I was livid at the officials. As I have said many times before, no good ranting and raving on the touchline; best to have your say in private in the referee's room after the game, which I did, accusing the referee and the linesman of not being up to standard for this level of football and an important cup tie. I cannot remember all of their response but I believe they told me that they had been invited over from Ireland at the request of the F.A. to take charge of some games.

They did admit that perhaps the game was a bit above their experience. What more could I say?

I was shell-shocked, but you have to move on and so now we come to the following Saturday, the 14th of September 2002, and the first qualifying round away at Chipstead. I felt another different approach would be needed before the game from myself, so we gave the players a night off from training and decided to have a couple of beers and a pool competition and an informal chat about our progress so far, as we had played quite a few games in a short space of time and being a new side, it was good to see everyone together in a relaxed atmosphere. I remember spending a bit of time that evening on a one to one basis with Pat Massaro, who hadn't scored in the last two games but was on 10 goals already. I just tried to restore some of his confidence back, as he was one of those players who, being a prolific scorer, felt that that was his only contribution to the game. I assured him that he had other values too, but of course, that was his prime role in the side.

Now to the game itself with Chipstead and the chance to make some club history if we were successful, as it was some twenty years or so since the club had last reached the second qualifying round, and also only the third time in the club's entire history. We made the short journey to Chipstead and were playing on a surface which could only be described as pristine and was crying out for football. What a day it turned out to be, as we brushed aside a very good Chipstead side with our 3-5-2 formation, which brought us goals from Scot Langridge, a debut goal from Nathan Pullen, who came on as a substitute, and Pat Massaro (so our little chat did have some effect).

It was a great game and a great result, 3-1, and we were £7,500 richer. So now we waited for that all-important Monday second qualifying round draw and our fourth game so far in the F.A. cup. We came out of the hat blessed with a home tie, but with really tough opposition in Aveley from the Ryman division one north side, and although our league form took a bit of a dip after our win at Chipstead, we felt that we were in with a chance against our Ryman opposition. We had our usual pre-match F.A. cup light training night, which included a game of pool and darts and a good chat amongst ourselves about using our F.A. cup formation of a 3-5-2. F.A. cup day arrived, and there was a good crowd and a cracking game, which saw us take the lead when Tony McKenzie scored after only 4 minutes, a lead which we held until half-time. The second half saw Aveley draw level and then a very bad refereeing decision (and I'm not moaning again) by Kent-based referee, David Buck, who awarded Aveley a penalty for a reason I will never know for all my life as our player got to the ball first inside the box. I turned round to Chick in the dugout and said, "Fuck me, he's going to cost us the game now, after all this work". I was not down and out and made my allowed number of substitutes to try and breathe a new lease of life into the side as we were playing now against twelve men (eleven plus the ref.). We gave as good as we could and Aveley finished us off with 5 minutes to go, when we fully deserved a replay at least. As for the referee in this game and the Godalming game in the F.A. Vase, if there had been V.A.R, we would not have come off the pitch until at least midnight, there were so many wrong decisions in both games. Although defeated, it left me very proud of our players and how they had adapted themselves and made a bit of history, despite some racial taunts from the Aveley fans which made the newspaper who covered the game, but there was no action taken by the ref or county officials, so, you see, this stuff was going on even then, 17 years ago!

Nothing could have prepared us for what was going to happen on the 1st of March 2003, away at Sidlesham, in which the home side decided to use racial tactics on the field and from the bench to gain a win over us, or so it seemed when they were hell-bent on making remarks about our captain, Steve Roberts and his colour and his dreadlocks. Steve reacted in what I would call a calm way by simply saying to them, "I will see you then in the car park after the game,", but would you believe, the referee, Mr Paul Preston sent Steve off for the threat he made and let the game get completely out of control, leaving us with ten men! Thank you, ref. As I mentioned before, we had a very good youth side and they managed to get to the second round of the F.A. youth cup and were given a great tie away at Cardiff City, to be played at their famous Ninian Park ground. I must say that this game took me into another area of my football career, as it started my scouting career that would last me many years. I decided to ring up Torquay United, who had played Cardiff City youth team in the earlier round, and asked their youth team manager if he could fax me up some details about Cardiff which he kindly did. While I was on the 'phone, he said, "Have you got a minute, because the first team gaffer wants a word with you?" So next thing I'm on the 'phone talking to Leroy Rosenior(ex-West Ham, a tv football pundit, and M.B.E)who asked me, being a non-league manager, if I would do a job for him and go to watch Boreham Wood, a non-league club, and give him a report. I said I would do that for him and they respected it and duly beat Boreham Wood 5-1 at home. He rang me on the Monday and thanked me for the report and asked if I would be able to do some more work for him when needed. I said yes to that and that started my like for scouting.

So, there we are, that's the next step in the book but a lot of water has to go under Three Bridges yet. Back to the youth team and their game against Cardiff and with my notes given to the youth team manager, they went down to Cardiff on a Sunday and despite losing 3-1, they put up a great show and even equalised with a Pat Dunning strike and it stayed like that until 8 minutes from time when Cardiff were feeling a bit nervous and slung on two of their subs who had had first-team experience. Consequently, they had a big influence on the two goals that finished the young Bridges off, but it was a great day for the boys, the team management and the club.

So now back to earning my bread and butter with the league and the continuing work to build a side and climb the table, and also doing my day job and still writing the newspaper column. Good old non-league football is a way of life, or to people like me, a drug you are just hooked on, and maybe that is why I let chairmen of football clubs be dishonest with me with their promises and it was about to happen at Three Bridges, but it took time and it was done very deceptively using my personal life, although that could not be hidden sometimes.

It certainly made headlines when, after entering my house on the Thursday before the Peacehaven game, I heard an almighty crash at the front of my house. I opened the front door to see my neighbour's car embedded under my front window and into the brickwork and her body half out the car! It is a wonder no one was killed, but there was not even a scratch on any person, just loads of structural damage. The headlines in the paper read 'Car comes calling through Micky's front door' and you guessed it, I was back in the dugout 48 hours later to oversee our fine victory at Peacehaven.

I still carried on my work to bring the football club up as a real challenger in the league for promotion, if not this season, it would be next season 2003/4. Because of our cup run and the weather, we were falling behind with games but we still had a good run, losing only 4 games out of 10 and Phil Gault and Pat Massaro were climbing the league's goalscoring charts with away wins at Peacehaven and Telscombe, 7-0, Littlehampton Town 5-0, and home to Horsham YMCA 3-2 in the local derby. During that period, I brought some more class to the club and at no extra money, just wanting to buy into what was turning out to be a very good side and a bright future with myself and Chick, Paul Smith (Scholsey), Seb Favata, who had been at A.F.C. Wimbledon, the phoenix club, and Martin Beard, a Carshalton 1st team player and one of the Surrey County F.A. players. The problem was, our training facilities were poor unless we could get onto the pitch, which secretary Martin Clarke hated, so sometimes I had to make alternative arrangements which included one night I remember well when I decided to ask Phil Gault if we could use the private leisure club where he worked to do some weights and exercise bikes.

We also held the Three Bridges swimming gala. What a great night we all had and of course, me having been a very good swimmer although my legs and spine are fucked, I fancied myself against the players in all the races as I still do at least 50 lengths three times a week. However, I was in unknown company as far as swimming was concerned, and took a lot of stick from the lads when I was beaten in a couple of races, but when it came to the butterfly, no one could get anywhere near me.

We had such a team spirit that it would not matter what comments players made to each other and that night proved to be no exception, as Sean Campbell, one of my black players and a great lad and a good player who I had brought to the club from St. Leonards, decided to wear a brilliant white, tight swimming cap, so you can imagine the lads when I shouted to Sean, "You look like a fucking boiled egg without the top!" at which the rest of the players fell about laughing, even Sean! You see, that is what I had created within the squad; no player, black, white, foreign, small or tall was ever singled out in the dressing room because of their differences, and I can honestly say that if I was in a trench fighting for my life, I would take great pride in having them alongside me knowing I had a good chance of survival. Sure, they were never without a bollocking if they had not put a shift in but again a statement often used in non-league football - what goes on in the dressing room stays there. Even our boisterous physio, Paul O'Donnell and his wife Jan kept to that rule and we also would not let any fans use abuse to upset our game.

Those players knew myself and Chick were genuine football people and wanted the best for them and the club, but as the season went on, I began to feel something was not right. It certainly was not the way we were playing or any of the other managers at the club, and in Barry Mealand, our football director, we had the nicest bloke you would ever want to meet, (sadly he passed away six years ago on Easter Monday 2013), so despite us having a good season, our first in charge, the penny dropped when Chick made a comment to me during one of our home games. "Have you noticed, Mick, that when we are winning, the chairman always leaves the stand during the game, but when we are losing, he stays to the end to give us his comments?" I turned to Chick and said, "You are right! Chairman Alan Bell does not want us here, but we will have a meeting with him soon and front him up," as there were rumours flying about from my players regarding my job and a certain Mr Sammy Donnelly (who, funnily enough, I was to work alongside in the future at Eastbourne Town).

I must say, I always had good and fair press and was lucky to have such good reporters working for the Crawley Observer, Andy West, Graham Carter, and the Sussex Argus's Howard Griggs, who I used to talk to when I was boss at St. Leonards. I think Graham and Howard are now sports editors. Here are some of the quotes from me that they wrote: I was asked about how small I was and I replied "I might be small, but I was a better player than Papa Smurf!; when asked about the Christmas party, "We have to play Pagham first before our Christmas fancy dress party, so I hope the players don't get confused as I don't want Pat Massaro running onto the pitch dressed as Spiderman! I was also questioned over the fact that I had used 50 players in the first team this season, to which I replied, "Yes, but not all at once during a game!" Thanks, lads, for the fun.

Pat and Phil Gault were banging in goals for fun and also Phil's game had more about it than Pat just putting the ball in the net. He possessed a great quality of being there at the right time and had that extra ability where he could see things that were about to happen and would make the run. When I left the club, they had 50 goals between them, the best in the league, but we still struggled defending as we had only kept 6 clean sheets all season.

However, we were working on that and towards the end of the season, we were still scoring but not conceding, and if we did it was only the one goal. We were looking good and I could see a top-five finish, but as I have said, I felt there were problems off the pitch and felt good that no players were involved. I was waiting for the right time to see the chairman about my concerns over my future, which was funny, as it seems I did not have to wait long because I had a phone call from Alan Bell, the chairman, on a Monday, inviting me out to dinner on the Thursday evening and he said, "Let Chick take the training as I have some ideas to go over with you for next season." Well, talk about a bolt out of the blue! He had never rung me all season, so could I be that mad to think this was going to be pleasant, or was I to choke on a bone or spill my soup all down my clean white shirt? Hands up how many non-league managers feel that a dinner invite from the chairman will end up in tears, with one of the chairs at the table left vacant before the meal is finished? So, drinks were ordered and it was no expense spared, so I ordered what I wanted so as to mellow myself down somewhat. As we started to talk about the season and the future, I went straight for jugular saying, "I understand you want Sammy Donnelly to take over as first-team manager? After all the fucking work I have done here, £9,000 in the F.A. cup and sponsorship, with new warm-up tops for the players and staff and also the advert in the programme from a company I deal with, and 8 hard months of work to bring you a very good team and a future that will see us as champions next season?" I was so near to walking out, but you see, he never denied my statement, but kept on about my health and the concern he and the club had over it and that he did not want to be responsible if anything happened to me while I was managing the club. He also mentioned my work on my Ryman round-up newspaper column, so my reply was quite quick and to the point, as I said, "It is very kind of you to consider my health, but no one in my family is that worried, and neither are any of my doctors, as this condition known as SVT is not life-threatening and needs just a simple procedure to control it, so I think you are using this to bring Sammy in as you quoted that you have been waiting for two years to get him on board as I know he throws a bit of his own in with certain players to keep them."

The chairman, now on the back foot, tried to tell me that he would give me 48 hours to think about it and the home game against fourth in the table Ringmer, and then I could take a seat on the board as director of football and we would get someone in to work with Chick. He then said, "It is my job to know people and I know you will take that job so I will see you after the game Saturday." I then pointed out if I wanted a fucking job as director, I could have one in the Ryman Premier league now, but I wanted to manage football teams! With that, I got up and walked out before he had the chance to say, "Would you like to see the dessert menu?" leaving, like I said, the now vacant chair at the table. Early on Friday morning, Chick rang me and said, "All the boys were training, but I was asked afterwards by one of the committee if I would work with a new manager, but Micky, I did not know what had gone on with you and the chairman, so I thought you had resigned. Then they mentioned Sammy Donnelly, which seemed strange!" I told Chick the truth and he just said, "Okay, after Saturday, we will have it on our toes and away and we will have to tell the players after the game." We agreed on this and left it until the Saturday, the 29th of March 2003, a week after my 55th birthday.

Meanwhile, on the Friday, I went up to see my great and loving friend and my Merlin, Robin Denman and told him all about it, and despite Robin being terminally ill with throat cancer, he got his brother to bring him to the game on that Saturday to support me and although not able to speak, he had written on his notepad, 'You have lost one of the best managers you will ever have, as he would have got you that first title ever next season'. That was my Merlin, always up there with his opinion whether you liked it or not. Fuck knows what he would have made of all the politicians that have tried to ruin our country over the last three years with Brexit!

The Saturday came and myself and Chick arrived at the ground very early to decide what to say to the lads after the game. We also wanted to go out in style against a very good Ringmer side. The players arrived as normal and our physio, Paul O'Donnell and wife Jan had no idea of what was going to happen come 5 pm. It was all about the game first and a good display and the result, and I must say now the players never let us down with either as they set about Ringmer in the type of fashion we had been working on and built on slick passing, movement, crossing and making yourself available for each other, combined with midfield flare and finally, a defence that had good shape. Ringmer were shell-shocked as we took the lead with a trademark goal from Massaro, turning his man on the edge of the box and scoring from all of 20 yards, but Ringmer got the equaliser just before half-time, giving them, some hope. However, on that day, our team were a class above in all departments, as the papers said and when Seb Favata scored a great goal with an overhead kick some 12 yards out, it was all over except for Phil Gault scoring a trademark goal for him, pulling, as we had coached him, off the far post to score our third. I looked at Chick and said what a great display we had from the team and how sad we both were when all the players had already pledged themselves for next season and that fucking stupid chairman had gone and ruined everything, but I was so happy for the players as they were going to be remembered for this display and had warmed the hearts of the fans looking to the future.

This was not to be, though. They may have had their Sammy Donnelly in the end, and had a couple of cup finals, but even

Sammy failed to deliver that league title which we would have done, I'm sure, because anyone at that ground for the Ringmer game, our last in charge, would have seen that. I was proved right, as it was going to be 8 years more before they got that title and promotion to the Ryman league.

Now came the worse bit, having to tell the players after the game, but before we did that, we made sure they had their wage packets in their hands and we then explained what had happened and that this was our last game in charge of the team. What happened next was quite astonishing, as some of the players didn't even shower, they just said, "We are not playing if you are not our manager," and made for their cars, leaving at most three players behind. I showered and went to make for my car, but Alan Bell, the chairman, stopped me and asked me what I was doing. I replied, "You know, Alan because you told me you know what people will do. Well, you don't know Micky fucking Taylor, that's for sure, so stick the club up your arse. I've gone; it's the end, and by the way, so has Chick and most of the players!" He did not know what to say to me, but he had plenty to say to the papers which I have kept all these years which really showed the man up for what he was. So, it was Three Bridges, but a bridge too far! I had a laugh when it was said after I had gone that the football was so bad, you paid £5 to get into the ground and £8 to get out of it, but on the whole of the club and its goings-on has been another tale to tell, which makes the non-league rollercoaster the exciting ride it is unless of course, you want to get off......

CHAPTER FIFTEEN

2003 - 2012 the roller coaster stays on track, despite being vandalised.

First, I had to deal with the local papers as they were shocked about what had happened at the club. I have to say they were very good to me, giving my side of the story and of course, at the same time, having to listen to the excuse being used to get me to step down. My thanks go to journalists Andy West, Graham Carter, and Howard Griggs. Also, more importantly, I had to find clubs for some of the players, one of them being Seb Favata who, by a stroke of good luck, was to get another chance back at A.F.C. Wimbledon, helping them climb the leagues. In fact, he went on to play for them 53 times during the 2003/4 season, not missing a game; that's how good he was. To think it could have been Three Bridges, as he had pledged himself to me and the club for another season at least.

So back to my enforced break and Alan Bell trying to do his best to derail my rollercoaster had quite the adverse effect on me. I had some time to think and was still doing some work for Leroy Rosenior at Torquay, so I kept busy. I also had to help Phil Gault to get away from Three Bridges, as he was unhappy and did not want to play under any other manager, so I took him to Whyteleafe so my great friend, Bernie Donnelly and manager Lee Richardson could have a look at him. He trained with them and they even tried to buy him out of his contract, but Alan Bell was acting like some little kid, trying to stop a player progressing. You could say that I was the one to put him on a contract in the first place, but there was a good reason for that because I had to ensure that Phil was going to stay with the football club, at least all the time I was there. I could not understand why you would want a player at a football club who did not want to be there.

Alan Bell did not get things all his own way. I must admit, I did manage to get Phil a couple of games in Whyteleafe's reserve side, and went down to watch him play against Fleet Town. He stood out a mile, showing his class and of course, my good friend, Colin Turner was at Whyteleafe at the time, and he was a great one for non-diplomacy as he said, "Let's fucking play him and fuck Three Bridges". Obviously, we couldn't do that and Phil just went through the motions back at Three Bridges and went on to have a great career in the Sussex County league after getting out of his contract. I still say to this day that lad would have gone on to be a pro.

I joined the scouting team at Whyteleafe and my first job in the 2003/04 season was to go and watch Wick F.C., who Whyteleafe were playing in the F.A. Cup. I did a good report on them. I actually travelled down to watch the game at Wick and felt quite pleased with my report as Whyteleafe put them to the sword, winning 5-0 and putting themselves in the first qualifying round. So that's where I spent my season, working along with Colin Turner, Bernie Donnelly, and Lee Richardson. Again, I learnt very quickly this scouting business at non-league level was really a very frustrating job.

I can now give you one instance and it was with Whyteleafe. They had been drawn away to Sittingbourne in the first qualifying round. The week before they were due to play Sittingbourne, I went down to watch them. I cannot remember who they were playing at the time but funnily enough, I bumped into a couple of the committee from Three Bridges, who were watching the opposition for their F.A. cup tie, one of them being my good friend who I mentioned earlier, Barry Mealand, who started to apologise to me for the behaviour of some of the members. My reply to Barry was, "No need to talk about it; you never know, one day I might write a book"! How prophetic is that?

Back to Whyteleafe and my report on Sittingbourne. I must say, as a scout, my reports were quite in-depth and had enough information, not too much information. I took this report down to the club on the Tuesday evening, handed it to Bernie and Lee and said, "Right, okay, you've got all you need there, I'll look out for the result on Saturday." Just to make sure, on the Saturday morning I decided to 'phone Bernie while they were travelling to Sittingbourne and asked, "Have you gone through everything with Lee? To which he replied, "I'm sorry, Turk, I've left it at home!" My reply to him was a bit more restrained than it would be to anyone else because he was and still is a great friend of mine and the family. Of course, I waited for the result, and would you believe, they went and got beat 1-0! Now I was fucking furious because they were quite a beatable side and Whyteleafe had a decent team, there was no way they should have lost that game. If you don't take any notice of what scouts do for you then it is a pointless exercise. Rather than do reports from then on in for Whyteleafe, I decided to just be around the club if they needed any player to be looked at and enjoy the company of the management and the players alike. Of course, I could take in any game I wanted to, as long as it was non-league and that's really how things were to be as the rollercoaster was slowing down, but again, you never know what's around the corner or what the next 'phone call will bring.

That proved to be right as my next football 'phone call was a disappointing one, to say the least, but very understandable. It was from Leroy Rosenior at Torquay, asking me if I would carry on scouting, but the problem was that the board had decided that, although the playing budget could be or might be increased, they were not willing to pay other expenses, such as scouting, amongst other things. I replied, "So are you telling me that I will have to pay to get into games, pay for my own travelling? Because that's all I ever asked for!" There was one perk that made me laugh when he said I wouldn't need to pay if I wanted to come down and watch a home game, and I thought, fuck that for a game of soldiers. A 350-mile round trip and of course the train fare? He was a charming fellow, and in a nice way, said to me, "I would like you to carry on, but that is the situation". I nearly let my love of football run away with me but had to decline his offer because no way was I going to pay all those expenses myself. That was my brush with scouting for professional clubs. Good old non-league football, you can't beat it.

So as you can see, the season was beginning to be bits and bobs for me, just watching loads and loads of non-league football matches and of course, carrying on again with my Ryman round-up in the South London Guardian, to which I could devote a bit more time instead of ringing the managers up on a Sunday to get their views so I could meet Mondays deadline. I made a point of going to a game every week and making that my headline game, which kept me in touch with all the people I knew in non-league football because believe me, you can soon be the forgotten man in football when you are not involved at a club.

The phone does go silent to a certain degree, and at first, it is like a blessing not being bothered by players while at work or watching the tv, and even to the point of going fishing with the phone in one hand and the rod in another and missing a good fish. You might think what was I moaning about? After all, he seems to have the attitude of 'fuck the football, there are better things to do than have all the aggro from players and chairman alike'. Well, nothing could be further from the truth! Football just became a part of life and the one thing that I did learn from it, was to be careful who you trust in the world of non-league football if you are going to be a manager or a player!

So, the rollercoaster goes on, but at the moment, carrying no passengers. I'm sure it won't be long before it does and away we go again, and meanwhile, I spent time watching lots of football from step 6 upwards and seeing some good talent and good matches. I always liked going to watch Dulwich Hamlet, as you never know what you are likely to come across. They always produced good players and a good manager in Gavin Rose, who, after 10 years, has the blood of dark blue and pink running through his veins. I always look for their results. In my column in October 1999, I did cover Whyteleafe's 1st round home tie against football league side Chester City, in which the Leafe had most of the game and had Chester on the back foot. They should have won the game when given a penalty near the end, only for Steve Lunn to bring a save out of the keeper and blast the rebound over the bar and with it the tie. The frustration on their faces told the story! I always say you only get the one chance against league opposition and that proved to be the case as Chester won the replay 3-1, and the dream was all over.

As I have said, writing for the newspaper kept me in touch with all of the managers and players, some who had played for me over the years, but that was soon to come to the end after nearly 8 years when I moved out of Croydon to the southeast coast to Bexhill in late 2006. I was still travelling back to Croydon three times a week to my window and joinery business, in which I was joint director with Mark Lilly, who still runs the company to this day.

I always had a link with Hastings, as you know from my managing days at St. Leonards and my caravan, so I will take you back to December 2004 and the departure of Steve Lovell from Hastings United and the appointment of a complete legend, not only on Merseyside in the blue corner but also in his beloved Wales, none other than Neville Southall, one of the best goalkeepers ever. You might be thinking why have we gone back, so I will explain, I had a phone call from Hastings chairman,

Dave Walters, who told me that Neville had been appointed first-team manager to replace Steve, as he was a free agent after being sacked by Dover after only 16 games in charge and would I like to do some scouting for him on players and teams they were going to play, as he had no knowledge of the Ryman league at all. So, I said, "Okay, I will have to meet with him first, though," which I did down at the ground. Well I had shaken the hand of Dave MacKay and that was bad enough, but when Neville shook my hand, it was like my bones were going to be crushed! He had hands like a shovel, but was a really nice bloke, speaking with his broad Welsh accent, explaining to me what he would like me to do on the scouting side as he already had his coaching staff at the club, which suited me fine. He also informed me that Dave Walters had told him that at Hastings United, he will have a job for life. You can guess my reply to him. I said, "Neville, you have already been hard done by at Dover and despite what the chairman has told you, I am telling you now that at the moment, you are a novelty here, with the fans having photos done with you and of course, the newspapers loving it as you are such a celebrity, but these fans down here are unforgiving; if you start fucking up results you will be out the door!"

To be fair, he started quite well but he had a bad run of results in October/ November 2005. I remember one game in particular I did for him in 2005 when things were not going well and he needed wins, I was asked by Neville to go and watch Tooting and Mitcham v Newport I.O.W and they had a front player called John Hastings, who was more than just very good, he was clever, played with his back to goal, gave little reverse passes and found space to get it back and pull the trigger, so in my report, I explained that it was no use going zonal, you have to man to man mark him so close that your player needs to be able to tell you the washing instructions inside the player's shirt! As usual, I faxed him over the report and told him I would be at the game on Tuesday as I lived in Croydon and Tooting's ground was a stone's throw away from me. Well, I watched on in astonishment as John Hastings was getting the freedom of the park and no player was marking him close enough and because of that, the Hastings United back central defenders were getting pulled about all over the place and they paid the price with John Hastings scoring a hat trick. I never said anything after the game as I felt wouldn't be right to do so; all I did was give him a nod and said I would ring him tomorrow and left it at that. I was quite taken aback when speaking to him the following day and I asked him why John Hastings was allowed the freedom of the park when on my report I had clearly stated how good he was and how he should deal with him and to be fair, he gave an honest reply by saying he had left the report at the ground and therefore he had not been aware of the threat the player posed and also the way that the team play up to him, but he realised that if he had read the report, his game plan would have been different and the result also. He was a great bloke (no big-time Charlie) and I carried on doing bits for him until one day I had a phone call from him to say, "Micky, they have just sacked me!" So that was the end of Neville and like others before him, including myself, he was not given enough time and I was glad that assistant manager, Terry White, followed him out of the door in support for him, but he was back with Hastings United sometime after and he is still there today. I see that he plays the odd charity game, but I don't think he is involved anymore. Who could blame him? One day I must ring him.

At that time, I kept thinking it is time to turn it in and go horse racing instead. Although I am not a gambling man, I love going horse racing as I find it very exciting, especially over the jumps, and to put the icing on the cake there is a nice picture of me with A.P. McCoy, which you will have seen in this book (I don't do things by half).

The rollercoaster which this book is all about was again out of action for some time, as far as having a role to play in a club, but it gave me a chance to get out and take in more non-league games and meet with people in the game. As always, I would turn up in collar and tie, which always got you noticed and also, more importantly, it got you a team sheet rather than trying to fill in the team changes over those sometimes terrible tannoy systems which sounded like the announcer was underwater. Everyone at every non-league club was trying to do their best, but most of them were volunteers. Before I knew it, the rollercoaster was running again, but not for long.

I was back into football again after a phone call from my old mate, Wally Petty, who asked me if I would be interested in managing Lingfield F.C. in the Sussex County league division 3, along with Des McCarthy. So, we both agreed to give it a go and went down to see the committee and look at facilities. The playing surface was okay and they had floodlights, but I could see danger as experience is a great thing to have, and as soon as they mentioned the cricket section, I began to think it wouldn't work, but we started our jobs as it was in the middle of the season and of course, cricket was still lying in bed waiting for the summer to arrive. We prepared the team for a division 3 cup game under lights at home and Wally had recruited some players for us. To be fair, we played quite well, despite losing the game just minutes from the end, which left us disappointed given the way we had played, so at least there was some hope to build a team on, or so we thought. But as the weeks went by, I could see Des getting more frustrated, to the point where you arrive thinking if it does not improve on Saturday, that's it.

Well, that day did arrive and we were away to Uckfield Town, who had nice changing rooms but the pitch was awful. This made our coaching fly out of the window as you could not pass the ball. It was just both teams playing long balls, hoping for a mistake or a knock-on, which they could do better than us. The final whistle blew and we both looked at each other and said, "No fucking more of this!" To rub salt into the wound, as we were making our way back to get changed, I was met by Gary Bowyer, the ex-Carshalton player/manager who also had a short stay managing at St. Leonards after I had gone from there. He said, "Micky, what the fuck are you doing here at this place, and Des as well? The only Lingfield you should be interested in is the racecourse and having a bet on a Saturday. You both must be mad and I am glad I have met you today to tell you that, Please tell me you will turn it in!" to which we both replied, "You are dead right there, Gary," and so after the game, we gave them our notice to quit and it also meant that we did not have to engage with the cricket committee and it was goodbye to Lingfield F.C. We did feel a bit sad for Wally as he had now taken us to two clubs, Haywards Heath Town and Lingfield, and we had resigned from both of them.

Now the rollercoaster is again in the workshop for repairs. It is important for you to realise that, apart from a few clubs north of the water, this book is mostly about non-league clubs in the south of England, because apart from the national league, all our leagues are regionalised and that includes the early stages of the F.A. Cup, Vase and the trophy. Managers, therefore, do not move to clubs long distance as they do in league, championship, and premiership football, where they move home and family in the majority of cases. That is why sometimes, although in name only, the Vanarama National League is looked upon as being non-league football. I think it is fair to say that it is not, but simply division 3 of the football league and I believe one day it will be part of the football league.

With the rollercoaster tucked away and a few years of stepping back and having a rest yet still watching plenty of games and the odd mission of scouting, I was fast approaching my 60th birthday. Of course, this was going to be more of a football reunion than a birthday and it was going to take some organising and a lot of my time. I chose one of my old clubs, Whyteleafe Football Club to host the event and also on my 50th birthday, for some unknown reason my uncle Les Harrington had bought me a cup for my birthday; as if I needed one as my trophy cabinet was full to the brim. I decided, in his memory, to play this game and call it the Harrington Cup. I wanted as many of the old players that I had played with, managed, and associated with to be at that birthday reunion. It was a great day on Easter Sunday 2008 and I had arranged a game but it was put in serious doubt because we had a snow storm shortly before the game. Now you must remember that these players, some of whom I had played with over 40 years ago, were out there playing alongside me and it was a good game, although I would not say it was the fastest game in the world. The game ended with a penalty shoot-out and it was quite funny really because there is never such a thing as a friendly game of football. I remember quite clearly Billy Paterson missing his penalty and walking off in disgust as I calmly stepped up and tucked mine away to win the cup. One lovely thing to come out of all this was not only to see all the players and managers from down the years but when the Sussex Argus pink on Saturday evenings gave me a full page with photos and the headlines 'Taylor makes final appearance at 60. Colourful ex-saints boss pulls on his boots one last time' (or so they thought). I remember training for the game by doing quick sprints up and down my garage and on my exercise bike at my bungalow, thinking this was going to get me fit. I pulled more fucking hamstrings doing that than I had ever done during my playing and coaching career!

It was also great to have my son playing on the same pitch as his dad, although typical goalkeeper; as good as he was in goal, he wanted to play out on the field. We raised some money for charity as the bottles of malt whisky were sent round and the food I had paid for was laid out along with money behind the bar which was well-appreciated after a hard-fought game. Also, I knew Alan Pardew, who was then manager at Newcastle United, through his non-league days with Morden Nomads and Richard (Simmo) Simpson, along with Lee Richardson and Bernie

Donnelly. Alan could not make the party or the game but sent down a signed Newcastle United shirt which raised a lot of money when I raffled it. There was also a great gesture from my great friend Bernie Donnelly, which was to have the match ball signed by all the players and my birthday card signed by all the guests. Funnily enough, my good friend Tommy Power, who recently, sadly, passed away, won the shirt in the raffle and one of the players who was at Croydon when we won the double, my good friend and a top-class centre back mark, Geordie Dickinson, was very lucky when Tommy took the shirt over to him and gave it to him. I remember Tommy's words which showed his kind of humour; "What would a Spurs fan want with a bloody Newcastle shirt?" Geordie thanked him but that was Tommy all over.

So, with the party having taken quite a bit of time up, I was again watching games, doing little bits and pieces for different managers, but nothing to warrant bringing the rollercoaster out. It almost got to the point where the indoor slippers and the pipe came out, watching the racing on Saturday afternoons and Coronation Street and EastEnders during the week. It was going to be a long time before the 'phone rang again, but I kept involved doing little jobs for some of my ex-players who had become managers. One example was doing a bit for John Crumplin, who had the bad luck of being manager at Walton and Hersham, and also Graham Harps playing as a wing-back. I say bad luck for John because of his chairman, Alan Smith, who went through managers like you would toilet rolls having swallowed ten Senokot laxative tablets all at once! Mind you, John saw the light and resigned in 2010, but I had warned John because myself and Des McCarthy decided to go and watch Walton at Ashford United and say hello, so we spoke before the game and then took our place in the stand right below the chairman, Mr Smith, who did nothing but slaughter John and the team throughout the 90minutes, so we made him aware. Job done, and another fucking non-league football chairman thinking he was God.

CHAPTER SIXTEEN

2013-2019: Rollercoaster gets new lease of life and a new lick of paint.

Now I was beginning to organise my 65th birthday, to be played again at Whyteleafe, but this time I was a lot fitter and would play a bigger part in the game. Quite a few of the players from the past were there and this time, I was playing in the same team with Eddie Mark who I had played alongside at Addiscombe Social F.C., some 42 years earlier. Also on my side, I had Mr John Domfe (former West Ham United) who did nothing but moan all of the first half. So I said, "Give it a rest, John, it's my fucking birthday, or you won't get any cake," but John was not treating this as a birthday game, so at half-time, we were 3-2 down and he wanted some shape to our side and pass the ball to each other. Well, something worked because we were like Real Madrid in the second half and soon raced into a 5-3 lead. Eddie Mark had got his trademark hat trick and I had scored 2. We went on to win 7-4 and with a hat trick for me and 4 for Eddie. What a combination we were! But the best for me was when, faced with only Geordie to beat, I nutmegged him and smashed the ball into the top corner of the net, and I thought not bad for 65 years old! That was going to be my last game as a player although I had said that to the press when I was sixty, but what a way to finish your playing days on a hat trick and after all those years being a winger and the provider. Funny old game, this football! So, I lifted the Harrington Cup again (thanks again Uncle Les). On a last note, I did suffer after scoring that goal, as, lying on the floor in celebration or exhaustion, all of my team jumped on top of me! I tell you I was fucking bruised for days after; game over!

So the party after the game, one of my old players, Graham Harper (Harps) who was assistant manager to Tommy Williams at Carshalton Athletic, asked me if I would be interested in being their chief scout for the season 2013/14, as they had just escaped relegation from the premier division of the Ryman league through Tommy's appointment late in the season. I agreed to meet with Harps and Tommy one night before they started training, at a pub in Motspur Park. I found Tommy to be a most likeable young man and very knowledgeable of his football. I remember him saying these words to me, "Micky, as a scout with me you are part of the management team and whenever you attend a game with Carshalton Athletic, I will want you in the dressing room and in the dugout." I really felt chuffed by those words and it was almost as though I had turned the clock back to 1999 when my old boss, Ken Jarvie, had said the same thing to me at Croydon F.C. I remember thinking again these are the type of young men that I want to work for and I will give them the best I can give. I must say football scouts really are never mentioned much, and if you get a chance, there is a book that my son bought me which sums up the scouting world. It's by a chap called Michael Calvin and is simply called The Nowhere Men, but that would never apply to me with Tommy and Graham.

Out came the rollercoaster, again full of energy. I knew it was going to be a tough season as Tommy had a small budget and a young side which were going to have to stand up to the likes of Maidstone United, Margate, Hendon, and Dulwich Hamlet to name a few, but we did have some good young players like Tommy Bradford, and Harold Odametey. Tommy stayed at the club and is doing well there, but Harold followed

Tommy Williams to Kingstonian and went on to Hampton and Richmond and is now playing at Dagenham and Redbridge. The one player who I could not make out at Carshalton was Adriano Moraes, a young defender who had no control over his playing mood at all and could turn and do something stupid at any time during a game. He was a good defender but always a thorn in Tommy's and Harps' side.

The season got underway and we were well beaten away at Wingate and Finchley, a game I missed as I was watching Maidstone United at the Gallagher Stadium and also looking forward to meeting Bill Williams who was their chief executive and talking about the old days when he had Dover Athletic and I had St. Leonards which we did have a good chat about. But on to my mission for Tommy and Carshalton and it was a good game in front of a very big crowd and finished in a 1-1 draw against a very good Wealdstone side, who I thought would go very well, but little did I know they were to end up champions that season!

It was Maidstone I was interested in, as we had Maidstone at home on the Tuesday. They had a long throw expert and two lethal forwards in Frannie Collin and Zac Attwood and a superb goalkeeper in Lee Worgan, who became a legend there. That night we were as good or even better than them, but when a draw looked on the cards, the long throw caught us out and they got the winner right at the death (do footballers ever listen to information?). But there was hope for us in the way we played and nearly got something from a very good side so the future looked okay. We lost our next game, but something was to happen on the Tuesday 20th of august 2013 as we made our way down to East Sussex on the team bus to face Bognor Regis Town on their usual pristine playing surface. Harps was away on holiday and our other assistant, Luke, made it to the ground but his car was playing up and he was not able to leave the car to help Tommy, so I was asked if I would take up the role instead. I jumped at the chance to work in the changing room again and having a say in the game, which I duly did when Tommy asked me before the start if, at half-time, I would also talk to the players. Whether that night I had a magic wand or what, I don't know, but being 2-0 down at half-time was going to make it a tough dressing room and when Tommy asked me if I had anything to say, that was it! I was up and running and I remember saying to the lads, "You may be 2-0 down, but you can beat this lot if only you would remember that the night sky was for the stars and the moon, not the fucking ball, and the grass was for you to play on. So, pass and keep the ball and shoot at every opportunity you have around the box and I am sure you will come in after the game having won 3 or 4 goals to 2!" Out they went and that is exactly what they got - a great win against a good Bognor side! It was then when one of the players, young Harold Odametey, said to me, "How did you know the score?" to which I replied, "You have to believe in your own ability and do what you are instructed to do, which you all did and that wins games." What was also nice was to meet and have a chat to Jack Pearce, who is one of the most respected men in non-league football. It was a good night all round and looking forward to the season, but it was back to scouting for me and I would be a liar if I did not hope that another chance would come my way with Tommy and Harps. Although, as I have said before, I was always welcome in that changing room giving one to one advice, as some players need that, but to be fair, things were not good in terms of results.

There was also one incident involving that player Adriano Moraes, which did not help matters, when during a game against Harrow Borough, he had been getting some stick from the Harrow manager, Dave Anderson and his response to the verbal was to leave the pitch and attack their bench, which led to a straight red and down to ten men and the loss of 3points, so like I said, you may be a good player but you must control your temper. In my case as a player, this was always a problem, so

I know how wrong it is as you let your team and manager and the fans down.

That incident aside, in senior or any football, it is a results game that keeps chairmen happy, but in Tommy's case, he had saved Carshalton from relegation and deserved better from the club as he was a loyal manager and a good one as well. However, the axe fell in October 2013 and although I was asked if I would carry on as scout, I would not work there unless Tommy was the boss. He had taken me there and I have loyalty as well - one out, all out, so the rollercoaster was going in for repairs again, or so I thought.

However, that was never going to be the case because I was watching a game one night at Tooting and Mitcham when my good friend and former player, Tony Reid, came and sat next to me and asked me if I would go and join him on the coaching staff and bring along Des McCarthy with me as he was manager at Eastbourne town in Ryman division one south. I spoke with Des and we both agreed we would take him up on his offer. We both lived around Hastings, which was okay for us. Tony was another up and coming manager who was learning the ropes and he also had on his staff, Sammy Donnelly, who you know took my job over at Three Bridges, but I had to live with that if it was going to work at Eastbourne Town. I must say they had a nice ground called The Saffrons and a good playing surface which always helps the passing game, which we all preached, and more important to me, I was happy there.

Being the goalkeeper coach for someone so small seemed strange, but of course, I had learned so much when my son at 14 years old was at Crystal Palace and Chelsea as a goalkeeper. and I used to make notes on the coaching methods. Another thing that made me want to be part of the set up was that we had some very good players, and a certain player called Rocky Baptiste and I said I would be meeting this player again and so it was to be, but never would I have thought for one moment it would be at Eastbourne Town! Rocky had another reputation, apart from being a goal scorer. He was shown on YouTube as the Miss of the Century. When playing for Harrow Borough against Waltham Abbey, he ran from the halfway line, beat all in front of him including the keeper, and then smashed the ball wide of the goal, but later in the game, he showed what he could do by smashing the ball home from all of 30 yards into the top corner of the net and that video has had more than 4 million hits on it!

Back to Eastbourne and our league form which, to be fair, was a bit up and down, but our chairman, Dave Jenkins, gave Tony a chance and never put a lot of pressure on him, and although our playing budget was small, Tony did manage to attract the players. We had another forward by the name of Billy Medlock, who had a reputation for scoring goals but for some reason, he was not my cup of tea. He had a lazy side to him that stood out when we played the good teams. One such game was the F.A. trophy at home to Ryman premier side East Thurrock United, although he was not the villain in this game. That was down to a certain Mr Rocky Baptiste because, with the clock running down, we were awarded a penalty which would put us through to the next round. So up steps Rocky to take it; not a problem until he blasted the fucking thing over the crossbar and the covered terrace onto our training pitch! I loved him, but I thought, fuck you Rocky; thanks for that. We now have to go to East Thurrock for a replay and I can tell you now that no John Coventry side lets you have a second bite of the cherry! That proved to be the case, as we were smashed 6-2 in the replay on a cold windy wet night at Rookery Hill.

That is where I saw the bad side of Billy Medlock in turning his back on the game and being lazy, despite several bollockings from coach Des McCarthy and one almighty bust-up in the dressing room after the game. This incident saw Des depart from the club as Billy was the chairman's golden boy and he could see him do no wrong in any game. So, we now had got player power, which does go on a lot in non-league football, as quite a few managers do not have contracts, and the old saying still stands - managers lose games and players win them. But Tony Reid was a strong manager and he knew how to keep the dressing room his way, which I hope I had something to do with, having been managed by me in the Dr Martens league which required players to be tough and a good grounding if you were ever to think of being a manager at some stage.

As for the league, we were doing okay and everyone at the club was behind us, although the fans were a bit subdued at times, not like they are now down at Eastbourne Town. They have a great fan base and they travel away as well, which I can bear witness to. When they played away at Crowborough Athletic in the F.A. Vase last season, 2018, their fans were great banging drums and chanting, and Eastbourne manager, John Lambert, who I know quite well said to me after the game, "They are worth a goal to us every game!" Although they did get knocked out and the Wembley dream was over, just as it is this season when they lost away at Leighton Town. So, fans help, but can't win you games.

Anyway, back to Tony Reid now, and our season was about to get worse as we had only 1 win in 9 games before that dreaded night in the new year, the 8th of January to be precise. It was a midweek home game against Sittingbourne. Like most non-league managers, we have jobs and Tony's job involved a lot of travelling, which made the managing of senior football clubs sometimes very tiring, so although I make no excuses for his actions that night, I do understand that sometimes you can go over the top and that is what led to the incident that cost him his manager's job. Sittingbourne F.C. were no angels in all of this and nor were we, having had a player sent off, so the game became very angry and there were some racial comments flying about during the game, which we lost 4-2. But it did not end there- further comments were made to Tony as he walked to the players' tunnel and unfortunately for a Sittingbourne player, Tony lashed out and gave him a few of his boxing days' right-handers which left the player in a bit of a state, so after it had all calmed down, I remember saying to Tony, "You will get the sack for what you have done, but I understand why you have done it. But the chairman will not it; is as simple as that," and he was taken into the boardroom and sacked. Had he not been, then his dressing room control may have suffered. I often speak to him about it and he always puts it down to 'live and learn from it' which he has done quite well as manager at Westfield in the Isthmian BetVictor league south central division, where he is just outside the play-off places at the moment. We all left Eastbourne Town and John Lambert took over, but could not save them from dropping down into the Sussex County league and no wonder, with the club using over 75 players, and I will say that relegation was not down to Tony as John lambert had enough games to lead the team to safety, but in 2020 he looks like he will take them back up to the Isthmian league, so I wish him all the best for that.

So now, from my point of view, it was time to get off the rollercoaster, put it in for repairs again and see what happens next, and in the meantime, it was watching games including the eating of hot dogs and drinking the tea and meeting football people and the pen and paper ready just in case some player caught my eye, but the problem with that was I would always be moaning that there were never any team sheets given out before the game. But things were jogging along okay until April 2014, when I had a phone call from Tommy Williams who informed me that he had been given the manager's job at Kingstonian, along with Graham Harper as his assistant and would I take up a job as chief scout? Well, what else could I do but take up the offer and get the rollercoaster out again, but this time it was on the tracks at such a big non-league club and at Kingsmeadow, a football league stadium, the home of A.F.C. Wimbledon and of course, the chance to work again with two great blokes, but during our first meeting I made it quite clear that if I was not away on some scouting mission, just being in the dressing room during match days was good enough for me. I didn't have to be in the dugout anymore, but he still let me have my one to one with the players in terms of advice as opposed to giving instructions.

What a great set up it was; the stadium was the best in the Ryman league and the playing surface invited you to play football on it! When I arrived at the ground, the stewards would always have time for a chat as they kept watch on the players' entrance. It all felt so great to be involved! I also thought that if this is the last job I get in football, then that will do me, and I wanted Tommy and Harps to do so well and I would give them all the help I could. It was going to be a hard job to follow Alan Dowson, who was a favourite with the fans, so it was very important that they got out of the traps and showed the fans what they could do in the 2014/15 season, on what you would describe as an average playing budget for that league. but with some new players and some that had stayed.

So how about a trophy to start with, when we won the Corinthian Casuals' Geoff Harvey Memorial Vase tournament and our first Ryman league game 5-2 away at Enfield Town. Not bad for starters! The following 7 games were unbeaten until we met title favourites, Maidstone United, away in a midweek fixture. I had seen them on the Saturday away at Tonbridge Angels and they lost 1-0, but they were a good side and they also had the plastic pitch which not many clubs had acquired at that time and had little time to prepare for. However, no excuses, we were beaten 4-1, but we still had players moaning how it affected their play. We had good players and I fancied our chances of a playoff place, but we suffered a massive blow when our prolific goal-scorer, Andre McCollin decided during October to leave us for national league side Aldershot Town and go full-time. He had already made his mark by scoring 7 goals in 11 starts, but despite the blow, Tommy had some very talented players such as Josh Casey, Dan Sweeney, Aaron Goode, Elvis Hammond, Charlie Penny , keeper Rob Tolfrey, and our Spanish lad, Pico Gomez Pelayo, but despite the talent we had and without making excuses, we did miss McCollin a lot.

We also missed 2 classy central players in Sam Page and our skipper Alan Inns, who could deal with defending but it was the scoring of goals that let us down, scoring only 63 in the league but conceding 56, which was good enough to get a playoff place, but we failed to win in any of our last five games which cost us dearly. We were disappointed with our F.A. cup venture, as we were knocked out at home by a strong Eastbourne Borough side. Also, the F.A. trophy went horribly wrong as we lost away to Barkingside from a lower division. The league cup went the same way, except we made the quarter-final losing away to Margate and also to cap it all, we went out in the 1st round of the Surrey Senior Cup.

So, there you have it; first season in charge for Tommy and Harps, and as far as the league, a top-half finish in 11th and only 8pts from the playoffs. If we'd had a good run in and taken some points, we would have made it, but I had this feeling that although Kingsmeadow was a great place to be at for non-league football, I started to wonder whether it turned the other sides on to play at such a stadium, because at quite a few home games, while the lads were warming up, I would hear the staff from the opposition say their players would fancy this. Sometimes, your home is not your fortress, as Spurs found out when they used Wembley, but with our lads, you would like to think that they would be saying to themselves, I must play well as I want to be playing at this stadium every other week. I know I would have been wanting to, although Bromley was a nice stadium.

We only managed 7 home wins and 9 home draws and 8 defeats all that first season, so my thoughts were not far off. But there was plenty to build on for the following season 2015/16, and the fans I think were okay with what Tommy was trying to build for the future, but fans can turn on you at any time, as Tommy was to find out in the future.

There were some memories for me that season in the dressing room but unfortunately, there was also a memory on the pitch as well, which was going to bring the club and our goalkeeper, Rob Tolfrey, some very bad press nationwide and of course YouTube showing the video of the event. Now, don't get me wrong; I am not saying what Rob Tolfrey did was right, but again, you had to be there to understand why it happened. It also involved the character of the player, who was always disciplined in his manner, otherwise he would not have been playing for Tommy Williams. The home game against Bognor Regis Town on Monday 23rd of February 2015 was being played in a normal manner with both sides trying to win the game, but the Bognor supporters were giving Tolfrey some stick behind his goal in the second half of the game. They could not do it in the first half, because the seated end behind the other goal was always closed off except for ball boys. The final whistle went; we had lost 2-1, but Rob decided to jump over into the Bognor fans and start laying into them for the insults he had been subjected to. Then all hell broke loose, with both teams now involved with fans as well and the stewards trying their best to restore order before the police arrived. I think Rob should have kept his head as he was going to get a long ban and also a hefty fine, but we all have something in us that will trigger us into doing something drastic if we are provoked to such a degree, and this happens in the premiership as well, and not only in non-league football, as a certain Mr Eric Cantona will vouch for.

Back to the dressing room now and my observations; it was great to sit there and watch players as Tommy got working on his tactic board for corners, free kicks, attacking and defending, the game plan, and so on until Harps took over and delivered his many words of advice. I used to look around and you could tell with some players it was in one ear and out the other, as their minds were so fixed on the game. The one exception was our Spanish lad, Peko. I used to say to him quite often as he stood in front of the mirror combing his hair, "Son, you are going out to play football, not to go on a date with some fucking girl, and there is a player next door who will do all he can to fuck your looks up, so don't bother putting your aftershave on either!" I will always remember how he used to look at me with a big smile as much as to say, 'what the fuck is he on about', but I was right. If he could have got braver, he would have scored a lot more goals, but at least our kit man, Paul Ferrie, did not have to wash his shirt that often, and also our physio, Jamie Street did not get his hands too dirty if he had to treat him during or after a game.

At this point, I should give some credit to our chairman, Mr Anderson, after his quick reaction when, during the F.A. cup tie away at Romford, our keeper, Rob Tolfery, suffered a nasty head injury and with only the goalkeeping coach Matt Lovett to take over, we managed to get by with a draw. Matt did not want to play in the replay and our only other keeper, Ben Dudzinski, who was registered, was at Durham University, so the chairman paid his rail fare and had him picked up from Kings Cross, taken to the ground, and after the game which we won, he had him taken back again; a nice gesture I thought at the time.

As the season ended, the building for the 2015/16 started and Tommy had lined up some great pre-season games at home. We played the likes of Millwall, Chelsea, A.F.C. Wimbledon, and Hastings away, which could not have been better for me living a mile from the ground. We had lost some players and also gained some, and all were going to get a chance to show what they could do against class opposition, and that is what we did. All three games were close, and against Chelsea, they had a certain young player called Tammy Abraham, who is now in Chelsea first team and has full England caps. He scored their goal against us in a 1-0 victory, but something else happened that night and just by chance really, as sometimes during home games I used to go up the players' tunnel and use the toilet in our own changing room. As I was coming back out, who should come out of the Chelsea dressing room but Mr John Terry! We spoke for a while and he complimented us on our performance so far. I asked why he was not in America with the first team and he just laughed and said, "I'm too old for that now and I love watching the young kids play." He wished us the best of luck for the season and we parted company. So many miles apart in terms of football, but we were the same human beings. Someone asked me why I did not get his autograph and I replied, "Well, he never asked for mine!" and that is a typical non-league football answer. Without us, those top pros may never have made it at all!

Because Kingstonian was a big-name club, you never knew who would turn up to watch. During one game, I was sitting in the director's area, as always, with pen and paper, making my notes, when this big bloke came and sat next to me and I asked him who he was. It turned out to be Martin Offiah MBE., the great rugby league player who was a legend in his own right at Wigan! We talked during the game and he was a great bloke, a right good east London boy. I asked him about his life in rugby and he truly was interested in non-league football and Kingstonian. Funny thing is that I never found out who he was connected with to be at our game, but it's a good memory to keep.

It was our first league game away at Leiston. We were missing Rob Tolfrey, our goalkeeper, who was banned following that game against Bognor. Although stand-in keeper, Elvijs Putnins, did okay, we lost 2-1 and the next game 3-0. Then, just as you think the wheels are coming off the rollercoaster, it rights itself and something out of the blue turns up. That came in a 7-0 home win over Met Police in what I must describe as one of the best footballing displays I have had the privilege to see, let alone be involved with, although when I was manager at Croydon

Athletic, our 6-2 win over champions-elect, Ford United, and the 9-1 win with three hat tricks against Tring Town come very close. As does the Surrey F.A. County win over Liverpool in the F.A. County cup.

On to the season ahead and it was going to be another 'so near, yet so far away', including an F.A. cup exit away to Dunstable Town and another exit in the F.A. trophy, this time at home to a very strong Truro City. That came after wins against Leatherhead and Dorchester Town after a replay, so we had to give it a go, but in the league, we could not seem to get that consistency you need, first beating Lewes regarding promotion. Even the Met Police got revenge for that thrashing earlier in the season by beating us 2-1 at Imber Court. we also re-signed Andre McCollin, who made a quick impact with 9 goals in as many games, but he got injured so our goal threat had gone again. That seemed to be just our luck, but every cloud has a silver lining and ours came by lifting the Alan Turvey league cup, beating Faversham Town 5-0 at Carshalton Athletic, much to the delight of the fans and the chairman and of course, all of the staff, and so you would think that would spur us on to a play-off finish, but not us! We went in the other direction, performing poorly in our last five league games. Talk about a rollercoaster! What a ride this was becoming.

However, we were looking forward to the 2016/17 season and the return of another Kingstonian favourite, Ryan Moss. Yet, the talking point before we even got started was this to be the club's last season at Kingsmeadow and where were we going to ground-share? Not only that, but all boardroom stuff going on in the background as to where our future was taking us can cause disruption among the staff and the players, but you can't make too many excuses. We certainly could not excuse our exit from the F.A. cup when we got beaten 4-1 away from home to a lower league side, V.C.D Athletic, which saw Tommy's budget cut very early. Our league form was 'win a couple, lose a couple', so as far as cups go, we had lost the Charity Shield to Hampton and Richmond Borough 1-0, as well as the F.A. cup and it was only September. We did have a good start in the F.A. Trophy, first beating Lewes and then Tonbridge Angels after a replay, giving us what we all thought was a passage to the next round away at North Leigh, but we soon realised that this was going to be a very hard tie to win and it proved to be as we lost 1-0.

We could have been having a trip to Tranmere Rovers if we had got through and beaten South Park from the Ryman division below us, which was all possible and I believe that Tranmere was the chairman's team when he was younger. So, now we have the situation where the chairman is unhappy about not playing Tranmere, and the fans were getting fed up, beginning to pick on Tommy and Harps as we moved into 2017. It was then that I realised that the fans did not have a clue what Tommy was trying to do at the club, working very hard at making it a top club once again, as he met with the younger players and watched the academy play on several occasions. Also, he had good contacts and more importantly, he was Kingstonian through and through, having won promotion with the club. Okay, we were being hit and miss at times but that sometimes is the case when you are trying to build a side on a small budget. We had very good young players in the side who were looking up to a great player and a perfect gentleman on and off the pitch in Alan Inns, our captain, George Wells, who was a super left side player, Youssef Bamba and Joe Turner, and some of the academy were getting a chance on the bench. However, the fans were having none of it and kept calling for his head every time we played. I felt the board let Tommy down by not showing their loyalty and confidence in his and Harps' ability to turn things around, and were bowing down to the fans, who I know pay their money, but it is the chairman and the board that run the club.

Even now, I find it hard to think that the board and the fans thought that Tommy could not have pulled that team away from the threat of relegation and would have made that club great again. I know he would have done so! I have had the experience of 60 years in this non-league game and he would, and still might, make a top-class senior manager. I would be the first to ask him if I can work with him again if and when he lands another job. So, the board gave way and on Sunday the 26th of March 2017, the day after we lost at Burgess Hill, Tommy Williams and Graham Harper were sacked and I, of course, walked with them out the door. I wonder if they really knew what they were doing; after all, clubs like Dulwich Hamlet have stood by their manager, Gavin Rose, and also Tonbridge Angels with Steve McKimm and in the end, they delivered promotion and on a far bigger budget than Tommy. They also had a far bigger fan base, but their fans kept calm and also stood by their manager. By the way, Steve McKimm played for me in the rep side when he was at Raynes Park Vale. I wish the club no bad times following our departure, as they once gave me a half-page spread in the programme and the players and fans helped me raise money for cancer research after my swimathon, so they were not all bad people. I always look for their results and hope they find a permanent home one day, and with it, another decent manager, who has played the game at a decent level, to take them forward.

As for me, well, the rollercoaster that has been the theme of this book was now going to have a well-earned rest until who knows what might happen? I started to prepare for my 70th birthday game, which was to be played once again at Whyteleafe F.C., but this time on the G3 surface and yes, you are right, I brought out the rollercoaster just for this game which was to take place on the 1st of April 2018. This was still a year away but it takes a lot to get all the players from down the years together again, so after the Kingstonian episode which left me a bit fed up with the game, I spent that year before my birthday just looking at games and watching my grandson George play for Crowborough under 13s, where he was scoring goals for fun, and to be honest, I was quite happy just giving advice and covering the odd game for anyone who picked up the phone and required me to do that! I also spent time looking back on all of those years and gathering the information and a lot of research to do this book, which the love of my life, Jacqui, inspired me to do.

So, now to my 70th birthday game and what a great day it was, seeing all the old faces again, including my old mate from years ago, Steve Kember the ex-Palace, Chelsea, Leicester City player who was also manager at the Palace for some time. We also had a photo taken at the party of myself, Colin Hoare, Dave (Eggy) Exel and Phil Quickenden, as we had played for Woodside Albion in a cup final some 55 years ago. This made me question how we were still going strong, when 5 of my players had been taken before they even turned forty.

I decided to auction some of my non-league memorabilia along with some framed team photos and stuff and the proceeds from the matchday programme to raise money for prostate cancer. I had a lovely letter back from them thanking me for using my 70th birthday to raise money, but it was about the football first and it was obvious that the 5 years since my 65th had taken its toll on some of the players, including myself, as the legs had gone, but they still turned up to watch the game and enjoy the party. As I have said, the rollercoaster came out as I put my manager's hat on again for what surely must have been the last time. There were some very good players that turned up and it was great to see at least 4 of the Croydon F.C. double winning side turn up to play. We also had some of the Surrey County F.A. Youth boys, so in order to show no fiddling of the teams, we decided to put all the players names, except the 2 goalkeepers, into a hat and make a draw for the teams with both my grandson, George, and Barry Kingsford's younger son picking out the players. I was going to manage one team, and my son, Daniel, player-managed the other team.

I looked at my team on paper and thought, we could get a good hiding here, but as those who know me can always be assured, above all I will have discipline in my dressing room and a balanced side as best as I could, which on that day took some sorting out. I did have James Wastell in goal and one of the Ryman league's prolific goal scorers and ex-Canvey Island legend, Simon Liddle upfront and Harps and Marc Crome, but not Mr John Domfe, which I was pleased about. He could moan at his own side now, not mine! Now, preparation counts for a lot in this type of games and I sat all the players down in the dressing room while, next door, they were all shouting and laughing and going out onto the pitch in dribs and drabs. Not my team - we all knew where we were playing and got ourselves a formation and were ready to go when the bell went, shirts tucked into shorts, socks rolled up properly and we came onto the pitch looking like a team. And by fuck did we play like one! We raced into a 2-0 lead with our neat passing game and me bellowing out instructions from the dugout. We did play some good football and won the game 7-4, but the proudest moment for me was to see my son, Daniel, my grandson, George, and my son's two godfathers Bernie Donnelly and Graham Whant playing as well. So, there it was - 3 birthdays, 3 wins and the Harrington Cup was to stay in the family and is at rest in my son's house now.

And what about the rollercoaster? You On that subject I have to say the ride is now finished unless something or someone comes calling... .A couple of weeks after the game, my great friend, Bernie Donnelly, presented me with a photo book of the day's events which I will keep forever, but to finish this chapter and my footballing life in non-league football, I use a very famous saying. Someone said at the party, "Micky, it seems that with all the time you have given to the game, this non-league football must seem like it's a matter of life and death to you," and I just simply replied, "No, you are wrong. It is far more important than that"!

CHAPTER SEVENTEEN

Reflections, the teams, and my views and thanks.

Well, this may be the finishing touch to my book, but I think it will be the hardest to write, as these are just thoughts and opinions which some of you may agree or disagree with. I must say that the non-league paper, for me, has been and still is, a great read and does keep all fans from over the country in touch with the rest of the non-league, systems 1 to 6 and also Scotland and Wales. Of course, years ago, we did have the Non-League Monthly and the best of all, Team Talk which was the forerunner to the paper today. I am sure Tony Williams is involved with that, but for me, Tony and his Non-League Yearly Club Directory is the non-league bible. I have many copies and have featured in a few myself.

Nowadays, clubs and leagues have their great websites that keep you up to date with scores on match days, and YouTube showing highlights of the smallest of clubs, so in that respect, the game off the field has improved beyond belief. Also, the introduction, to the clubs that can afford it, of the 3G all-weather playing surface has enabled clubs to bring the community closer to them and also generates extra income with the stadium being used almost every day for all the club's junior sides and other clubs that need to get a game played. I am not so sure I like the fan forum on some sites, as I believe there are so-called fans that hide behind this, giving stick to the board and the manager but won't address them face to face. The word for them is cowards.

In my opinion, ground grading has got out of hand. There are some smaller clubs who cannot afford to have a stadium brought up to, say, a capacity of 3,000 fans when their average gate is no more than 400 at best. That, to me, has to be relaxed, or let some of the premiership clubs bloody well help out. But I do however feel that toilet facilities should be improved and of course, disabled access. Other than that, for fuck sake, what can you expect for £10 admission, the bloody Royal Opera House?

The time has come to recognise that the national league is not non-league football, as most teams are full-time anyway, and surely has to join forces with football league division 2 sometime soon. We could have division 2 south and north, as the cost of travel is so great for clubs, players and fans, and you would have some great local derbies to go to. I know, having managed in the Dr Martens league, that the north v south games were very good fixtures and fans loved them, but it was always hard to find players to travel and give up their Saturday nights on part-time wages. I know it would be costly for clubs who have 3G to have to go back to grass surface, but surely you can still have that on the outside of the stadium and still create income?

Agents should be banned from non-league football and not receive any money at all. They only ponce on clubs and 'their player' as they call them, who would be quite able to agree his own terms, I'm sure of that. My grandson, George, won't need any agent if he makes the grade, as his grandad will make sure no one takes the piss out of him and pays him what he is worth!

This next part may cause quite a few fans to disagree; it is really about the non-league in the south of England which I have said before, and my book follows those lines too, but it still makes for great reading for any non-league manager/player/fan anywhere.

So, it is on to managers now, and I would like to first say that my top ten are not in order of anyone being the best; it is just on what, in my opinion, I feel they have done for their non-league clubs over a period of time. They have not come from pro clubs to manage a side; they have all taken the clubs onwards and upwards, some from grassroots backgrounds. I have also not included myself.

1) Billy Smith - Carshalton Athletic, Crawley Town
2) Gordon Bartlett - Wealdstone
3) Chris Kinnear - Margate, Dover Athletic
4) Gavin Rose - Dulwich Hamlet
5) Gary Wilson - Eastbourne Borough
6) Jay Saunders - Maidstone United
7) Jack Pearce - Bognor Regis Town
8) John Rains - Sutton United
9) Geoff Chapple - Kingstonian, Woking F.C
10) Neil Cugley - Folkestone Invicta
11) Ted Hardy - Dagenham and Redbridge

All of those managers I mention have been a great advert for the non-league game, as are so many more managers, but I can't name them all.

I am going to finish the book with a type of Micky (Turka) Taylor roll call so now onto some of the best Sunday park footballers I have played with.

Goalkeeper:
Dickie Vincent- Addiscombe Social.
Defenders: -
Jimmy Dunne, Roy Kilby, Billy Lennox, - Addiscombe Social
David Blake, Martin Whant -Thornton Heath United
John Botting - Waddon Athletic
Midfield:
Kenny Bourne, Micky Vaughan - Addiscombe Social
Forwards:
Eddie Mark - Addiscombe Social

Bernie Donnelly, Billy Patterson, Jimmy Fitzpatrick, Steff Tomm, Richard (Shaft) Simpson – Thornton Heath United

I can assure you that there were some great players and I mean great players, among those boys. They could have all made it in top non-league!

I want now to go on to my playing days in senior football and some of those who I also had the privilege of being on the same park with. First, some players at Bromley FC where I started my senior career:

Ray Scrivens
Ian Wigham
Stuart Scott
Doug Springett
Pat Brown

Then on to Whyteleafe:

Malcolm Gates
Les Browne
Danny Bacon
Vic Burge
Micky Bannantyne
Syd Maddox
Barry Smith
Tony Lidbury (goalkeeper)

Then at Epsom and Ewell:
Eddie Mark
Bobby Langton
Willy Bennet

Then it was off to Merstham:
Micky Povey

Peter Lewis

Charlie Buckman

So, there you are - not the greatest well-known non-league players, but nonetheless still as good as what is about today.

We move onto the rep sides now and my managing of players, so I will pick some of the best from both the Surrey Intermediate team and Surrey premier rep sides:

Tony Williams- R.A.S United

Kevin Simpson, Andy Munslow, Steve Lake, Ron Luffman, Alan Bessom, Terry Thoroughgood (goalkeeper)-Frinton Rovers

Steve Parker, Tony Hermitage, Alan Dorill – Reedham Park

Andy Hilton (goalkeeper) - Hersham R.B.L

Randolph Payne – P.O Telecom

Simon Liddle, Alan Smith, Peter Steer, Bruce Martin - Kingswood Wanderers

Paul Ottoway, Chris Jones (goalkeeper) - Croydon M.O

John Richards -Springfield Hospital

Gary Flatt - Battersea Park Rovers

Glen Kieley - St Luke's, West Norwood

Gary Butler - Coney Hall

Derek Laing - Ottershaw

That was some of the squad over 5 years that played under my management and won so many trophies which you will have read about. Also, there was the Morden and District Sunday rep side and what a Sunday league that was; one of the best in the country, as Ranelagh Sports proved when they won the F.A. Sunday cup in 1994, beating Hartlepool Lion Hotel 2-0 in the final, and I am not joking when I say some, if not all non-league premier league teams would have had to be at their best to cope with teams like Wrythe Athletic, Cenward, Crown

Meads, Ranelagh Sports, Morden Nomads, Manor Athletic, and Thornton Heath United.

Some other names I would like to mention here:

Tony Dunne, Bernie Donnelly, Billy Patterson - Thornton Heath United
Jack Goldie, Kenny Bernard - Ranelagh Sports
Ray Coombes, Sean Dalton - Crown Meads
Chris Chapman (goalkeeper) Brian Duke- Wrythe Athletic
Dave Tippits - Manor Athletic

These are only a few of the names, but of course, there was also the work with the Surrey County F.A. under 16s and 18s. I have combined my pick out of the squads of the young future non-league players during my time on the management team, but not when I was county chief scout. Some of these players went on to be good professional footballers and earned a decent living, some made a good standard in non-league and some just simply went away from football, but here is a list of some of my best lads and remember, it is always in my opinion only:

Stewart Vaughan (goalkeeper), Steve Hall - Banstead Athletic

Tony Chin - Dulwich Hamlet
Barry Kingsford - Carshalton Athletic
Dan Burgess, Jamie Sinclair (goalkeeper), Elliot Dell, Leon Raishbrook, Danny Tanner - Sutton United
Kojo Ohene, Steve Kabba - Croydon Athletic
Gary Holloway - Walton and Hersham
Desmond Boateng, Kevin Betsy, Andy Carroll, Aiden Kilner - Woking F.C.
Gavin Holligan - Aldershot Town

There would be many more players if I was to include the time when I was county chief scout and also, we decided not to include any players from the pro clubs as they did not like their players involved. Some players even felt that it was not good enough for them and I will never know why, as your next step, if recommended while playing for the County Youth F.A., is a trial for the England Youth F.A. team; there is nothing in between.

On to my next list now and these are the pick of some of the players I managed at senior level, including my time as director of football at Croydon F.C.:

Terry Gayle, John Fowler, Simon Mitchell, Gary Thornton, Paul Muir, Andy Wareing, Tony Brown, Shane Dutfield, Simon Rollinson, Leon Maxwell - Croydon Athletic

Ben Judge, James Wastell, Graham Harper, Nic Mcdonnell, Craig Dundas, Mark (Geordie) Dickinson, Eben Allen, Ali Reeve, Chris (Dicko)Dickson, Jamie Ndah (the brother of George), Simon Liddle, Omari Coleman - Croydon F.C.

John Crumplin, Sean Campbell, Adam Flanagan, Danny Fletcher, Dominic Barclay, Jason Davy, Des Boateng, Simon Fox, Tony Reid, Michael O'Callaghan. Carleton Chatelier, Gavin Ramsden - St. Leonards F.C.

Alan Mansfield (goalkeeper), Steve (Robbo) Roberts, Martin Beard, Danny Punt, Paul (Scholesy) Smith, Seb Favata, Pat Massaro, Phil Gault, Marc Hudson, Jamie Edwards - Three Bridges F.C.

Now it's time to move on to a rather small list of managers that I considered worth a mention and who I enjoyed being managed by and if you're not on this list, you will know why!

Johnny Mark, Alf Kilby - Addiscombe Social
Les Browne, - Whyteleafe
Micky Ackland - Bromley F.C.
Fred Setters - Merstham F.C.

I must say at this point there is one manager that I would have loved to have been managed by and that is, believe or not,

George Borg, because I was a right little bastard handful as a player and I could see us having some great fun on the park and off it, as George would never bully me. I would have been ready for him but he would have loved my wing play I'm sure.

Now we come to the last list of non-league players that will, I'm sure, cause some controversy. Here are some of the best non-league football players who have not come down from the pro club ranks, but if anything, have gone from non-league to pro football league, championship and premiership and I have seen many over sixty years:

John Swannell (goalkeeper) - Hendon, 50/60s
Uncle Roy Law, Eddie Reynolds - Wimbledon 1960s
David Sadler - Maidstone United, 1960s
Laurence Batty (goalkeeper) - Woking F.C., 1990s
Chris (The Lip) Kelly - Leatherhead, 1970s
Cyrille Regis - Hayes F.C., 1970s
Stuart Pearce - Wealdstone,1970/80s
Ian Wright, Greenwich Borough, 1980s
Les Ferdinand - Hayes, 1980s
stan Collymore - Stafford Rangers, 1990s
Gary Abbott - Aldershot Town, 1990s
Jimmy Bolton - Carshalton Athletic, 1990s
Steve McKimm - Hendon, 1995
Ben Strevens - Wingate and Finchley, 1998
Geoff Wood - Ford United 1998
Jon Keeling - Purfleet, 2001
Ben Judge - Croydon, 2001
Chris Smalling - Maidstone United, 2006/8
Erhun Oztumer - Dulwich Hamlet, 2012/14
George Purcell - A.F.C. Hornchurch, 2014
Alfie May - Hythe Town, 2014/15

Josh Casey - Woking, 2019

George Wells - Slough Town, 2019

Lee Worgan, (goalkeeper) - Maidstone United 2013/18

Craig Dundas - Sutton United, 2007/2018

The list could go on and on but those players listed are some of the best I have seen. I will leave all the others to those who do stats and ground-hop, but I will say that despite all my travels and the games I have seen and some outstanding players, there are 2 players that played for Whyteleafe and my Sunday side, Thornton Heath United, Billy Patterson /right-wing and Bernie Donnelly / left-wing. I have never seen any wingers anywhere as good as those players, so how they were never pros and made the big time, I will never know. Sometimes great quality is just under your nose but you fail to see it; or is it you just don't want to lose them?

Depression in non-league is never noted much in the media, but I can tell you it happens as I have suffered from it on many occasions. It is not all about not doing well or the press having a go at you, but it is the football and your working situation, the lack of sleep and the time lost with loved ones. You see, us players and managers do not get much financial reward in non-league; only the big ego, which within two games can go down the pan, so why do pro footballers on massive big money go whingeing to the press saying they can't cope? I have a message for them; you want to come and spend some time in non-league with a job to keep down and a family to feed, let alone a chairman that thinks you should be like Real Madrid. Then you can fucking moan or say you are so-called depressed. Be like I was and man up to it, or the other choice is fuck off out the game! I think I know the answer to that and that is my views on football depression. Howard Wilkinson, the manager of Leeds United, was furious one frosty morning when his players were complaining about the cold. He went and got the local coach company to send a coach round to take his players to the local coal mine to see the mineworkers come up from the coal face, their faces and hands grimed in coal dust, and he said, "Those lads pay to come to watch you on a Saturday, and how would you like to do their job? So, don't ever complain to me you are fucking cold again, because they would swap jobs with you anytime!"

CHAPTER EIGHTEEN

Hold on a minute; the rollercoaster is coming out and going to Spain 2020!

Can I not even have a holiday without football? The answer to that is no, as was proved this year, 2019. For the first time, myself and Jacqui decided to go to the annual fiesta in our much-loved little town of Cala-en-Porter on the island of Menorca in Spain. We went to see the horses, but I soon found out that there was to be an annual football match at the small G3 surface football stadium, between the Spanish bar owners and waiters and the English bar owners and visitors, so I went to watch the game, not having a clue how serious the game would be. I soon found out when the Spanish were in their national team shirts and England also in theirs; they even played the national anthems before the game which, unfortunately, England lost 5-2, so after the game and later that evening, I was sitting in one of my favourite bars when this chap who I had never seen before came up to me and said, "Are you Micky, the football man?" to which I replied, "Yes, can I help?" He replied, "Not fucking much! Did you see that game today and the Spaniards lift that cup? Well, can you get a side out here next year, 2020? We want that cup back! we will look after you for the weekend." I was in the middle of making notes on the book and thought this football will never leave you now and if you get involved, what next? We will have to see, but it looks like Cala-en –Porter, 2020, here we come!

Let's finish the book on a joke and some sound advice. What about Croydon Athletic, when Hayden Bird stabbed me in the back to take my job? To mark his first season as manager, the club decided to make a video, such was their season, but not to show off their 100 best goals. Instead, they showed their 100 best throw-ins!

And now for my advice to all clubs and managers: Winning must be a habit, but losing will always be a curse and you must never forget that the road to success is always under construction, no matter what!

I hope you have enjoyed reading this book as much as I have enjoyed writing it, although I wish that my love for football and the rollercoaster journey it has taken me on these last 60 years had been given to me in a different way other than on February 6th 1958, seeing my dad crying at the tea-table on hearing the news that seven Man United Busby Babes were lying dead after their plane crashed on a Munich runway then Duncan Edwards to make it eight two weeks later. I was to spend a big part of my life in non-league football, as I went to see 'uncle' Roy Law play non-league football for Wimbledon F.C. and I was hooked. So, on that note, all that remains to be said is - no matter what non-league side you support, may your team go with you! Micky (Turka) Taylor

The End

Near to completion of this book I learnt of the sudden death of my good friend and footballer, Martin Beard

R.I.P. Martin

Acknowledgements

It is time now to thank all the football clubs and their helpers and players and everyone else who has made this book possible for me to write, some who are no longer in existence:

Woodside Albion
Waddon Athletic
Bromley F.C.
Whyteleafe F.C.
Red Star F.C.
Merstham F.C.
Epsom and Ewell F.C.
Thornton Heath United
Frinton Rovers
Addiscombe social
Reedham Park F.C.
Netherne F.C.
Croydon Athletic
Croydon F.C.
St Leonards F.C.
Haywards Heath Town
Three Bridges F.C.
Lingfield F.C.
Hastings United F.C.
Eastbourne Town F.C.
Carshalton Athletic F.C.
Torquay United
Kingstonian F.C.

Representative manager of the following:

Surrey Intermediate league

Surrey Premier league

Surrey F.A. County Youth

Morden and District Sunday league

My thanks also to the following newspapers:

The Non-League Paper

Sussex Argus

Hastings and St Leonards Observer

Time now for my choice of non-league (this does not include national league):

Best ground - Kingsmeadow, the former home of Kingstonian

Best playing surface - B.A.C. Weybridge, Surrey Senior league

Best player - (uncle) Roy Law - Wimbledon

Best team I have seen - Aldershot Town when they were playing in the Ryman league

Best ground I have played on - Craven Cottage, home of Fulham F.C.

Best player I have played in the same team with - Bernie Donnelly - Thornton Heath United Best player played against – Ray Coombes - Crown Meads - Morden and District Sunday league (former player for Bishop Stortford F.C., amateur cup winners 1974

Best team played against - Farnborough Town – Surrey Senior league

There you have it - my choice - and not open for discussion!

Lightning Source UK Ltd.
Milton Keynes UK
UKHW040714050320
359822UK00001B/49